JOURNAL FOR THE STUDY OF THE NEW TESTAMENT
SUPPLEMENT SERIES
55

Executive Editor, Supplement Series
David Hill

Publishing Editor
David E. Orton

JSOT Press
Sheffield

THE
PURPOSE
OF ROMANS

A Comparative
Letter Structure Investigation

L. Ann Jervis

Journal for the Study of the New Testament
Supplement Series 55

Copyright © 1991 Sheffield Academic Press

Published by JSOT Press
JSOT Press is an imprint of
Sheffield Academic Press Ltd
The University of Sheffield
343 Fulwood Road
Sheffield S10 3BP
England

Typeset by Sheffield Academic Press
and
Printed on acid-free paper in Great Britain
by Billing & Sons Ltd
Worcester

British Library Cataloguing in Publication Data

Jervis, L. Ann
    The purpose of Romans
    1. Christianity. Scriptures
    I. Title   II. Series
    227.106

    ISSN 0143-5108
    ISBN 1-85075-304-0

CONTENTS

Acknowledgments   7
Abbreviations   8

Chapter 1
THE PROBLEM OF THE PURPOSE OF ROMANS   11
  A. Defining the Problem   11
  B. Proposed Solutions to the Problem   14
      1. Paul's Purpose is Theological   14
      2. Paul's Purpose is Missionary   19
      3. Paul's Purpose is Pastoral   22
  C. Summary   27

Chapter 2
COMPARATIVE LETTER STRUCTURE ANALYSIS AND
ITS RELEVANCE FOR THE PROBLEM OF THE
PURPOSE OF ROMANS   29
  A. Justification of the Methodological Approach   29
  B. Previous Letter Structure Studies   36
  C. The Structure of a Pauline Letter   41
      1. The Value of Various Letter Structure Sections
          for Determining the Function of Romans   42
      2. The Opening and Closing Sections of a Pauline
          Letter   47
  D. Some Preliminary Critical Considerations   55
      1. The Authenticity of Paul's Letters   55
      2. The Integrity of Some of Paul's Letters   57

Chapter 3
THE PAULINE OPENING FORMULAS   69
  A. A Comparison of the 'Identification of Sender' Unit
      in Paul's Letters   69
  B. The 'Designation of Recipient' Unit   80

C. The 'Greeting' Unit   83
D. Comparative Observations   84

Chapter 4
THE PAULINE THANKSGIVINGS   86
   A. Paul Schubert's Work on the Structure of the Pauline
       Thanksgivings and a Proposal   86
   B. Analyses of the Respective Thanksgivings   91
   C. Comparative Observations   107

Chapter 5
THE PAULINE APOSTOLIC PAROUSIAS   110
   A. The Boundaries of the Pauline Apostolic Parousias   110
   B. An Expansion of R.W. Funk's Structural Analysis   112
   C Analyses of the Respective Pauline Apostolic
       Parousias   114
   D. Comparative Observations   127

Chapter 6
THE PAULINE CONCLUSIONS   132
   A. The Functional Units of a Pauline Conclusion   132
   B. The Boundaries of the Pauline Conclusions   134
   C. Analyses of the Respective Conclusions   140
   D. Comparative Observations   155

Chapter 7
TOWARDS A RESOLUTION OF THE ROMANS DEBATE   158

Bibliography   165
Index of Biblical References   180
Index of Authors   184

ACKNOWLEDGMENTS

It is my joy to acknowledge some of the people who have been partners in various ways during the course of my studies: my supervisor
Dr R.N. Longenecker inspired devotion to the task and provided guid-
ance and care throughout; Dr J.C. Hurd gave graciously of his precise,
thorough and thoughtful scholarship; and Adrienne Taylor and Gayle
Ford significantly supported my efforts with their research acumen.

Without Shirley, Bev, Erin, Pam, John, Robin, Kathy, John, Jean,
Bob, Jo, Don, Terry, Kevin, Michael and Douglas, the years spent on
this project would be remembered with far less fondness, laughter and
serenity.

The balance which Peter and our children Dylan and Bronwen give
to my life has proved to be the greatest help in my work. For with
them I share the 'stuff of life' for which the academic pursuit exists.

ABBREVIATIONS

AnBib	Analecta biblica
ANRW	*Aufstieg und Niedergang der römischen Welt: Geschichte und Kultur Roms in Spiegel der neueren Forschung* (Berlin: de Gruyter, 1972–)
ATR	*Anglican Theological Review*
AUSS	*Andrews University Seminary Studies*
BDF	Blass, F. and A. Debrunner, *A Greek Grammar of the New Testament and Other Early Christian Literature* (trans. and rev. R.W. Funk; Chicago: University of Chicago Press, 1961).
Bib	*Biblica*
BibT	*The Bible Translator*
BJRL	*Bulletin of the John Rylands Library*
BN	*Biblische Notizen*
BR	*Biblical Research*
BS	*Bibliotheca Sacra*
BT	*Bible Today*
CBQ	*Catholic Biblical Quarterly*
ETL	*Ephemerides theologicae lovanienses*
EvTh	*Evangelische Theologie*
EQ	*The Evangelical Quarterly*
ExpT	*Expository Times*
HNT	Handbuch zum Neuen Testament
HTR	*Harvard Theological Review*
IB	*Interpreter's Bible*
IDB	G.A. Buttrick (ed.), *Interpreter's Dictionary of the Bible*
IJT	*The Indian Journal of Theology*
Int	*Interpretation*
ITQ	*Irish Theological Quarterly*
JAC	*Jahrbuch für Antike und Christentum*
JBL	*Journal of Biblical Literature*
JBR	*Journal of Bible and Religion*
JETS	*Journal of the Evangelical Theological Society*

JR	*The Journal of Religion*
JSNT	*Journal for the Study of the New Testament*
JTS	*Journal of Theological Studies*
LQHR	*The London Quarterly and Holborn Review*
NovT	*Novum Testamentum*
NTS	*New Testament Studies*
OJRS	*Ohio Journal of Religious Studies*
RB	*Revue biblique*
RelSRev.	*Religious Studies Review*
RSR	*Recherches de science religieuse*
RQ	*Restoration Quarterly*
SBL	Society of Biblical Literature
SC	Studia Catholica
SR	Studies in Religion
ST	*Studia theologica*
TB	*Tyndale Bulletin*
ThLZ	*Theologische Literaturzeitung*
ThV	*Theologia Viatorum*
TJT	*Toronto Journal of Theology*
USQR	*Union Seminary Quarterly Review*
WTJ	*Westminster Theological Journal*
ZKR	*Zeitschrift für Katholische Theologie*
ZThK	*Zeitschrift für Theologie und Kirche*
ZNW	*Zeitschrift für die neutestamentliche Wissenschaft*

Chapter 1

THE PROBLEM OF THE PURPOSE OF ROMANS

Romans occupies a unique position in Pauline studies. Its Pauline authorship is beyond dispute[1] and the ideas it expresses are considered quintessentially Pauline. Yet the purpose(s) for which Paul wrote his letter are significantly more obscure than for any of his other communications. At the end of the last century F.J.A. Hort commented: 'That the problem [of the original purpose of Romans] is not very simple may be reasonably inferred from the extraordinary variety of opinion which has prevailed and still prevails about it'.[2] And Hort's comment remains valid today. But so also does his encouraging challenge that the problem of the purpose of Romans 'is worthy of any pains that can be taken for its solution; for so long as the purpose of the Epistle remains obscure, the main drift of its doctrinal teaching must remain obscure also'.[3]

A. *Defining the Problem*

The question as to the purpose of Romans was articulated for the modern study of Paul by F.C. Baur,[4] who assumed that, since the other

_____

1. C.E.B. Cranfield says: 'The denial of Paul's authorship of Romans by such critics as E. Evanson (1792), B. Bauer (1852), A.D. Loman (1882) and R. Steck (1888) is now rightly relegated to a place among the curiosities of NT scholarship. Today no responsible criticism disputes its Pauline origin' (*The Epistle to the Romans* [Edinburgh: T. & T. Clark, 1975], pp. 1-2).

2. *Prolegomena to St Paul's Epistles to the Romans and the Ephesians* (London: Macmillan, 1895), p. 5.

3. *Prolegomena to St Paul's Epistles*, p. 5.

4. Über Zweck und Veranlassung des Römerbriefs und der damit zusammenhängenden Verhältnisse der römischen Gemeinde', *Tübinger Zeitschrift für Theologie* 3 (1836), pp. 59-178; *Paul the Apostle of Jesus Christ* (trans. from 2nd German edn, ed. E. Zeller, rev. A. Menzies; London: Williams & Norgate, 1876), I, pp. 308-65.

'authentic' Pauline letters were written from the 'imperious pressure of circumstances',[1] Romans must have originated in a similar way. So Baur asserted that the meaning of Romans—as, indeed, of any document—could be determined only when its original historical circumstances were understood. This conviction that Romans must be understood from a historical, as opposed to a dogmatic, point of view bequeathed to students of Romans a challenging problem.[2]

The question took on further definition with the discovery and publication of the non-literary papyri found in Egypt.[3] Study of these documents produced important new information regarding both lexicography[4] and letter genre. Of the three most significant scholars working on these materials at the turn of the century—G. Milligan,[5] J.H. Moulton,[6] and G.A. Deissmann[7]—it was the latter whose observations have had the most direct bearing on the problem of the purpose of Romans.

Through a comparison of Paul's letters with these ancient non-literary papyrus letters, Deissmann made a distinction between 'epistles' intended for public use and 'true letters' intended for personal use. 'True letters', according to Deissmann, were hastily written and rela-

---

1. *Paul*, I, p. 314.

2. Cf. Baur: 'The origin and aim of the Epistle are generally determined from the purely dogmatic point of view. Scholars have failed to inquire carefully into the historical occasion and the circumstances in the Roman Church on which the Epistle proceeds, and to make these the starting point of their discussions; as if the Apostle had had no other motive for writing than a desire to give a connected and comprehensive view of his whole scheme of doctrine, to furnish, as it were, a compendium of the Pauline dogmatics in the form of an Apostolic Epistle' (*Paul*, I, p. 310).

3. E.g. F.G. Kenyon, *Greek Papyri in the British Museum* (1893); *Ägyptische Urkunden aus den Königlichen Museen zu Berlin: Griechische Urkunden* (Berlin: Weidmann, commenced in 1895); B. Grenfell and A.S. Hunt (eds.), *The Oxyrhynchus Papyri*, I (London: Egypt Exploration Fund, 1898). For background, see R.N. Longenecker, 'Ancient Amanuenses and the Pauline Epistles', in *New Dimensions in New Testament Study* (ed. R.N. Longenecker and M.C. Tenney; Grand Rapids: Zondervan, 1974), pp. 218-97 (pp. 281-82).

4. See comments by C.F.D. Moule, 'Form Criticism and Philological Studies', *LQHR* 27 (1958), pp. 87-92 (p. 90).

5. *Selections from the Greek Papyri* (Cambridge: Cambridge University Press, 1910).

6. *From Egyptian Rubbish Heaps* (London: Kelly, 1916).

7. *Bible Studies* (trans. A. Grieve; Edinburgh: T. & T. Clark, 1901); *Light from the Ancient East* (trans. L.R.M. Strachan; London: Hodder & Stoughton, 1910); *St Paul: A Study in Social and Religious History* (trans. L.R.M. Strachan; London: Hodder & Stoughton, 1912).

tively formless, which conclusion encouraged a continuing lack of scholarly interest in the form of the Pauline letter. Yet Deissmann's emphasis on Paul's letters as actual communications to real addressees served to focus again the historical question. For Deissmann considered that the subject of Paul's letters was 'always problems of the individual soul or of the Christian community in a definite peculiar situation'.[1]

Prior to the insights of Baur and Deissmann, the fundamental question was this: since Paul's letters are doctrinal in nature and intent, why are the Corinthian letters and Galatians so unlike Romans? After Baur and Deissmann, however, the question was reversed: if all the letters of Paul are real communications, why is Romans so unlike the Corinthian correspondence and Galatians?[2]

Needless to say, historical contingency and letter function are today vital factors in the study of all of Paul's letters. J.C. Beker describes Paul's letters as 'eminently particular and occasional. . . a substitute for the dialogical directness of the apostolic word *"hic et nunc"* '.[3] M.L. Stirewalt simply says, 'a letter is a substitute for conversation'.[4]

---

1. *St Paul*, p. 14.
2. Cf. Baur: 'The Epistle to the Galatians and those to the Corinthians . . . give us a very different notion of how the Apostle came to write an Epistle. What led him to write these ones were special circumstances and needs. Nor was it that he used these as a peg on which to hang a doctrinal treatise which he had in his mind already; it is the imperious pressure of circumstances which calls and forces him to write, at the risk of seeing his work destroyed. We cannot but suppose that there was something of this sort in the case of the Epistle to the Romans' (*Paul*, pp. 313-14).

See also Deissmann, who states that Romans 'is a letter, and not a book . . . the saying, popular with many German students of St Paul, that it is a compendium of Paulinism, and that the apostle has here laid down his dogmatic and ethical system, is, to say the least, very liable to be misunderstood . . . [Paul] does not contemplate as his readers the literary public of his time, nor even Christendom in general; he addresses himself to a handful of people resident in the more modest quarters of Rome' (*St Paul*, p. 22).

3. 'Contingency and Coherence in the Letters of Paul', *USQR* 33 (1978), pp. 141-51 (p. 142). Cf. D.J. Selby, *Toward the Understanding of St Paul* (Englewood Cliffs, NJ: Prentice–Hall, 1962), p. 239; W. Doty, 'The Epistle in Late Hellenism and Early Christianity: Developments, Influences and Literary Form' (Dissertation, Drew University, Madison, NH, 1966), esp. p. 179.

4. 'Paul's Evaluation of Letter-Writing', in *Search the Scriptures. New Testament Studies in Honor of Raymond T. Stamm* (ed. J.M. Myers, *et al.*; Leiden: Brill, 1969), pp. 179-96 (p. 179).

And R.W. Funk regards the letters of Paul as substitutes for his apostolic presence.[1]

The question as to the original purpose of Romans, however, still lacks today a consensual answer. The reason for such a *vexata questio* is the unique tension that exists in Romans between letter genre and content. As a Pauline letter, Romans appears to be a real communication, a substitute for conversation—in short a 'particular' or 'circumstantial' letter. Yet it is difficult to propose any particular occasion or purpose for Romans that makes sense of its content. Its epistolary genre, in fact, seems to be at odds with its content.

B. *Proposed Solutions to the Problem*

Three main proposals as to the purpose of Romans have been offered: (1) the purpose of Romans is theological, stemming from Paul's desire to lay out his gospel—perhaps in the light of his forthcoming trip to Jerusalem; (2) the purpose of Romans is missionary, stemming from Paul's concern about the extension of his missionary work; and (3) the purpose of Romans is pastoral, to set right certain errors either of doctrine or behaviour at Rome.

1. *Paul's Purpose is Theological*

(a) *A theological tractate.* The view that the purpose of Romans is to expound Paul's theology in a general, non-particular way was dominant from the late Middle Ages until F.C. Baur. Along with much of the rest of Scripture, Romans was regarded as part of a 'complete and beautiful story. . . [that] sets forth all the articles of God's being; of human weakness; of law; of sin and punishment; of promise; of the Redeemer, the Son of God, and his suffering. Resurrection, and reign; of grace and righteousness; of the gathering of the Church; of eternal blessedness and eternal punishment'.[2] So Romans was interpreted as a particularly well organized, complete, and effective doctrinal statement; as one of Paul's most powerful theological discourses. For Luther 'the whole purpose and intention of the apostle in this epistle is to break down all righteousness and wisdom of our own, to point out

---

1. 'The Apostolic "Parousia": Form and Significance', in *Christian History and Interpretation: Studies Presented to John Knox* (ed. W.R. Farmer, C.F.D. Moule and R.R. Niebuhr; Cambridge: Cambridge University Press, 1967), pp. 249-68 (p. 249f.).

2. *Melanchthon on Christian Doctrine* (trans. and ed. C.L. Manschreck; New York: Oxford, 1965), p. xlviii.

again those sins and foolish practices'.[1] Melanchthon, interpreting Romans within the category of rhetoric, viewed it as a systematic theological argument.[2] Likewise Calvin saw Paul's purpose in Romans as being to expound justification by faith in a methodical fashion.[3]

The interpretation of Romans as a theological exposition of the gospel has continued today among many, perhaps most vocally by Karl Barth. In reaction to analytical historicism, Barth called for a 'theological exegesis' as opposed to an 'historical exegesis'. And his subsequent hermeneutic of 'exposing the Word in the words', of penetrating the document so that it 'seems hardly to exist as a document',[4] resulted in understanding Romans as a 'dogmatics in outline'—a summary of the essence of Paul's thought.[5]

Such an understanding makes sense of Romans' content without accounting for its historical contingency.[6] It does not then provide a role for its letter function. A number of scholars, in fact, have effectively played down the *briefliche* character of Romans.[7] In particular, A. Nygren maintains that 'the characteristic and peculiar thing about Romans, differentiating it from the rest of Paul's epistles, is just the

---

1. *Luther's Works. Lectures on Romans* XXV (ed. H.C. Oswald; St Louis: Concordia, 1972), p. 3 n. 1.

2. See T.H.L. Parker, *Commentaries on The Epistle to the Romans. 1532–1542* (Edinburgh: T. & T. Clark, 1986), pp. 5-6.

3. *The Epistle of Paul the Apostle to the Romans and to the Thessalonians* (Grand Rapids: Eerdmans, 1961), p. xxiv.

4. *The Epistle to the Romans* (London: Oxford University Press, 1933), p. 8.

5. As J.C. Beker underlines in *Paul the Apostle. The Triumph of God in Life and Thought* (Philadelphia: Fortress, 1980), p. 59.

6. Beker points out that Barth's approach 'bypasses the historical issues' (*Paul the Apostle,* p. 65).

7. E.g. J.A. Bengel, who calls Romans a statement in the abstract, *Gnomon of the New Testament* II (trans., rev., and ed. A.R. Fausset; Edinburgh: T. & T. Clark, 1873), p. 2; See also R. Haldane, *Exposition of the Epistle to the Romans* (Edinburgh: Oliphant, 1874), p. 703; C.A.A. Scott, *Saint Paul: The Man and the Teacher* (Cambridge: Cambridge University Press, 1936), p. 17; A. Feuillet, 'Le plan salvifique de Dieu d'apres l'Epître aux Romains', *RB* 62 (1950), pp. 336-87, 489-529, esp. p. 336; A. Schlatter, *Gottes Gerechtigkeit: Ein Kommentar zum Römerbrief* (Stuttgart: Calwer, 1952), p. 11; E. Brunner, *The Letter to the Romans* (London: Lutterworth, 1959), p. 10; W. Lüthi, *The Letter to the Romans* (Edinburgh: Oliver & Boyd, 1961), p. 211; W.G.T. Shedd, *A Critical and Doctrinal Commentary on the Epistle of St Paul to the Romans* (Grand Rapids: Zondervan, 1967). S. Sandmel says that the purpose of Romans is to give an 'an orderly statement' on major matters (*A Jewish Understanding of the New Testament* [Cincinnati: Hebrew Union College Press, 1957], pp. 90-91).

fact that it was not, or was only in a slight degree, aimed at circumstances within a certain congregation'.[1]

Continued adherence to an understanding of Romans that focuses on its theological content apart from its letter genre is partly the result of the weighty influence that biblical theology has exerted in this century. The concern in contemporary Pauline studies to locate the *Mitte* of Paul's thought[2] has lessened the impulse to keep each of Paul's letters distinct so as to interpret the content of each letter in terms of its unique historical circumstances. While there are positive features in such a biblical theological approach, there needs to be constant sensitivity to this basic exegetical issue: that the material substance of a letter is conditioned by its own particular original purpose.[3]

The understanding of Romans as a theological tractate appears also in two somewhat more nuanced forms that take into account, at least to some extent, issues having to do with historical circumstance and letter genre. One version understands Romans as a circular letter. Another sees Romans occasioned by Paul's concern over anticipated controversies at Jerusalem. Both of these views, however, consider Paul's purpose in Romans to be the setting forth of his gospel in written form, whether as a circular letter or in anticipation of his Jerusalem visit, and so may legitimately be seen as advocating primarily a theological rationale for the letter.

(b) *A circular letter*. E. Renan and J.B. Lightfoot both advanced a circular letter theory for Romans. Renan held that the letter was

---

1. *Commentary on Romans* (Philadelphia: Muhlenberg, 1949), p. 4.
2. As in e.g. A. Schweitzer, *The Mysticism of Paul the Apostle* (trans. W. Montgomery; New York: Holt, 1931); R. Bultmann, *The Theology of the New Testament* (New York: Scribner's, 1951); R.N. Longenecker, *Paul, Apostle of Liberty* (New York: Harper & Row, 1964); H.N. Ridderbos, *Paul. An Outline of His Theology* (trans. J.R. de Witt; Grand Rapids: Eerdmans, 1966, 1975); E. Käsemann, *New Testament Questions of Today* (trans. W.J. Montague; London: SCM, 1969); *idem, Perspectives on Paul* (trans. M. Kohl; Philadelphia: Fortress, 1971); E.P. Sanders, *Paul and Palestinian Judaism* (Philadelphia: Fortress, 1977); and Beker, *Paul the Apostle*.
3. N.A. Dahl writes: 'To the apostle himself, letters to particular churches written on special occasions were the proper literary form for making theological statements. Of this fact both exegesis and theology, not to mention preaching, have to take account.' ('The Particularity of the Pauline Epistles as a Problem in the Ancient Church', in *Neotestamentica et Patristica. Eine Freundesgabe, Herrn Professor Dr. Oscar Cullmann zu seinem 60. Geburtstag überreicht* [Leiden: Brill, 1962], pp. 261-71 [p. 271]).

addressed simultaneously to Christians at Rome and to three other churches: Ephesus, Thessalonica, and an unknown church; and that it was meant to be a resumé of Paul's theological teaching.[1] Lightfoot, struggling with the textual difficulties of Romans, suggested that the letter was originally sent to Rome, but that when Paul was in Rome he prepared a shortened form for publication.[2]

T.W. Manson was also concerned with the textual difficulties of Romans, particularly those of 1.7 and 15 and the ending at 15.33.[3] Accepting the 'Ephesian hypothesis' of David Schülz and what he considered the conclusive evidence of P[46], Manson proposed that Rom. 1.1–15.13 was 'a record made by Paul and his clerical helpers of a real discussion',[4] the substance of which (comprising issues that arose in Galatia and Macedonia concerning relations between the law and the gospel and between Judaism and Christianity) stemmed from an earlier time, and did not involve Rome. Though 1.1–15.13 did not involve Rome, it was sent to Rome, along with a statement of Paul's future plans, so making up what we now have as Rom. 1.1–15.33. Rom. 1.1–16.23, however, was sent to Ephesus. Paul evidently wanted the church both at Rome and in Asia to benefit from hearing his 'manifesto'.[5] And so, Paul's original purpose was to write a letter that would have significance for the church as a whole.[6]

(c) *Written in view of a trip to Jerusalem.* Another version of the 'theological purpose' theory is that Romans originated in connection with Paul's impending trip to Jerusalem: that Paul sought in Romans to sum up past controversies and conclusions in preparation for his Jerusalem trip where he would present the Gentile offering. G. Bornkamm, for example, sees Romans as Paul's theological reflection in the light of an anticipated debate at Jerusalem.[7] It is more than a record of past controversies, it is a polemical letter directed to the

1. *Saint Paul* (trans. I. Lockwood; New York: Carleton, 1869), p. 481.
2. *Biblical Essays* (London: Macmillan, 1893), pp. 352, 374.
3. 'To the Romans—and Others', in *The Romans Debate* (ed. K.P. Donfried; Minneapolis, MN: Augsburg, 1977), pp. 1-16.
4. 'To the Romans—and Others', p. 15.
5. 'To the Romans—and Others'.
6. Cf. R. Jewett who also suggests that Romans was a general doctrinal treatise addressed to more than one congregation, but with the intention of enlisting assistance for his western mission (*Paul's Anthropological Terms* [Leiden: Brill, 1971], p. 48).
7. 'Paul's Last Will and Testament', in *The Romans Debate*, pp. 17-31.

Jews with their distinctive understanding of salvation. 'Behind the letter to the Romans stands the history of the life, work, preachings and
struggles of Paul. . . a history of his theological thinking.'[1] So the
letter is Paul's summary statement—and, whether he knew it at the
time or not, his 'last will and testament'—in which, motivated by his
trip to the Jewish capital, Paul summarizes and develops the major
thrusts of his gospel.

Other New Testament scholars have proposed that Romans is, in
effect, Paul's 'trial run' that presents his case in anticipation of the
impending Jerusalem controversy. J. Jervell proposes that 'Paul is
writing Romans mainly for himself as practice for his defence speech
in Jerusalem'.[2] R.E. Brown and J.P. Meier nuance this approach
somewhat: Paul is writing to Christians at Rome who 'had been shaped
by the Jerusalem Christianity associated with James and Peter', and as
he 'hones what he will ultimately say to Jewish Christians of the same
persuasion in Jerusalem'.[3]

The recapitulative character of Romans has often been accentuated.
F.J.A. Hort,[4] C. Gore,[5] and W. Sanday and A.C. Headlam, for
example, regarded the letter as 'the ripened fruit of the thought and
struggles of the eventful years by which it had been preceded'.[6] Many
recent scholars, in fact, have viewed Paul as having written Romans at
a turning point in his life, when he set his face toward the threatening
trip to Jerusalem.[7] In particular, E. Fuchs maintains that the reason
Paul deals so extensively with the Jewish/Gentile question is because
'Jerusalem is the hidden address of the Epistle to the Romans'.[8]

---

1. 'Paul's Last Will and Testament', p. 29.
2. ' The Letter to Jerusalem', in *The Romans Debate*, pp. 61-74 (p. 74).
3. *Antioch and Rome: New Testament Cradles of Christianity* (New York: Paulist, 1982), pp. 110-11.
4. *Prolegomena to St Paul's Epistles,* pp. 49-50.
5. *St Paul's Epistle to the Romans* (London: Murray, 1899).
6. W. Sanday and A.C. Headlam, *The Epistle to the Romans* (New York: Scribner's, 1920), p. xlii.
7. E.g. D.W. Riddle, *Paul, Man of Conflict* (Nashville: Cokesbury, 1940), p. 1; E.J. Goodspeed, *Paul* (Nashville: Abingdon, 1947), pp. 153f.; M. Black, *Romans* (London: Marshall, Morgan & Scott, 1973), p. 20; N. Perrin, *The New Testament: An Introduction* (New York: Harcourt, Brace, Jovanovich, 1974), p. 106; U. Wilckens, 'Über Abfassungzweck und Aufbau des Römerbriefes', in *Rechtfertigung als Freiheit: Paulusstudien* (Neukirchen-Vluyn: Neukirchener, 1974), pp. 110-70, (p. 139).
8. *Hermeneutik* (Bad Cannstatt: Müllershön, 1954), p. 191.

2. Paul's Purpose is Missionary

Another proposal as to the purpose of Romans is that in this letter Paul is addressing the needs of his mission. Because Paul wants to use Rome as a base for his missionary travels westward, he needs the sympathetic support of the Roman Christians. So, in the hope of garnering a firm base of support, Paul writes to the Christians at Rome—either to introduce himself or to exonerate himself from certain false perceptions that they may have.

(a) *A letter of self-introduction.* The view that Romans is primarily a self-introduction seeking the support of believers at Rome is based on a certain reading of the letter 'frame', especially 1.8-17 and 15.14-32. In these verses Paul states: (1) that he has repeatedly been prevented from fulfilling his heartfelt desire of coming to Rome, where he expects to encourage and to be encouraged in the faith, and to preach the gospel; (2) that his intent is to come as soon as he has delivered the collection to Jerusalem; and (3) that he looks forward to seeing the Roman Christians as he goes on his way to Spain. In preparation for his visit, Paul writes this letter of self-introduction, with the hope that it will till the ground for a fruitful response on the part of his addressees to his Spanish mission.

R.A. Lipsius[1] and B. Weiss[2] were early representatives of this view. Recently D.E. Aune has written: 'Paul's main purpose in writing Romans was to present the gospel he proclaimed (Rom. 1.15) as a means of introducing himself and his mission to the Roman Christians because he intended to pay them a visit (1.10-15; 15.22-29), and use Rome as a staging area for a mission to Spain (15.24)'.[3]

---

1. *Briefe an die Galater, Römer, Philipper* (Freiburg: Mohr, 1891), p. 75.
2. *A Commentary on the New Testament* III (trans. G.H. Schodde and E. Wilson; New York: Funk & Wagnalls, 1906), pp. 1-2.
3. *The New Testament in Its Literary Environment* (Philadelphia: Westminster, 1987), p. 219. See also A. Wikenhauser, *New Testament Introduction* (Freiburg: Herder, 1958), p. 407; P. Feine and J. Behm, *Introduction to the New Testament* (14th rev. edn by W.G. Kümmel, trans. A.J. Mattill, Jr; Nashville: Abingdon, 1966), p. 221; O. Cullmann, *The New Testament: An Introduction for the General Reader* (trans. J. Bowden; Philadelphia: Westminster, 1966), p. 701; A.F.J. Klijn, *An Introduction to the New Testament* (Leiden: Brill, 1967), p. 77; K.H. Schelke, *An Introduction to the New Testament* (Cork: Mercier, 1969), p. 141; B.N. Kaye, ' "To the Romans and Others" Revisited', *NovT* 18 (1976), pp. 37-77, (pp. 37 and 42); J.A.T. Robinson, *Wrestling with Romans* (London: SCM, 1979), p. 8; S.K. Williams, 'The "Righteousness of God" in Romans', *JBL* 99 (1980), pp. 241-90,

R. Jewett,[1] building on the work of C.J. Bjerkelund[2] and A. Suhl,[3] and taking into account W. Wuellner's 'epideictic theory',[4] argues that Romans belongs to the epistolary type of 'ambassadorial letter'.[5] The point of such a letter is to affirm values held by the audience, thereby nurturing community with its readers so as to increase and encourage co-operation. The purpose of Romans, therefore, as Jewett sees it, is 'to advocate in behalf of the "power of God" a co-operative mission to evangelize Spain'.[6] Jewett's suggestion attempts to reconcile letter genre with content.[7]

The 'introduction theory' is continued, though with a slightly different nuance, among those who stress that Paul's purpose in writing was to prepare for his coming by instructing his readers in the essentials of his gospel. S.K. Stowers's conclusion is that Romans is Paul's self-introduction as 'teacher and preacher of the gospel'.[8] His purpose was to instruct believers at Rome in the major tenets of the Pauline gospel,

---

(p. 245); C.E.B. Cranfield, *Romans: A Shorter Commentary* (Grand Rapids: Eerdmans, 1985), p. xiii. E. Käsemann calls Romans Paul's 'theological report' intended to introduce himself and win his readers over to his gospel so that they will help him both with his westward mission and act as 'rearguard protection in relation to Jerusalem' (*Commentary on Romans* [trans. G.W. Bromiley; Grand Rapids: Eerdmans, 1980], p. 404).

1. 'Romans as an Ambassadorial Letter', *Int* 36 (1982), pp. 5-20, (p. 19).

2. *Parakalo: Form, Funktion und Sinn der parakalo-Sätze in den paulinischen Briefen* (Oslo: Universitetsforlaget, 1967). Bjerkelund determined that the function of the 'parakalo' clause in a Pauline letter was diplomatic, suggesting that, though Paul considered himself to have official status to command, he used a form of diplomatic exhortation.

3. 'Der konkrete Anlass des Römerbriefes', *Kairos* 13 (1971), pp. 119-50. Suhl concurred with Bjerkelund's interpretation of the function of the 'parakalo' clause in Paul.

4. 'Paul's Rhetoric of Argumentation in Romans: An Alternative to the Donfried–Karris Debate over Romans', in *The Romans Debate*, pp. 152-74 (p. 166). Wuellner claimed that Romans falls within the purview of 'epideictic oratory'. The intent of this form of oratory is 'to strengthen the disposition toward action by increasing adherence to the values it lauds' (quoting from Perelman and Olbrechts-Tyteca, *The New Rhetoric* [Notre Dame, IN: University of Notre Dame Press, 1969], p. 51).

5. 'Ambassadorial Letter', p. 16.

6. 'Ambassadorial Letter', p. 9.

7. Cf. on the other hand M. Dibelius who argues that Romans is Paul's introduction and announcement but says it is 'almost like a dissertation' (*A Fresh Approach to the New Testament and Early Christian Literature* [London: Nicholson and Watson, 1936], p. 161).

8. *The Diatribe and Paul's Letter to the Romans* (Chico, CA; Scholars Press, 1981), p. 182.

and in so doing to encourage openness to his gospel for 'his intended tenure with them as the teacher of the Gentiles'.[1] This view also depicts Paul as wanting believers at Rome to 'thoroughly understand his position before they pledge their support'.[2]

(b) *A letter of self-defence.* Some scholars have proposed that Paul's intended readers were people whom he regarded as being either hostile, or potentially hostile, towards himself. The Roman Christians had heard (or possibly would soon hear) negative things about Paul's antinomian gospel. So Romans is an 'apologia' for Paul's preaching and missionary practices.[3]

Erasmus suggested that in Romans, Paul is laying out the substance of his case before the Christians at Rome in advance of the critical judgments that he expects will reach them from Galatia and Corinth.[4] M. Goguel proposed that Romans is a 'balance-sheet' of Paul's ideas

1. *The Diatribe and Paul's Letter to the Romans*, p. 182.
2. R. St John Parry, *The Epistle of Paul the Apostle to the Romans* (Cambridge: Cambridge University Press, 1921), p. xiii. So also T. Zahn, *Introduction to the New Testament* (trans. J.M. Trout *et al.*; Edinburgh: T. & T. Clark, 1909), I, p. 436; H. Lietzmann, *Einführung in die Textgeschichte der Paulusbriefe: An die Römer* (Tübingen: Mohr, 1919), p. 28; C.R. Erdman, *The Epistle of Paul to the Romans* (Philadelphia: Westminster, 1925), p. 8; C.H. Dodd, *The Epistle of Paul to the Romans* (London: Hodder & Stoughton, 1932), p. xxv; E.F. Scott, *The Literature of the New Testament* (New York: Columbia University Press, 1932), p. 155; K.E. Kirk, *The Epistle to the Romans* (Oxford: Clarendon, 1937), p. 25; R.M. Hawkins, 'Romans: A Reinterpretation', *JBL* 60 (1941), pp. 129-50 (p. 132); C.B. Williams, *A Commentary on the Pauline Epistles* (Chicago: Moody, 1953), pp. 225f.; V. Taylor, *The Epistle to the Romans* (London: Epworth, 1955), p. 11; F.W. Beare, *St Paul and His Letters* (London: Black, 1962), p. 97; Selby, *Toward the Understanding of St Paul*, p. 289; J.P. Pritchard, *A Literary Approach to the New Testament* (Norman, OK: University of Oklahoma Press, 1972), p. 253; F.F. Bruce, *Paul: Apostle of the Heart Set Free* (Grand Rapids: Eerdmans, 1977), p. 12; R. Aus, 'Paul's Travel Plans to Spain and the "Full Number of the Gentiles" of Rom. xi 25', *NovT* 21 (1979), pp. 232-61. N.A. Dahl thinks that Paul's focus is on the reception of the collection in Jerusalem and that 'the Christians in Rome needed to know what Paul taught and how he understood his own mission if they were going to ally themselves with other Pauline churches and intercede for a favorable reception of the collection' ('The Missionary Theology in the Epistle to the Romans', in *Studies in Paul* [Minneapolis, MN: Augsburg, 1977], pp. 70-87 [p. 77]).
3. So J.W. Drane, 'Why Did Paul Write Romans?' in *Pauline Studies: Essays Presented to F.F. Bruce on his 70th Birthday* (ed. D.A. Hagner and M.J. Harris; Exeter: Paternoster, 1980), pp. 208-27 (pp. 223-24).
4. See F. Godet, *Commentary on St Paul's Epistle to the Romans* (trans. A. Cusin; New York: Funk & Wagnall's, 1883), p. 53.

written in the interest of curtailing the influence of his opponents' views, which views were beginning to reach Rome.[1] And W.L. Knox wrote that Paul 'expects his readers to feel some doubt as to his action in abandoning the Law'.[2]

3. *Paul's Purpose is Pastoral*

J.C. Beker serves as something of a bridge to the pastoral purpose view of Romans, for he argues that the occasion of Romans is 'both in Paul's concrete situation and in that of the Roman church'.[3] Thus Paul writes both to introduce himself so as to secure a new mission base and to deal with issues in the Roman church. In this view it is the paraenesis (chs. 14–15) that reflects the actual problems at Rome, revolving, as it does, around the Jewish/Gentile question. The rest of the letter focuses on helping the Romans be unified and understand the priority of Israel in the gospel, so that the Roman church may be an adequate mission base for Paul's Spanish mission.[4] This conception of a 'dual occasion' for Romans is shared by G.P. Wiles,[5] C.J. Roetzel,[6] R.P. Martin[7] and J.A. Ziesler.[8]

A.J.M. Wedderburn also suggests that there is no single reason for Paul's writing of Romans. Paul writes because of a combination of various needs that he perceived in the Roman church and as a result of his own particular circumstances. In Romans he addresses himself to two different Christian groups who were divided over the law. Paul

1. *The Birth of Christianity* (trans. H.C. Snape; London: Allen & Unwin, 1953), pp. 316-17.
2. *St Paul and the Church of Jerusalem* (Cambridge: Cambridge University Press, 1925), p. 260 n. 26. See also J. Knox, 'Romans. Introduction', *IB* (New York: Abingdon, 1954) IX, pp. 355-72 (pp. 361-63); A.M. Hunter, *The Epistle to the Romans* (London: SCM, 1955), pp. 14f.; E. Best, *The Letter of Paul to the Romans* (Cambridge: Cambridge University Press, 1967), p. 6; J. McKenzie, *Light on the Epistle* (Chicago: Thomas More, 1975), p. 87.
3. *Paul the Apostle*, p. 71.
4. See also Beker's 'Paul's Theology: Consistent or Inconsistent?', *NTS* 34 (1988), pp. 364-77 (pp. 371-77).
5. *Paul's Intercessory Prayers* (Cambridge: Cambridge University Press, 1973), pp. 74-76.
6. *The Letters of Paul: Conversations in Context* (Atlanta: John Knox, 1975), p. 59.
7. *Reconciliation: A Study of Paul's Theology* (London: Marshall, Morgan & Scott, 1981), pp. 127-28.
8. *Paul's Letter to the Romans* (London: SCM, and Philadelphia: Trinity Press International, 1989), pp. 15f.

wanted to communicate to the group who adhered to the Jewish law that the law had now been fulfilled in Christ, yet nevertheless God acts consistently. The gospel, in fact, reveals God's eternal righteousness. On the other hand, Paul wanted to encourage the law-free group to appreciate their Jewishness and to remember that the gospel demands righteousness. Paul's own needs were for the support of the Roman church, both for his journey to Jerusalem and for his future visit to them. He wrote in order to answer criticism of his gospel and ministry, which criticism might prevent the Roman Christians from fully endorsing his taking the collection to Jerusalem.[1]

Others, however, propose that Paul's aim in Romans is entirely pastoral. Advocates of this view delineate the problems to which Paul addresses himself as either errors of doctrine or errors in behaviour.

(a) *A letter addressing errors of doctrine.* The earliest expression of the view that Romans is a pastoral letter addressing errors of doctrine is found in the Marcionite Prologue, which says that in Romans, Paul 'recalls them to the true evangelical faith' since the Roman Christians had been deceived by false prophets who had led them 'astray to the Law and the Prophets'.[2] And this view was prominent among the Fathers, perhaps even dominant in the Middle Ages.[3] Augustine, for example, argued that Romans was occasioned by a dispute among Jewish and Gentile Christians at Rome concerning 'whether the Gospel. . . comes to the Jews alone because of their merits through the work of the Law, or whether the justification of faith which is in Christ Jesus comes to all nations without any preceding merits for works'.[4]

In more recent times, H. Preisker has proposed that Paul speaks in Romans to a situation where there was discord between Jewish and Gentile Christians: disagreements over the merits of their different

1. *The Reasons for Romans* (Edinburgh: T. & T. Clark, 1988).
2. Quoted from W.G. Kümmel, *The New Testament: The History of the Investigation of its Problems* (trans. S.M. Gilmour and H.C. Kee; London: SCM, 1973), p. 14. See also J. Finegan, 'The Original Form of the Pauline Collection', *HTR* 49 (1956), pp. 85-103 (p. 89).
3. See J. MacRory, who maintains that this patristic view passed into the *Glossa Ordinaria* and thereby became the generally accepted view of the Middle Ages ('The Occasion and Object of the Epistle to the Romans', *ITQ* 9 [1914], pp. 21-32).
4. *Augustine on Romans: Propositions From the Epistle to the Romans, Unfinished Commentary on the Epistle to the Romans* (trans. P.F. Landes; Chico, CA: Scholars Press, 1982), p. 53.

24   *The Purpose of Romans*

backgrounds, the proper use of the Old Testament, eschatology, and obedience to the state.[1] J. Marcus suggests a similar occasion for this letter: that Paul writes because of conflicts among the Jewish and Gentile Roman Christians over questions of the law.[2] Others have thought that Paul's purpose was to unmask a heretical interpretation of the gospel held in Rome—viz., a distorted understanding of the place of the law that came about because of Gentile Christians having been evangelized by Jewish Christians—and that Paul, aware of the problem, writes in order to correct this obliquity.[3]

F.C. Baur proposed that Paul wrote to Jewish Christians at Rome, who, having a dualistic Ebionite view of the world, stood in need of Paul's gospel.[4] So Paul sends his letter to these Christians because they need to be brought to the 'true Gospel faith'.[5] K. Lake wrote that while there probably was 'not a majority of Jewish Christians in Rome... there were Jewish Christians who preached strongly the position of the Jerusalem school of thought, and did not accept the teaching of the liberal Antiochene movement'.[6]

F. Watson's proposal is that Paul wrote to a city in which there existed two separate congregations, one Jewish Christian and the other

1. 'Das historische Problem des Römerbriefes', *Wissenschaftliche Zeitschrift der Friedrich-Schiller-Universität Jena* 2 (1952–53), pp. 25-30.
2. 'The Circumcision and the Uncircumcision in Rome', *NTS* 35 (1989), pp. 67-81.
3. So W.J. Coneybeare and J.W. Howson, *The Life and Epistle of St Paul* (London: Longmans, Green, 1873), p. 498; A. Jülicher, *An Introduction to the New Testament* (trans. J.P. Ward; London: Smith, Elder, 1904), p. 112; W. Lütgert, *Der Römerbrief als historisches Problem* (Gütersloh: Bertelsmann, 1913); G. Harder, 'Der konkrete Anlass des Römerbriefes', *ThV* 6 (1954), pp. 13-24; W.G. Kümmel, *Introduction to the New Testament* (rev., ed. and trans. H.C. Kee; Nashville: Abingdon, 1975), pp. 312-14.
4. *Paul,* I, p. 345.
5. *Paul,* I, p. 352.
6. *The Earlier Epistles of St Paul* (London: Rivingtons, 1930), p. 412. D. Patte thinks Paul's goal in Romans is to convince the Jewish Christians of the validity of the gospel that gives equal status to the Gentile Christians (*Paul's Faith and the Power of the Gospel* [Philadelphia: Fortress, 1983], pp. 246-50). L. Gaston, on the other hand, after accepting M. Barth's thesis that the term 'works of law' indicates 'God-fearing' Gentiles (*Ephesians* [Garden City: Doubleday, 1974], pp. 244-48), portrays Paul's intended readers as Gentiles who had adopted certain Jewish practices as a means of self-justification. 'Recognition of such legalistic Gentile Judaizers is an important part of the background for understanding Paul's polemic' (*Paul and the Torah* [Vancouver: University of British Columbia Press, 1987], p. 25).

Pauline Christian. Paul's purpose in writing was 'to convert the Jewish Christian congregation in Rome to Paulinism'.[1]

(b) *A letter addressing errors of behaviour.* A second type of 'pastoral purpose' theory represents Paul as focusing on errors of behaviour in the Roman church. P.S. Minear thinks that the paraenetic chapters of Romans reveal several problems in the Roman congregation—in particular, five warring groups at Rome at the time of Paul's writing: (1) those 'weak in faith', who condemned the 'strong in faith'; (2) those 'strong in faith' who scorned the 'weak in faith'; (3) the doubters; (4) the weak in faith who did not condemn the strong; and (5) the strong in faith who did not condemn the weak.[2] The purpose of the letter, therefore, is to bring about the 'obedience of faith' (1.5 and 16.25f.)— to achieve harmony among these factions. So as Minear views matters: 'The need in the Roman church for a stronger, more obedient faith' is the reason Paul writes.[3]

Chrysostom anticipated this interpretation. For, commenting on the fact that Romans appears different from Paul's other letters, Chrysostom said that even so its purpose is 'to bring the men to good order'.[4] Likewise, W. Marxsen,[5] H.-W. Bartsch,[6] W.S. Campbell[7] and W. Wiefel[8] take a comparable stance. For Marxsen, Paul's primary goal is peace in the Christian community at Rome.[9] The paraenetic chapters provide the clue to the problems by their reference to the 'strong' and the 'weak'.[10] Bartsch interprets the absence of the designation 'church' in the letter's address to mean that there was division among believers

1. *Paul, Judaism and the Gentiles. A Sociological Approach* (Cambridge: Cambridge University Press, 1986), p. 100.
2. *The Obedience of Faith* (London: SCM, 1971), pp. 8-17.
3. *The Obedience of Faith*, p. 1.
4. *The Homilies of St John Chrysostom on the Epistle of St Paul the Apostle to the Romans* (trans. J.B. Morris; Oxford: Parker, 1841), p. 4.
5. *Introduction to the New Testament* (trans. G. Buswell; Philadelphia: Fortress, 1968).
6. 'The Historical Situation of Romans', *Encounter* 33 (1972), pp. 329-39.
7. 'Why Did Paul Write Romans?', *ExpT* 85 (1974), pp. 264-69.
8. 'The Jewish Community in Ancient Rome and the Origins of Roman Christianity', in *The Romans Debate*, pp. 100-19.
9. *Introduction*, p. 62. Cf. W.B. Russell who thinks that Paul's main purpose is Gentile/Jewish unity among the Christians at Rome ('An Alternative Suggestion for the Purpose of Romans', *BS* 145 [1988], pp. 174-84).
10. *Introduction*, pp. 95-97.

at Rome, caused by anti-semitism.[1] Campbell sees the letter as directed to a Gentile Christian majority in Rome which is resisting fellowship with Jewish Christians.[2] And Wiefel finds historical evidence to support his claim that Romans was written to combat anti-semitism among Gentile Christians towards their Jewish Christian brothers and sisters.[3]

(c) *A letter asserting apostolic authority.* Another version of the 'pastoral purpose' theory has it that Paul's purpose was to bring the Roman church under his apostleship. A. Fridrichsen contends that Paul's chief motive in Romans is to assert his apostolic authority in the Roman Church.[4] G. Klein regards the 'non-interference clause' in 15.20 as critical and argues that Paul, in order to write this letter, must consider the Roman Christian community lacking in the 'fundamental kerygma', since he has stated that his policy is to preach only where Christ has not been named.[5]

(d) *Excursus.* W. Schmithals maintained that Romans is a composite of two letters to Rome, to which have been added fragments of both Pauline and non-Pauline origin.[6] Thus there are two different purposes and two different occasions evident in Romans as it now stands. Letter A (1.1–4.25; 5.12–11.36; 15.8-13) was motivated by a desire to bring Gentile Christians, who had a decided leaning towards Judaism, into a Pauline understanding of the gospel. Letter B (12.1-21; 13.8-10; 14.1–15.4a, 7, 5f., 14-32; 15.21-3; 15.33) was written later, in the

1. 'The Historical Situation of Romans', pp. 330-31. Cf. J. Dupont, 'Appel aux faibles et aux forts dans la communauté romaine (Rom. 14.1–15.13)', *Studiorum Paulinorum Congressus Internationalis Catholicus 1961* (AnBib 17–18, 1963), pp. 1, 357-66.
2. 'Why Did Paul Write Romans?', pp. 268f.
3. 'The Jewish Community in Ancient Rome and the Origins of Roman Christianity', p. 119.
4. 'The Apostle and His Message', *Uppsala Universitets Årsskrift* 3 (1947), pp. 1-23 (p. 7). Cf. Godet, *Commentary on St Paul's Epistle to the Romans*, pp. 56-57.
5. 'Paul's Purpose in Writing the Epistle to the Romans', in *The Romans Debate*, pp. 32-49, (p. 44).
6. *Der Römerbrief als historisches Problem* (Gütersloh: Mohn, 1975).

light of their acceptance of the Pauline gospel, urging them to be more tolerant of othei believers who were not so enlightened.[1]

C. *Summary*

The existence of this wide range of proposed solutions to the problem of the purpose of Romans invites us to question the type of evidence on which these proposals are based. For the obvious lack of consensus suggests that there may be a methodological problem at the root of such a profusion of differing theories.

The predominant methodology of the solutions proffered involves making a decision as to which emphasis in the content of Romans is especially significant. Some proposals are supported by reading a large part of the content of Romans in a certain way. The 'theological purpose' proposal and the hypothesis that Paul is addressing various errors of doctrine at Rome, for example, rest on a certain reading of most of chapters one to eleven. The first reads these chapters as Paul's summary statement of his theological thought. The other finds in these same chapters Paul's direct address concerning several doctrinal matters about which he considers his readers to be misguided.

Other proposals rest on a certain reading of a relatively small portion of the content of Romans. For example, the hypothesis that Paul is introducing himself in order to establish a missionary support base at Rome is based on evidence from a few verses near the end of the letter—though, of course, it then finds supporting evidence in much of the letter-body to strengthen its case. The same part of the content of Romans also provides the foundation for the theory that Romans is in reality Paul's letter to Jerusalem.

Other theories, for example those of J.C. Beker and A.J.M. Wedderburn, incorporate more than one emphasis based on various parts of the letter's content.

So we are brought face to face with the need for standard controls in reading the content. In the majority of cases a proposal's worth may be measured only by weighing the clarity of the argument in favour of the importance of that particular emphasis from the letter's content

---

1. See also J. Kinoshita, who determined that there was an original letter (chs 1; 2.6-16; 3.21-26; 5.1-11; 8; 12; 13; 15.14-33) and that the rest is secondary. Kinoshita claims that there are two different emphases because there are two different audiences. The original letter was directed to Gentiles and the secondary additions to Jews ('Romans—Two Writings Combined', *NovT* 7 [1964], pp. 258-77).

upon which it rests. There is a need for a more disciplined approach to this important problem beyond that of merely arguing the relative merits of the contents of one passage over that of another, and so it is to the methodological question that I shall turn in my next chapter.

Chapter 2

COMPARATIVE LETTER STRUCTURE ANALYSIS AND ITS RELEVANCE
FOR THE PROBLEM OF THE PURPOSE OF ROMANS

A. *Justification of the Methodological Approach*

The proposals outlined in Chapter 1 focus almost exclusively on the
content of Romans in constructing a hypothesis regarding its purpose.
The assumption of these hypotheses is that Paul's purpose may be most
clearly seen through a convergence of clues from Romans' content.
Content alone, however, is not sufficient to describe authorial intention. Clues from the formal features of a text may, in fact, offer more
evidence of an author's purpose. For while the content may be what is
uppermost in the mind as a writer both contemplates writing and proceeds to write, functional intention determines the way that content is
communicated.[1] That is, the function of the communication, whether it
be to exhort, to explain, to encourage, to introduce, to admonish, or
whatever, determines the form in which the content is set.

For instance, in both Gal. 1.4 and Phil. 2.6-11 Paul speaks of
Christ's giving himself for the salvation of the world. While the content of both passages is similar, their form is very different as a result
of the particular function of each. The Galatian passage functions as
part of the letter's opening formula and is a noticeable addition to
Paul's normally straightforward wish for grace and peace. By under-
lining the work of Christ at this point Paul highlights one of the central themes of his letter's body. The brief and pointed presentation of
this content results, then, from the function of the passage—viz., to
serve as part of the overture for the letter.

1. Cf. R.W. Funk, who points to the fundamental relationship between authorial
intention and the text's formal characteristics when he writes about 'the marriage to
intention on the part of words, syntax, style and form' ('Saying and Seeing: Phenomenology of Language and the New Testament', *JBR* 34 [1966], pp. 197-213
[p. 202]).

The Philippian passage, on the other hand, occurs within the letter's body and serves to present Christ as the example the Philippians should follow in their personal lives. Its form is that of a hymn or carefully crafted poem concerning Christ's work, which is most likely pre-Pauline[1] being incorporated and edited by Paul as he wrote the letter. The hymnic form suggests that the passage's function is to exhort imitation of the humility of Christ and encourage meditation on Christ's example.

An author's purpose is, of course, wedded to the function the communication is meant to perform, and since function is tied closely to the formal features of a text, it is from the formal features that we may find indications of a text's communicative function and thereby of the purpose of the author.

The question I am pursuing has significance for the field of historical inquiry. A hypothesis about Paul's purpose in Romans is part of understanding more fully this communication's original historical circumstances.[2] On the other hand, answering my question is not a necessity for an adequate present-day encounter with the text of Romans. Any individual reader of Romans may, of course, understand it quite apart from a knowledge of the various hypotheses concerning authorial intention. Recently, in fact, several aspects of the 'intentional fallacy' have been exposed both in literary[3] and biblical studies.[4]

---

1. Originally proposed by E. Lohmeyer, *Kyrios Jesus: Eine Untersuchung zu Phil. 2, 5-11* (Heidelberg, 1928, 1961). See R.P. Martin, *Carmen Christi. Philippians ii. 5-11 in Recent Interpretation and in the Setting of Early Christian Worship* (Cambridge: Cambridge University Press, 1967) for an extensive review of the discussion. Also J.T. Sanders, *The New Testament Christological Hymns* (Cambridge: Cambridge University Press, 1971).

2. S. Brown writes: 'The historian listens in on the communication between the author and his addressee(s), in the hope of learning something about the historical circumstances in which the communication took place' (*The Origins of Christianity. A Historical Introduction to the New Testament* [Oxford: Oxford University Press, 1984], p. 29). The aspect of historical inquiry with which we are concerned is the author's intention in his communication as it may be gleaned from the functional character of that communication.

3. See e.g. W.K. Wimsatt, Jr and M.C. Beardsley, *The Verbal Icon. Studies in the Meaning of Poetry* (Lexington: University of Kentucky Press, 1954), p. 3.

4. G.B. Caird defines the 'intentional fallacy' as 'the error of supposing that a writer meant something other than he has actually written' (*The Language and Imagery of the Bible* [London: Duckworth, 1980], p. 61).

The recent shift in literary studies has been away from reading a text in order to find the meaning of the author towards an approach which considers that meaning results from the interest of the reader, regardless of authorial intention.[1] The main thrust of many studies on the nature and function of language is in the direction of how the *reader* understands certain complexes of language. It is this attitude about where meaning resides that produces a statement such as that by S. Doubrovsky who considers that a literary text 'is no more endowed with a single meaning than human nature is'.[2]

My investigation remains primarily within the realm of historical inquiry, while recognizing that it is not necessary to hold a hypothesis about Paul's purpose in Romans in order for the text of this letter to be meaningful to any particular reader. But despite that caveat we must not lose sight of the importance for a scholarly treatment of Romans of gaining as much knowledge as possible concerning Paul's purpose.

The intrinsic importance of authorial intention in gaining an understanding of a text is recognized by certain branches of linguistic scholarship. For instance, the discourse critics G. Brown and G. Yule write that one should regard the text as that thing 'in which language was used as an instrument of communication in a context by a speaker/writer to express meanings and achieve intentions'.[3] One of the most important aspects of acquiring meaning from a text, according to this field of study, is determining its 'communicative function (how to *take* the message)'.[4] Or as another discourse critic, R.E. Longacre, writes, 'the meaning of a discourse is not simply a subjec-

---

1. So S. Brown writes: 'If meaning is actually generated by the experience of reading, rather than residing "in" the text, then we must accept a Copernican revolution in our interpretive theory. For the reading experience is guided not by the "intention of the author", to which appeal is so often made, but by the interest of the reader.' ('Reader Response: Demythologizing the Text', *NTS* 34 [1988], pp. 232-37 [p. 232]).

2. *Pourquoi la nouvelle critique. Critique et objectivité* (Paris: Mercure de France, 1966), quoted from P.M. Wetherill, *The Literary Text: An Examination of Critical Methods* (Berkeley: University of California, 1974), p. 186.

3. *Discourse Analysis* (Cambridge: Cambridge University Press, 1983), p. 26.

4. *Discourse Analysis*, p. 225.

tive construct on the part of the reader but has a reality of its own in accordance with the author's intention'.[1]

The literary discipline of discourse analysis[2] has recognized that an attempt to grasp the speaker's or writer's intention is fundamental to a hearer's or reader's understanding of a communication. 'The reader (hearer), as he receives the discourse, will normally try to build a representation (his model) of the state of affairs communicated by the speaker.'[3] The reader/hearer does this by trying to determine the speaker's/writer's intended meaning.[4] Thus, discourse analysis, particularly as it relates to our investigation, 'assumes that the writers of the Biblical texts intended certain ideas to be gained from their compositions by the reading audience. It assumes further that the authors communicated their intentions successfully to their original audiences'.[5]

The particular problem of interpreting letters is the specificity of their original occasion. Full understanding of the contents of a letter is not possible for any other than the original intended readers, for only they are privy to the particular referent features of the conversation.[6] Yet the very specificity of the original occasion of letters calls for an attempt at reconstructing a letter's particular function so that its meaning may be more clearly understood. So scholarly interpretation of the meaning of a letter must include a proposal as to the author's intended purpose in writing to his readers.

Discourse analysis has recognized that communication is organized at a level more fundamental than grammar. This level it calls

1. 'Interpreting Biblical Stories' in *Discourse and Literature* (ed. T.A. van Dijk; Amsterdam: Benjamins, 1985), pp. 169-86 (p. 169).

2. The term 'discourse analysis' was first used by Z. Harris in a series of papers published in 1952 entitled 'Discourse analysis', *Language* 28/1 (1952), pp. 1-30, and 'Discourse analysis: a sample text' *Language* 28/4 (1952), pp. 474-94.

3. Brown and Yule, *Discourse Analysis*, p. 206.

4. Brown and Yule, *Discourse Analysis*, p. 225.

5. R.D. Bergen, 'Text as a Guide to Authorial Intention: An Introduction to Discourse Criticism', *JETS* 30 (1987), pp. 327-36 (p. 334).

6. Cf. P. Violi, who writes concerning letters that 'a complete understanding. . . is not open to the generic reader. On the contrary, only the specific individual to whom the letter is addressed is capable of 'co-operation' with the text, because only he possesses the necessary encyclopaedia to decipher the inferences it contains. . . [so that] the reader without the background knowledge required by the text is not able to complete the necessary inferences for a full comprehension of it' ('Letters', in *Discourse and Literature*, pp. 158-59).

'discourse'. Discourse is a functional level that organizes the grammatical units. The organization of functional units is what effects the intended communication process. For instance, the following is grammatically correct, but does not communicate coherent meaning:

A: What is your name?
B: Well, let's say you might have thought you hid something from me before but you haven't got it any more.
A: I'm going to call you Dean.
A: I feel hot today.
B: No.[1]

This has led to a recognition that the unit of language that provides the communicative function is not the clause or sentence alone, but a more basic unit of discourse, often called a 'functional unit'.[2] At the first level the determination of meaning involves both deciding on 'the meanings of words and structure of a sentence and build[ing] up a composite meaning for the sentence. . . [and] predicting on the basis of the context plus the composite meaning of the sentences already processed, what the next sentence is likely to mean'.[3] But the more basic functional units are what organize and convey meaning. These more basic units are realized in formal features of the text.[4]

Discourse analysis, then, recognizes that the process of communication occurs mostly at the 'subliminal level'.[5] That is, especially in written communication, subliminal factors are what carry much of the communicative weight. These subliminal factors are really formal features such as the size of the information units, the order of the pre-

1. W. Labov, 'The Study of Language in its Social Context', in *Studium Generale* 23 (1970), pp. 30-87, quoted from M. Coulthard, *An Introduction to Discourse Analysis* (London: Longman, 1977), p. 7.
2. Coulthard, *Introduction to Discourse Analysis*, p. 64.
3. Brown and Yule, *Discourse Analysis*, p. 234. Cf. C. Cherry, who writes: 'The syntactical constraints of a language ensure that, *to some extent*, we know already what will be said, or written, in a given situation or at a certain point in a speech or text'. (*On Human Communication. A Review, A Survey, and A Criticism* [Cambridge, MA: M.I.T. Press, 1966], pp. 117-18).
4. Coulthard writes that what discourse analysis seeks to show is 'how the functional categories are *realised* by formal items' (*Introduction to Discourse Analysis*, p. 8).
5. Bergen, 'Text as a Guide to Authorial Intention', p. 324.

sentation of the information, and the choice and use of particular parts of speech.[1]

Formal features, discourse analysts propose, provide the information which allows us to make judgments about authorial intention. Or as R.D. Bergen states it: 'Subliminal factors in human communication contain data essential for making judgments about authorial intention. Like the proverbial underside of the iceberg, most of the surface structural data in a text that is crucial in making judgments about an author's intentions is found in the portions of the communication process that are normally invisible to the reader . . . Subliminal factors must be studied to gain a more adequate grasp of authorial intention'.[2]

In agreement with discourse analysis, the conviction that formal features of a text can indicate its communicative function is what underlies the work of this thesis. So, through comparative analyses of certain formal features of Paul's letter to the Romans, we will seek to make a proposal about the intention of this letter—that is, about Romans' communicative function.

I shall generally use the word 'function' rather than 'purpose' to describe the problem with which I am concerned. Purpose denotes what Paul was thinking about and concerned with as he wrote. Function denotes the overriding intention of the communication without suggesting that one is peeking into Paul's mind. The concept of purpose stands further back from the text than the concept of function, which is that least visible aspect of the writer's relationship with his writing and at the same time the most determinative aspect of that relationship.

Another conviction that underlies this investigation is that a text is written in order to convey certain attitudes and information.[3] So in order to understand as fully as possible what is written it is important to gain an adequate understanding of what the author meant to convey.

While during this investigation the terms and categories of discourse analysis will not be used, my analysis will share its basic premises with

1. Bergen, 'Text as a Guide to Authorial Intention', p. 329.
2. Bergen, 'Text as a Guide to Authorial Intention', p. 329.
3. Cf. Jin Soon Cha, who writes that intention underlies texts and that intention 'refers to the communicative purpose of a text. That is, texts are constructed in order to explain something, in order to blame, praise, criticize, accuse, persuade, encourage, discourse or threaten someone or in order to do something else' (*Linguistic Cohesion in Texts: Theory and Description* [Seoul, Korea: Daehan Textbook, 1985], p. 134).

this field of study: that determination of the function of a communication is (1) based on an analysis of the communication's formal features, and (2) important for understanding the meaning of a communication.

It is my conviction that by a comparative investigation of certain formal features of the letters of Paul, the function of any particular Pauline letter can be distinguished. The method of noting variations and agreements between various writings is standard practice in New Testament research. Both form criticism and redaction criticism use this method as a fundamental procedure to formulate hypotheses about the occasion in which a pericope or an entire text originated, as well as to suggest a purpose for the author's writing. The chief difference between the method of the present investigation and that of form or redaction criticism is that the latter concentrate primarily on the content of comparable units while our study will focus chiefly on comparable formal features.[1]

Scholars involved in epistolary analysis recognize the importance of variation in the formal features of the text for hypotheses about function. J.L. White, for example, writes, 'the particular form of an individual phrase, or a certain combination of epistolary conventions, frequently signals the basic intention or occasion of the letter'.[2] P. Schubert has led the way in a comparative study of formal units in

1. Cf. T.Y. Mullins: 'The study of forms in the NT has proceeded in two different directions. On the one hand there has been the work of Form-Criticism, in the Gospels especially, in which the content of the 'form' has played a most important part and the structure has often appeared to be subordinated. On the other hand there has been the work of Literary Criticism: its approach to form marked by a tendency to let structure characterize a 'form' and to let the content contribute only functional elements' ('Petition as a Literary Form', *NovT* 5 [1962], pp. 46-54 [p. 46]). This latter approach is articulated by P. Schubert, who describes his methodological approach as one of 'observing homogeneous sections, determining their extent, discovering the significance of identical basic structure and function and accounting adequately for agreements as well as for individual variations' (*Form and Function of the Pauline Thanksgivings* [Berlin: Töpelmann, 1939], pp. 38-39).

2. *Light from Ancient Letters* (Philadelphia: Fortress, 1986), p. 19. For an example of this approach see S.N. Olson, who sets forth a proposal about Paul's purpose in 2 Corinthians (2 Corinthians is Paul's appeal for trust and functions with a view to restoring mutual confidence) on the basis of a comparative study of the formal features of Paul's epistolary 'confidence expressions' ('Confidence Expressions in Paul: Epistolary Conventions and the Purpose of 2 Corinthians' [Yale: PhD dissertation, 1976]).

Paul's letters.[1] And those following him have shared his conviction
about the significance of a comparative study of Pauline epistolary
forms for an understanding of the original purpose of a letter. As H.
Gamble says: 'The phenomenon of variations within a consistent pattern demonstrates the interaction of letter-styles and letter-situation'.[2]

Epistolary studies to date, however, have tended to analyse only one
or another letter section in isolation from others, and so have
restricted their scope. The proposals of H. Gamble and R.W. Funk
concerning Romans' function, for example, may differ so greatly
from each other largely because of each's restricted focus.[3] Study of
one letter section alone cannot provide adequate information for such
proposals.

The present investigation is concerned with the function of Romans.
So its comparative analysis will focus on the formal epistolary features
of Romans most directly indicative of its function.

B. *Previous Letter Structure Studies*

The establishment of the form of the Pauline letter began when Adolf
Deissmann compared Paul's letters with Greek common letters in the
then newly discovered papyri. Deissmann, in fact, as John White notes,
was the one who 'initiated a study of Paul's letters *qua* letters'.[4]
Deissmann's conclusion was that Paul's letters were not literary in
form but rather were written haphazardly under the stress of his great
responsibilities.[5] He considered that 'St Paul was not a writer of epis-

---

1. *Thanksgivings.*
2. *The Textual History of the Letter to the Romans* (Grand Rapids: Eerdmans,
1977), p. 83. Cf. C.J. Roetzel, who writes: 'It is the alterations he made that tell us
most about Paul's self-understanding, his intentions and his theology' (*The Letters of
Paul*, p. 17).
3. Gamble works with the Pauline conclusions and his investigation leads him to
posit that this is a 'letter sent exclusively, so far as we can tell, to the Roman church'
(*Textual History*, p. 136). Funk's study of the Pauline apostolic parousias produces
what he considers to be substantial evidence that Rom. 1.1–15.13 was a general letter
which could be 'particularized and dispatched, as the occasion demanded, to other
well-known churches which he had not founded or visited' ('The Apostolic
"Parousia", p. 268).
4. 'Saint Paul and the Apostolic Letter Tradition', *CBQ* 45 (1983), pp. 433-44
(p. 435).
5. *Light from the Ancient East*, pp. 240f.

tles but of letters; he was not a literary man. . . He wrote with absolute abandon'.[1] So, according to Deissmann, the Pauline exegete must do justice 'to the ebb and flow of the writer's temporary moods. The single confessions in the letters of a nature so impulsive as St Paul's were dashed down under the influence of a hundred various impressions, and were never calculated for systematic presentation'.[2] Such a conclusion, of course, retarded research into the formal features of Paul's letters. But Deissmann's basic insight that Paul was a writer of 'real letters'[3] and not of literary epistles served to stimulate comparative studies with other ancient non-literary letters that ultimately resulted in the recognition that, indeed, Paul's letters exhibited a formal structure.

In 1923 F.X.J. Exler produced a dissertation that clarified the basic parts of a Hellenistic letters: opening, body, and closing.[4] Exler focused primarily on the opening and closing where typical letter formulas are more prevalent, although he also identified some conventional phrases within the body.

Following Exler, H.A. Steen worked on formulas that occur principally in the letter-body.[5] Steen refers to epistolary formulas as clichés, by which he means those recurring phrases 'qui servent à atténuer ou à renforcer les expressions impératives'.[6] These stereotyped epistolary expressions, then, serve to nuance the imperatives in the letter-body. Steen saw his work as building on but moving beyond the work of Ziemann (*De Epistularum Graecarum formulis sollemnibus quaestiones selectae* [Halle, 1910]) and Exler, both of whom concentrated heavily on the opening and closing of letters.[7] Steen showed that also in the letter-body of Greek letters there are recurring formulas.

---

1. *Light from the Ancient East*, p. 240.
2. *Light from the Ancient East*, p. 241.
3. *Light from the Ancient East*, p. 234.
4. 'The Form of the Ancient Greek Letter: A Study in Greek Epistolography' (PhD dissertation, Catholic University of America, 1923).
5. 'Les clichés épistolaires dans les Lettres sur Papyrus Grecque', *Classica et Mediaevalia* 1 (1938), pp. 119-76.
6. 'Les clichés épistolaires dans les Lettres sur Papyrus Grecque', p. 125.
7. 'Les clichés épistolaires dans les Lettres sur Papyrus Grecque', p. 123.

H. Koskenniemi,[1] also building on Exler's work, examined ancient Greek letter theory as well as the letters themselves.[2] The 'idea' that Koskenniemi judged to be fundamental for the writing of ancient letters was the desire to turn *apousia* (separation) into *parousia* (presence).[3] The function of a Hellenistic letter, then, was the maintaining of personal contact and the imparting of information. Koskenniemi followed Exler's structural outline for an ancient Hellenistic letter: salutation, body, and closing.[4] He noted, however, that there are formulas particular to each part of a letter.

Other important works that detailed aspects of the form of ancient Greek letters were those by J. Sykutris and K. Thraede. Sykutris[5] provided both a summary of ancient letter theory and a categorization of ancient letters by literary and functional types, as well as by historical period. K. Thraede[6] investigated the distinguishing features and motives of the letter in pre-Christian literature, in the New Testament, and in later letters.

W. Doty's 1966 dissertation[7] surveyed both Hellenistic letters and the letters of Paul. In treating the form of a Hellenistic letter, Doty delineated the following structure: (1) an introduction, which includes sender, addressee, greetings, and often additional greetings or wishes for good health; (2) the text or body, which is introduced by characteristic introductory formulas; and (3) a conclusion, which consists of greetings, wishes (especially for persons other than the addressee), a final greeting or prayer sentence, and sometimes dating.[8]

---

1. *Studien zur Idee und Phraseologie des griechischen Briefes.*

2. A.J. Malherbe has expanded on this work ('Ancient Epistolary Theorists', *OJRS* 5 [1977], pp. 3-77).

3. Koskenniemi: 'Die gleiche Denkvoraussetzung, das Zusammenleben als Hintergrund für den Briefwechsel, spürt man bei der Antwort der Brieftheorie darauf, was die Aufgabe des Briefes sei. Es wird nämlich als die wichtigste Aufgabe des Briefes angesehen, eine Form eben dieses Zusammenlebens während einer Zeit räumlicher Trennung darzustellen, d.h. die ἀπουσία zur παρουσία machen' (*Studien zur Idee und Phraseologie des griechischen Briefes*, p. 38).

4. *Studien zur Idee und Phraseologie des griechischen Briefes*, p. 155.

5. 'Epistolographie', *Realencyclopadie der klassischen Altertumswissenschaft* (ed. A. Pauly, G. Wissowa, *et al.*, Suppl. 5; 1931), pp. 186-220 (pp. 218-19).

6. *Gründzuge griechisch-römisher Brieftopik* (Munich: Beck, 1970).

7. ' The Epistle in Late Hellenism and Early Christianity'.

8. See also Doty, *Letters in Primitive Christianity* (Philadelphia: Fortress, 1973), pp. 13-14.

Having attained a broad consensus concerning the standard form of a Hellenistic letter, scholars then focused on the classification of letter types according to their function and formal features. J.L. White articulated the impetus for this kind of study, saying that while previous studies 'have aimed at such a broad mass of undifferentiated material rather than at the formal analysis of isolable segments within the wider category... it now seems appropriate to turn attention to specific letter types'.[1]

Chan-Hie Kim identified the Greek 'letter of recommendation' as a letter with the following shape: opening; background (which gives the reasons and circumstances involved in the recommendation); request period; appreciation; and closing.[2] White worked on the 'official petition'.[3] M.L. Stirewalt studied the form and function of 'the Greek letter-essay',[4] considering fifteen documents and classifying them under this name. Stirewalt concludes that the function of the letter-essay was primarily to include and inform a third party.[5] R. Jewett, developing some of Wuellner's observations about Romans as a type of epideictic rhetoric, suggested a letter category that he called the 'ambassadorial letter'.[6] This was followed by the study of J.L. White and K. Kensinger[7] in which a portion of the Greek papyrus letters were categorized as to their functions (e.g. letters of request, information, order or instruction).[8]

---

1. *The Form and Structure of the Official Petition* (Missoula, MT: University of Montana, 1972), pp. 1f.

2. *Form and Structure of the Familiar Greek Letter of Recommendation* (Missoula, MT: University of Montana, 1972).

3. *The Form and Structure of the Official Petition.*

4. 'The Form and Function of the Greek Letter-Essay', in *The Romans Debate*, pp. 175-206.

5. 'The Form and Function of the Greek Letter-Essay', p. 206.

6. 'Romans as an Ambassadorial Letter'.

7. 'Categories of Greek Papyrus Letters' in *SBL 1976 Seminar Papers* (ed. G. MacRae; Missoula, MT: Scholars Press, 1976), pp. 79-92. Research into the form and function of the ancient common letter has continued. See White, 'The Ancient Epistolography Group in Retrospect', *Semeia* 22 (1981), pp. 1-14.

8. Work has also been done on other nationalities of letters. J.A. Fitzmyer surveyed several Aramaic letters and discerned the following structure: (1) *praescriptio*, (2) initial greetings, (3) secondary greetings, (4) body of the letter, and (5) concluding statement ('Some Notes on Aramaic Epistolography', *JBL* 93 [1974], pp. 201-25).

Much of contemporary epistolographic research, therefore, has concentrated on comparing Hellenistic letters with those of Paul and identifying Hellenistic letter types that could profitably be used in determining Pauline letter functions and forms.

Within this branch of the research scholars such as T.Y. Mullins isolated smaller units within the Hellenistic letter and so also identified smaller units within the letters of Paul. Mullins writes:

> The way to go about analysing the NT forms is first to establish the fact that certain forms which were in common use around the first century appear in the NT. Then you analyse points of agreement and disagreement between the common use and the NT use. Where the forms have a distinctive shape in the NT, you seek to determine how the distinctive shape came about. And finally you seek the interpretive significance of the form, following the common significance as far as possible, but taking into account the meaning of changes which produced a distinctive shape in NT use.[1]

Other studies concentrated more specifically on the form of the Pauline letter itself. In particular P. Wendland, in studying the forms of early Christian literature, brought the Pauline letter form into focus.[2] On the basis of the papyri available to him, Wendland noted the chief characteristics of the beginning and ending of a Pauline letter. He was the first to notice that 'nach dem Praskripte beginnt Paulus oft mit der Danksagung gegen Gott. . . z.B. Röm. 1.8 . . . , Phil. 1.3'.[3] And he recognized that 'an den Schluss des Briefes setzt Paulus mancherlei persönliche Bemerkungen, zuletzt die Grüsse'[4] and that 'jeder paulinische Brief wird abgeschlossen durch einen kurzen Segenswunsch'.[5] In this way, Wendland identified the shape of the opening and closing of a Pauline letter: salutation (sender, addressee, greeting), followed by a thanksgiving, and at the end, a doxology, greetings and a benediction.[6]

---

1. 'Formulas in New Testament Epistles', *JBL* 91 (1972), pp. 380-90 (p. 390).
2. 'Die urchristlichen Literaturformen', in *HNT* 1.3 (Tübingen: Mohr/Siebeck, 1912), pp. 191-357.
3. 'Die urchristlichen Literaturformen', p. 341.
4. 'Die urchristlichen Literaturformen', p. 342.
5. 'Die urchristlichen Literaturformen', p. 343.
6. This basic outline was foundational for R.W. Funk; see *Language, Hermeneutic and Word of God* (New York: Harper and Row, 1966), ch. 10.

Another pioneer 'in this type of comparative study was O. Roller,[1] who made use of information about the structure of ancient Greek letters to define letter structure in Paul.[2] Two dissertations by students of Dibelius, L. Champion[3] and G.H. Boobyer,[4] also used the approach of comparison between the Hellenistic materials and Paul, and in so doing further clarified specific structural elements in Paul's letters.

C. *The Structure of a Pauline Letter*

In recent years the studies of W. Doty,[5] J.L. White,[6] and R.W. Funk[7] have largely standardized our understanding of the Pauline letter form in light of the form of the common Hellenistic letter. The various Pauline letter structure sections have been identified both (1) through a process of comparative study with the Greek non-literary papyri, and (2) by a comparison of Paul's letters with each other. In this manner P. Schubert illuminated the Pauline thanksgiving periods,[8] C.J. Bjerkelund refined our understanding of Paul's *parakalo* clause,[9] J. White shed light on the letter-body,[10] H. Gamble elucidated the form of the Pauline conclusions,[11] and T.Y. Mullins clarified a number of smaller epistolary forms.[12] The structural sections of a Pauline letter

---

1. *Das Formular der paulinischen Briefe. Ein Beitrag zur Lehre vom antiken Briefe* (Stuttgart: Kohlhammer, 1933).

2. Roller's focus, however, was not primarily on formal features, but on determining the genuineness of Paul's letters.

3. 'Benedictions and Doxologies in the Epistles of Paul' (Dissertation, Ruprecht–Karls Universität, Heidelberg, 1934).

4. '*Thanksgiving' and the 'Glory of God' in Paul* (Borna–Leipzig: Noske, 1929).

5. 'The Epistle in Late Hellenism and Early Christianity', *idem, Letters in Primitive Christianity.*

6. E.g. *The Form and Function of the Body of the Greek Letter: A Study of the Letter-Body in the Non-Literary Papyri and in Paul the Apostle* (Missoula, MT: University of Montana, 1972).

7. *Language*, ch. 10.

8. *Form and Function of the Pauline Thanksgivings.*

9. *Parakalo: Form, Funktion und Sinn der parakalo-Satze in en paulinischen Briefen.*

10. *The Form and Function of the Body of the Greek Letter.*

11. *The Textual History of the Letter to the Romans.*

12. 'Ascription as a Literary Form', *NTS* 19 (1972–1973), pp. 194-205; 'Benediction as a New Testament Form', *AUSS* 15 (1977), pp. 59-64; 'Disclosure: A Literary Form in the New Testament', *NovT* 7 (1964), pp. 44-50; 'Formulas in

can now be identified as: the opening formula, the thanksgiving period, the body, the apostolic parousia, the paraenesis and the conclusion.

1. *The Value of Various Letter Structure Sections for Determining the Function of Romans*

This comparative study will concentrate not on finding a specific Hellenistic letter category into which Romans might fit, but on comparing the formal features of Paul's letters with one another. Such an approach is based on a recognition of the Pauline letter as a literary subsection of the broader *Gattung* of the real Hellenistic letter,[1] and therefore deserving of study not only in a broader context but also with a more restricted focus. All of the structural sections of a Pauline letter are not, however, of equal value in this quest for understanding the letter's function. The opening and closing sections are where Paul (re)establishes his relationship with his readers and where the function of each of his letters is most evident.[2] It is, then, these opening and closing sections of Paul's letters that are most promising for investigation. For even though it is the letter-body that conveys the specific reasons for writing,[3] the function intended by the information in the letter-body is indicated in the opening and closing sections. The opening and closing sections of Paul's letters serve to reaffirm Paul's relationship with his readers and to direct their attention to the main themes of the letters.[4] It is, therefore, in the opening and closing of Paul's letters that their functional characteristics are most clearly seen.

New Testament Epistles'; 'Greeting as a New Testament Form', *JBL* 87 (1968), pp. 418-26; 'Petition as a Literary Form'; 'Visit Talk in the New Testament Letters', *CBQ* 35 (1973), pp. 350-58.

    1. Cf. J.L. White, who regards 'the Pauline letter as a letter type within the Hellenistic world' (*Body*, p. xi).

    2. White writes that the opening and closing of the Pauline letter 'serve the same broad epistolary function, the communication of Paul's disposition in writing' ('Saint Paul and the Apostolic Letter Tradition', p. 437).

    3. So White, 'Saint Paul and the Apostolic Letter Tradition', p. 439.

    4. Cf. G. Lyons, who notes that in a speech or written discourse (which is essentially a refinement of the pattern of introduction, body, and conclusion) the introduction and conclusion are where the speaker makes his purpose explicit (*Pauline Autobiography. Toward a New Understanding* [Atlanta: Scholars Press, 1985], pp. 26-27). This observation is also applicable to a Pauline letter. The epistolary sections that enclose the body are where Paul encapsulates the material contained in the letter-body. P. Schubert has demonstrated this specifically in relation to the Pauline

Much of the letter-body will, therefore, be eliminated from the investigation. Yet it is important to note that the Pauline letter-body is a distinct part of Pauline letter structure. Prior to Funk, it was usually taken that the body of a Pauline letter was what was left over after identifying the letter's opening and closing sections.[1] Funk, however, both identified the body as a distinct letter structure section and drew a sketch of its shape: a formal opening, various connective and transitional formulas, a concluding 'eschatological climax', and a travelogue.[2] Funk's work concentrated on the travelogue—or what he was later to term the apostolic parousia.

As D.E. Aune notes, it is the body of the letter that 'has proved most resistant to formal analysis'.[3] Yet it is generally recognized that the body of a Pauline letter consists of three parts: a body-opening, a body-middle and a body-closing.[4] The body-opening is often difficult to identify. J.T. Sanders proposed that a formula of injunction following the *eucharisto* period is what serves to open the body of the letter.[5] J.L. White, however, argues that Paul used not just one formula to introduce the body of a letter (i.e. an injunction formula), but six formulas at various times: a disclosure formula, a request formula, a joy expression, an expression of astonishment, a statement of compliance, or a formulaic use of the verb of hearing or learning.[6]

The body-middle is even more difficult to describe. White suggests three reasons why this is so: (1) we lack comparative material from the papyrus letters; (2) the body-middle is very 'fluid' and therefore often difficult to distinguish from the body-opening and body-closing; (3) it is difficult to tell whether the transitions in the body are to major

---

thanksgiving, which he showed served as introduction to the material in the body (*Thanksgivings*).

1. White comments that the study of letter openings and closings contributed 'in a back-handed way' to an understanding of the extent of the body (*Body*, p. 1).

2. *Language*, p. 270.

3. *The New Testament in Its Literary Environment*, p. 188. Cf. J.L. White: 'Regarding the body portion of Paul's letters common features are less evident than in the opening and closing' ('Ancient Greek letters', in *Greco-Roman Literature and the New Testament* [ed. D.E. Aune; Atlanta: Scholars Press, 1988], p. 99).

4. White calls these the 'substructure of the Pauline letter-body' (*Body*, p. 46).

5. 'The Transition from Opening Epistolary Thanksgiving to Body in the Letters of the Pauline Corpus', *JBL* 81 (1962), pp. 348-62 (p. 348).

6. 'Introductory Formulae in the Body of the Pauline Letter', *SBL* I (1971), pp. 91-97.

sections or simply indicate a minor development of the present subject.[1] Nevertheless, White proposes that in every Pauline letter except Philemon it is possible to distinguish two body-middle parts: the first being a well organized theological argument; the second being an 'applicatory section', where in a less tightly structured section the principles just set forth are made personal for his readers.[2]

According to White, the body-closing of a Pauline letter has four main formulas: (1) a motivation for writing formula, (2) responsibility statements, (3) a courtesy request for a letter, and (4) a notification of a coming visit.[3] While no more than three of these four formulae occur in any one Pauline letter, the body-closing consistently begins with a motivation for writing formula and ends with a reference to an anticipated visit by Paul or one of his co-workers.[4]

Funk's delineation of the unit that concerns Paul's coming visit has proven to be a significant contribution to our understanding of the letter-body closing. Funk initially termed this section a travelogue—a section largely concerned with Paul's plans for a visit to his readers, either by himself or an emissary.[5] Later he called it the 'apostolic parousia' section. This section will be dealt with in more detail later, since its function, more than that of all the other parts of the letter-body, renders it particularly useful for the present investigation.

In addition to the Pauline letter-body opening and middle, as well as parts of the letter-body closing, the paraeneses in Paul's letters will not be included in our investigation. A paraenetic section, when it occurs,[6] is better described as a type of material than as a letter structure section.[7] It was M. Dibelius, one of the earliest form critics, who, in

1. *Body*, p. 102 n. 6.
2. 'The message introduced in the body-opening. . . is developed according to its theoretical and practical aspects' (*Body*, p. 97).
3. *Body*, pp. 160-62.
4. *Body*, p. 162.
5. *Language*, p. 270; see also Funk, 'Saying and Seeing', pp. 209-12.
6. Paraenesis occurs as a section only in 1 Thessalonians, Galatians, and Romans, though Paul exhorts behaviour appropriate to the new life throughout his letters.
7. Funk, on the other hand, comments: 'paraenesis. . . is not strictly speaking a literary form, but roots in oral instruction in wisdom, the sermon, the homily, the "lecture" of the philosophical schools, the diatribe'. Nevertheless, he holds that it is a formal structural element in the Pauline letter (*Language*, p. 256).

his commentary on James,[1] first identified paraenesis as a distinctive type of material. Building on the work of P. Wendland[2] and R. Vetschara,[3] Dibelius viewed material as being paraenetic if it were in 'a text which strings together admonitions of general ethical content' and if it spoke to a specific audience in the form of commands, for:

> Paraenetic sayings ordinarily address themselves to a specific (though perhaps fictional) audience, or at least appear in the form of a command or summons. It is this factor which differentiates them from the 'gnomologium', which is merely a collection of maxims.[4]

This type of material, Dibelius asserted, was traditional, and so was shared by several Christian missionaries. In fact, Dibelius held, in his paraeneses Paul 'produces very little that is new, but rather transmits older sayings material'.[5]

W. Marxsen agrees, in the main, with Dibelius. Paul's paraenesis is substantially traditional. Its arrangement is stylistic and its content largely interchangeable.[6] C. Roetzel, on the other hand, contends that though Paul uses traditional material, he applies it in specific fashion to various concrete situations.[7]

In his study of Paul's use of παρακαλῶ and παράκλησις,[8] C.J. Bjerkelund notes that παρακαλῶ 'in den Papyrusbriefen nicht als "terminus technicus" der Paränese vorkommt'.[9] And Bjerkelund concludes that:

> greifen wir noch einmal auf die Inschriften zurück, so boten sich uns da die diplomatischen Königsbriefe als die nächste Parallel zu den paulinsichen

1. *A Commentary on the Epistle of James* (11th rev. edn prepared by H. Greeven, ed. H. Koester, trans. M.A. Williams; Philadelphia: Fortress, 1976).

2. *Anaximenes von Lampsakos: Studien zur ältesten Geschichte der Rhetorik* (Berlin: Weidmann, 1905).

3. *Zur griechischen Paränese* (Smichow: Rohlicek & Sievers, 1912).

4. *James*, p. 3 col. 2.

5. *James*, p. 3 col. 1.

6. *Introduction*, p. 26.

7. 'I Thess. 5.12-28: A Case Study', in *SBL Seminar Papers* 2 (1972), pp. 367-83 (pp. 373, 377).

8. *Parakalo*. Bjerkelund investigates these terms and their synonyms (ἐρωτῶ, παραμυθέμαι, and μαρτύρομαι) in the papyri and in Paul. Earlier T.Y. Mullins recognized petition as a literary form. Through analysing the Oxyrhyncus Papyri, Mullins delineated four different types of petitions, three of which are found in Pauline letters ('Petition as a Literary Form').

9. *Parakalo*, p. 58.

Briefen an; —innerhalb der griechischen Schriftsteller sind es die diplo-
matischen Reden, die den Briefen des Apostels am nächsten kommen, wobei
zu bemerken ist, dass auch die diplomatische Rede brieflichen Charakter hat.[1]

The παρακαλῶ clause was used in such diplomatic types of letters
as a way of politely encouraging compliance with the wishes expressed
in the letter—a clause which 'handelt sich um einen würdigen und
urbanen Ausdruck der Aufforderung, dem alles Befehlende oder
Untertänige fernliegt'.[2] While it occurs most commonly in official
communications, these communications 'persönlichen Charakter
haben, d.h. in Schriftstücken, die sich den Privatbriefen nähern'.[3] So
Bjerkelund contends that Paul's παρακαλῶ exhortations reflect
diplomacy rather than a use of traditional paraenetic material, with his
purpose being to convey a trusting relationship between himself and
his readers.

The Pauline paraeneses have also been subjected to formal analysis
by D.G. Bradley,[4] who compares them with various 'topoi' drawn
from such materials as pseudo-Isocrates, Marcus Aurelius, Sirach and
Testament of XII Patriarchs. According to Bradley the 'topoi' found
in these materials are self-contained teaching forms whose connection
with their context is loose and arbitrary—their order being apparently
random, having been strung together by catchwords.[5] The subject
matter of the 'topoi', however, have one thing in common: 'they are
always related to the problems of daily life and give practical advice
on matters of thought and action which have general, if not universal,
applicability'.[6] Bradley identifies two blocks of 'topoi' in the Pauline
letters: Romans 13 and 1 Thess. 4.9–5.11, concluding that the Pauline

---

1. *Parakalo*, p. 87.
2. *Parakalo*, p. 87.
3. *Parakalo*, p. 110.
4. 'The *Topos* as a Form in the Pauline Paraenesis' *JBL* 72 (1953), pp. 238-46.
Funk notes that Bradley's study of the 'topos' as a form in the paraenetic material of
Paul is akin to previous studies on the 'Haustafeln' and the catalogues of virtues and
vices. For references to previous works, see *Language*, p. 255 n. 15. See also E.
Kamlah, *Die Form der katalogischen Paränese im Neuen Testament* (Tübingen:
Mohr/Siebeck, 1964). Kamlah divides the catalogues of the NT into two types of
forms: the descriptive (e.g. Rom. 1.18-32) and the paraenetic (e.g. Rom. 13.12-14,
Col. 2.20–3.17). These NT catalogues have Jewish and Hellenistic parallels.
5. 'Topos', p. 243.
6. 'Topos', p. 244.

paraenesis does contain the 'topos' form and that Paul's use corresponds to its use in Hellenistic ethical paraenesis.[1]

J.L. White has suggested that the function of paraenesis in Paul's letters is to appeal to general Christian tradition and/or previous instruction in order that Paul's apostolic presence may be underlined.[2]

Formal analyses of the Pauline paraeneses have, as we have seen, generally been able to deduce more about the function of the paraenetic material than about the formal features of such material. The formal features of the Pauline paraeneses, in fact, seem to cohere to the individual exhortations or maxims rather than to the section as a whole. The Pauline paraenetic sections do not appear to display specific formal characteristics, even though the paraenetic material contained within them does. On the other hand, the letter structure sections that are relevant for this work (i.e. the opening formula, the thanksgiving, the apostolic parousia and the conclusion) are, fortunately, those that exhibit the most regular formal features.

2. *The Opening and Closing Sections of a Pauline Letter*

(1) *The opening formula.* The opening formula of a Pauline letter identifies the sender(s), the addressee(s) and gives greetings.[3] The customary Hellenistic opening formula was A—B—χαίρειν, with the sender in the nominative and the recipient in the dative,[4] and with this the Pauline opening formulas agree. Paul's expansion of the typical Hellenistic opening formula, however, differs from all known Hellenistic letters, as O. Roller observed when speaking of the 'ungriechischen Lange der Paulinischen Superscriptionen'.[5] Likewise, Paul's letters differ from ancient Hellenistic letters where 'ganz selten

---

1. 'Topos', p. 246.
2. 'Saint Paul and the Apostolic Letter Tradition', p. 441. In another article White cites approvingly the suggestion of N. Dahl ('Paul's Letter to the Galatians: Epistolary Genre, Content, Structure', [unpublished paper presented at the annual meeting of the SBL, 1973], p. 75) that the paraenetic material functions in Paul's letters to indicate how responsible Paul felt for the spiritual maturation of his readers in accordance with the dictates of the new age and in advance of the parousia ('Ancient Greek Letters', p. 100).
3. First identified by Exler, *The Form of the Ancient Greek Letter*, pp. 13 and 23.
4. *The Form of the Ancient Greek Letter*, p. 133.
5. *Das Formular*, p. 58. Cf. Marxsen: 'There are no parallels in ancient literature to the way in which Paul expands his introductions' (*Introduction*, p. 25).

findet sich die erste oder zweite Person in der Superscriptio',[1] for Paul invariably opens his letters using the first person, and often also includes a reference to his co-workers.[2]

Recent studies have noted that the greeting was generally followed by a wish for health or a statement that the sender was constantly remembering the addressee.[3] And this may be, as White maintains,[4] what we have in the second half of Paul's normal salutation (χάρις ὑμῶν καὶ εἰρήνη)—viz., a surrogate health wish.[5]

b. *The thanksgiving.* The thanksgiving section of Paul's letters is parallel to similar sections in ancient letters where the gods are thanked on behalf of either the writer or the addressee. In Paul's letters, however, as White points out:

> The Pauline thanksgiving differs, formally and functionally, from its common letter counterpart. Unlike the thanksgiving of the common letter tradition, thanks to the gods does not depend upon safety from great danger. Further, the addressees play a much more positive role; they are cited as the cause of thanksgiving.[6]

The prevalent view of the thanksgiving section as a regular feature of Hellenistic letters has been contested. K. Berger, for example, argues that 'Danksagungen in hellenistischen Briefen sind vergleichsweise (!) selten und haben keinen vergleichbaren Inhalt'.[7] B. Rigaux also dismisses the thanksgiving period as a fixed Hellenistic letter element:

> The Pauline use of the thanksgiving form in his letters does not seem to owe its origin to some external influence. According to a Jewish custom, Paul

---

1. Roller, *Das Formular*, p. 434 n. 246.
2. P. Wendland noted the three elements of a Greek letter opening ('Die urchristlichen literaturformen', p. 340).
3. Cf. Doty, *Letters*, pp. 30f. This observation was anticipated by Exler, *The Form of the Ancient Greek Letter*, p. 134.
4. 'The Structural Analysis of Philemon: A Point of Departure in the Formal Analysis of the Pauline Letter', *SBL* (1971), pp. 1-48 (p. 33).
5. See also J.L. White, 'Saint Paul and the Apostolic Letter Tradition', p. 437.
6. 'The Structural Analysis of Philemon', pp. 30-31.
7. 'Apostelbrief und apostolische Rede: Zum Formular frühchristler Briefe', *ZNW* 65 (1974), pp. 190-231 (p. 219).

most likely simply used to begin his preaching with an expression of thanks-giving, a pattern which he later incorporated into his correspondence.[1]

There are, then, two opinions concerning the Pauline thanksgiving periods: (1) that the thanksgiving is a standard epistolary form in Hellenistic letter writing with a primarily literary function, and (2) that the thanksgiving is a personal Pauline epistolary feature reflecting the apostle's own prayers and stemming ultimately from the blessings and thanksgivings of contemporary liturgical practice, both Jewish and Christian (the background of which was the Hebrew Bible and other Jewish literature).

P. Schubert's study of the Pauline thanksgivings established the first line of thinking.[2] Schubert noted that all of Paul's letters, with the exception of 2 Corinthians and Galatians, 'exhibit (following the opening formula) a thanksgiving, and that all these thanksgivings exhibit certain identical and readily observable functional and formal features'.[3] Using the literary method suggested by R. Schültz,[4] Schubert based his structural analysis on the literary units of κῶλον and περίοδος. Through careful analysis of the εὐχαριστῶ periods (named for the principal verb and key-term of this period),[5] Schubert identified two structural types of Pauline thanksgivings. What he termed type 'Ia' is evident in Philemon, 1 Thessalonians, Colossians, Philippians and Romans, and is the more elaborate kind of structure. Type 'Ib' has a simpler structure and is found in 2 Thessalonians, 1 Corinthians and also in Romans. So by a comparison of Paul's use of εὐχαριστῶ periods with that of contemporary Hellenistic papyri and inscriptions, Christian literature of the first and second centuries, the Septuagint, Philo and Epictetus, Schubert concluded that 'the thanksgivings of the papyrus letters exhibit essentially the same essential,

---

1. *The Letters of St Paul. Modern Studies* (ed. and trans. S. Yonick; Chicago: Franciscan Herald, 1968), p. 122.

2. Cf. Schubert: 'To state the most important thesis of this study concisely: the Pauline thanksgivings are characteristically and basically epistolary in form and function' (*Thanksgivings*, p. 38).

3. Schubert, *Thanksgivings*, pp. 179-80.

4. R. Schütz (*Der parallel Bau der Satzglieder im Neuen Testament und seine Verwertung für die Textkritik und Exegese* [Göttingen, 1920], cited from Schubert, *Thanksgivings*, p. 11) developed his method from ancient grammarians and rhetoricians who identified literary units called κῶλον and περίοδος.

5. Schubert includes occurrences of εὐχαριστῶ, εὐχαριστία, εὐχάριστος.

structural characteristics as do the Pauline thanksgivings; both Pauline types (Ia and Ib) have their parallels in the papyrus documents'.[1]

Schubert drew several conclusions from his research: (1) that the thanksgivings in the Pauline letters are strictly epistolary in form and function;[2] (2) that these epistolary forms are 'an essential functional element within each letter';[3] (3) that the function of the thanksgivings is 'to indicate the occasion for and the contents of the letters which they introduce';[4] (4) that the structural variations among the thanksgivings are due 'generally speaking to the differences between the specific situations';[5] related to this, (5) that 'the Pauline thanksgivings. . . can be adequately understood only as products of vital attitudes and social situations. . . objective interpretation cannot but recognize this fact as extremely significant';[6] and (6) that Paul was in reality not just a Jew who was ' "exposed" to Hellenistic "influences", but that he was an indigenous Hellenist—an Ἑλληνίστης ἐξ Ἑλληνιστῶν'.[7]

Two main criticisms of Schubert's work have been advanced: (1) that he failed to take into account the Jewish character and background of the content of Paul's thanksgivings, and (2) that he left the 'impression that Paul's thanksgiving reports were *mere* literary devices'[8] with no real prayer intent at all.

J.M. Robinson and J.T. Sanders have proposed an alternative view concerning the Pauline thanksgiving sections: that the thanksgivings reflect both the prayers of the apostle and the liturgical practice of Jews and Christians in giving thanks. Robinson[9] stresses relationships

1. *Thanksgivings*, p. 181.
2. *Thanksgivings*, p. 183.
3. *Thanksgivings*, p. 25.
4. *Thanksgivings*, p. 27. Schubert's identification of the thanksgiving's function as introduction has been generally accepted. As White writes, the thanksgiving 'telegraphs . . . the letter's message' ('Saint Paul and the Apostolic Letter Tradition', p. 438).
5. *Thanksgivings*, p. 181.
6. *Thanksgivings*, p. 183.
7. *Thanksgivings*, pp. 184f.
8. P.T. O'Brien, 'Thanksgiving and Gospel in Paul', *NTS* 21 (1974), pp. 144-55 (p. 146).
9. J.M. Robinson, 'Die Hodajot-Formel in Gebet und Hymnus des Frühchristentums', in *Apophoreta. Festschrift für Ernst Haenchen* (ed. W. Eltester; Berlin: Töpelmann, 1964), pp. 194-235; *idem*, 'The Historicality of Biblical Lan-

between the Hebrew Bible, Jewish writings and the Pauline thanks-givings, noting particularly that the Pauline thanksgivings echo early Christian liturgical thanksgivings and blessings (*hodaya* and *beracha* respectively).[1]

J.T. Sanders regards the Pauline thanksgiving as an 'epistolary prayer' that is 'only slightly modified from the liturgical form of the prayers of the Christian community'[2] but which nevertheless fits within formal letter conventions. The Pauline thanksgivings, then, serve not merely the formal and functional requirements of Hellenistic epistolography, but Paul's desire to express faith and hope in a manner appropriate for worship.[3]

P.T. O'Brien's study of Paul's introductory thanksgivings identifies four functions for the thanksgiving periods: (1) an epistolary function; (2) a pastoral function that expresses concern for the addressees; (3) a didactic function (with the possible exception of Rom. 1.8ff.); and (4) a paraenetic function.[4] The thanksgivings, he points out, are integral parts of their letters, 'setting the tone and themes of what was to fol-low'.[5] O'Brien's study also takes seriously the factor of prayer in the Pauline thanksgivings. Likewise, G.P. Wiles writes that 'Paul's linking of thanksgiving with supplication or intercession was based not only in

guage', in *The Old Testament and Christian Faith* (ed. B.W. Anderson; New York: Harper & Row, 1963), pp. 124-58.

1. J.-P. Audet argued earlier that it was 'the Jewish "benediction" (*berakah*) which has been. . . the true parent of the Christian εὐχαριστία' (p. 646). Audet deals primarily with εὐχαριστία as a form in the gospel tradition (pp. 648ff.), especially in relation to the eucharistic prayers; yet he makes the general statement that '"the benediction" has proved to be one of the most deep-rooted literary forms to which the religion of the patriarchs, of Moses and of the prophets gave birth' (p. 648) and that therefore 'the Christian εὐχαριστία stands in direct succession from the Jewish benediction' ('Literary Forms and Contents of a Normal Εὐχαριστία in the First Century', *Studia Evangelica* 1 [ed. F.L. Cross and K. Aland, *et al.*; Berlin: Akademie Verlag, 1959], pp. 632-43 [p. 659]).

2. 'The Transition from Opening Epistolary Thanksgiving to Body in the Letters of the Pauline Corpus', p. 362.

3. So Robinson, 'The Historicality of Biblical Language', p. 149 n. 29.

4. *Introductory Thanksgivings in the Letters of Paul* (Leiden: Brill, 1977), pp. 262f.

5. *Introductory Thanksgivings*, p. 263.

epistolary convention, but more fundamentally in Jewish liturgical practice'.[1]

Recent studies have tended to synthesize the two opinions: that the form of the Pauline thanksgiving sections is largely Hellenistic, but that their content is influenced chiefly by Judaism. J.A. Fitzmyer, for example, suggests that while the Pauline thanksgiving 'resembles the Greco-Roman letter form, the sentiments uttered in it are often phrased in characteristic Jewish 'eucharistic' formulas and sometimes recall the Qumran Hodayot'.[2]

Whether the origin of the formal features of the Pauline thanks-givings is to be found in Hellenistic epistolary practice or in Jew-ish/Christian worship, the fact remains that there are several identifiable formal features that may be investigated. The contest as to whether the function of the thanksgivings is simply epistolary or to be seen as an expression of prayer has been won by those who contend for the latter.[3] For everything else we know about Paul as a letter-writer suggests his desire to communicate his apostolic concern for his readers, so that it is untenable that he would open a letter in an entirely formal fashion. At the same time, however, there is no doubt that Paul adapted an existing Hellenistic letter form in order to express his prayer concerns.

(c) *The apostolic parousia.* Funk describes Paul's purpose in the apos-tolic parousia sections as: (1) to make it clear that 'the letter is an anticipatory surrogate for his presence, with which, however, the let-ter is entirely congruent'; (2) to commend the emissary, whose role was to establish Paul's authority during his absence; and (3) to speak of Paul's coming visit or a visit that he prays will soon take place.[4] Funk says that it is in this way that Paul's 'apostolic authority and

---

1. *Paul's Intercessory Prayers* (Cambridge: Cambridge University Press, 1973), p. 160.

2. 'New Testament Epistles', in *The Jerome Biblical Commentary* (ed. R.E. Brown *et al.*; Englewood Cliffs, NJ: Prentice–Hall, 1968), p. 225; see also pp. 223-26.

3. So J.L. White writes that in the thanksgiving sections, 'Paul expresses thanksgiving to God because he has learned of some spiritual activity of his recipi-ents. Thereupon, he prays that his recipients' activity will result in their full spiritual maturation by Christ's return' ('Ancient Greek Letters', p. 98).

4. 'Apostolic "Parousia"', p. 266.

power are made effective'.[1] The apostolic parousia sections, then, function as a reminder of Paul's apostolic authority by making his presence felt either by reference (in ascending order of importance) to the letter, to the emissary or to a coming visit.

The apostolic parousia, as Funk lays it out, has five formal units and several sub-units: (1) 'I write to you' stating either Paul's disposition or his purpose in writing; (2) the basis of Paul's apostolic relation to the recipients; (3) implementation of the apostolic 'parousia', including either Paul's desire to see them, his hope to see them, an announcement or promise of a visit, or explaining his delay in coming and speaking of the dispatch of an emissary; (4) invocation of divine approval and support for the apostolic 'parousia'; and (5) benefit from the apostolic 'parousia'.[2] Funk bases his delineation of these items primarily on Rom. 15.14-33. Later I shall call this methodological tack into question and propose an alternative to his formal analysis.

(d) *The conclusion.* H. Gamble's study of the origin and development of the different forms of Romans provides valuable information regarding the Pauline epistolary conclusion.[3] Gamble denotes the structure of the Pauline conclusion as: (1) hortatory remarks, (2) wish of peace, (3) concluding greetings (3a greeting with the kiss) and (4) grace-benediction.[4] His investigation discloses that 'no matter what else occurs in the conclusions or which of these formulaic elements is omitted, the sequence as such is never violated. . . The epistolary conclusions, then, show a high degree of regularity in components and structure'.[5]

Gamble shows that the concluding 'hortatory remarks' have a different form from that of the παρακαλῶ clauses in the paraenetic sections of Paul's letters. The hortatory remarks lack the usual prepositional phrase (διά and genitive). Furthermore, their strict focus on the relationship between the community addressed and certain individuals or groups sets them apart from the paraenetic παρακαλῶ clauses.[6]

---

1. 'Apostolic "Parousia"', p. 266.
2. 'Apostolic "Parousia"' pp. 252-53.
3. *Textual History.*
4. *Textual History*, p. 83.
5. *Textual History*, p. 83.
6. *Textual History*, p. 80.

The 'wish of peace' is a standard part of the Pauline conclusions which echoes the prayer for peace in the openings of the letters.[1] White suggests that the wish of peace has an eschatological intent, noting particularly the eschatological orientation of 1 Thess. 5.23 and Rom. 16.20. He proposes that the wish of peace is based on Paul's expectation of his readers' obedience to his apostolic authority as outlined particularly in the preceding apostolic parousia and paraenetic sections.[2] The 'concluding greetings' exhibit normal epistolary practice. Exler had noted that 'during the Roman period it was a common custom to add greetings at the end of letters. These ἀσπάσασθαι phrases appear in various forms. At times an accumulation of such phrases is found in one and the same letter.'[3] Gamble observes that Paul shares the basic greeting formula with the Hellenistic letter (ἀσπάζεσθαι with the object) and that the greetings are a regular element in Pauline letter conclusions.[4]

Gamble suggests that the 'kiss of peace' is probably a sign of mutual greeting. He argues that 'a formal liturgical usage in any special connection cannot be determined'.[5] White suggests, on the other hand, that when Paul addressed his readers, he addressed them as if they were at worship when the letter would be read out, with the reference to a holy kiss being then the religious act enjoined by Paul as the officiant at the worship service.[6] The 'grace–benediction' that ends the letter is a particularly Christian type of farewell.[7] The fact that some of the Pauline conclusions contain an autograph (e.g. 2 Thess. 3.17) should

1. *Textual History*, p. 73.
2. 'Saint Paul and the Apostolic Letter Tradition', p. 442.
3. *The Form of the Ancient Greek Letter*, p. 136.
4. *Textual History*, pp. 73-74. Cf. Mullins, 'Greeting as a New Testament Form', and J.L. White, 'Epistolary Formulas and Clichés in Greek Papyrus Letters', *SBL Seminar Papers* 2 (1978), pp. 289-319 (p. 299).
5. *Textual History*, p. 76.
6. 'Ancient Greek Letters', p. 98. Cf. G.J. Cuming: 'The invariable placing of these phrases (i.e. greet one another with the kiss) near the ends of the epistles strongly suggests that they occurred near the end of the service at which the epistle was to be read' ('Service–endings in the Epistles', *NTS* 22 [1975], pp. 110-13 [p. 113]).
7. Cf. Wiles, who notes 'that these final benedictions replace a customary Greek epistolary salutation meaning "farewell"' (*Intercessory Prayers*, p. 114).R. Jewett suggests that 'the form of the NT benedictions and their function in their contexts tend to substantiate the hypothesis of homilectical use' ('The Form and Function of the Homiletic Benediction', *ATR* 51 [1969], pp. 18-34 [p. 34]).

also be noted.[1] White has suggested that the Pauline autograph functions somewhat like the 'illiteracy formula' of Hellenistic letters in which the dictator of the letter signs his name after the scribe has written the letter.[2]

D. *Some Preliminary Critical Considerations*

1. *The Authenticity of Paul's Letters*

In order to establish a standard form for the four parts of the Pauline letter that here concern us, we must deal first with the preliminary critical question as to what letters from the Pauline corpus are most relevant to our discussion.

The authenticity of Colossians and Ephesians is a matter of extensive and intensive scholarly dispute. These two letters, therefore, will not be used as examples of the form of a Pauline letter. Many scholars consider there to be a close relationship between Colossians and Philemon,[3] and suggest that since Philemon's authenticity is not disputed, we should regard Colossians also as an authentic letter of Paul, perhaps written at about the same time. Some also contend that if Colossians is regarded as authentic then probably Ephesians also is from Paul's hand. Yet to incorporate these letters into my analysis of the Pauline letter form would require a lengthy justification, since much of modern scholarship considers them to be 'pseudepigraphical documents that transmit Pauline traditions'.[4] The aims of this investigation are better served by dealing only with those letters of Paul that are widely accepted as authentic: Romans, 1 Corinthians, 2

---

1. For the role of the autograph and its relation to the use of an amanuensis see O. Roller, *Das Formular*; A. Eschlimann, 'La redaction des épîtres pauliennes', *RB* 53 (1946), pp. 185-96; G.J. Bahr, 'Paul and Letter Writing in the First Century', *CBQ* 28 (1966), pp. 465-77; *idem*, 'The Subscriptions in the Pauline Letters' *JBL* 87 (1968), pp. 27-41 (pp. 27, 32).

2. 'New Testament Epistolary Literature in the Framework of Ancient Epistolography', *ANRW* Series II.25.2 (1984), pp. 1730-56 (p. 1740).

3. Cf. J. Knox, *Philemon Among the Letters of Paul* (Nashville: Abingdon, 1959), p. 33; see also *idem*, 'Philemon and the Authenticity of Colossians', *JR* 18 (1938), pp. 144-60; R.P. Martin, *Colossians and Philemon* (London: Oliphants, 1974), pp. 32-40; L. Cope, 'On Rethinking the Philemon–Colossians Connection', *BR* 30 (1985), pp. 45-50.

4. Beker, *Paul the Apostle*, p. 3.

Corinthians, Galatians, Philippians, 1 and 2 Thessalonians,[1] and Philemon.

1. The debate over the authenticity of 2 Thessalonians is relatively equally balanced for and against. W. Wrede challenged its authenticity, asserting that the letter's literary parallels to 1 Thessalonians showed it to be a counterfeit of Paul's style (*Die Echtheit des zweiten Thessalonicherbriefes* [Leipzig: Hinrichs, 1903]. His conclusion has been followed by other scholars; e.g. C. Masson, *Les Deux Epîtres de Saint Paul aux Thessaloniciens* (Neuchâtel: Delachaux et Niestlé, 1957), pp. 9-13; R. Bultmann, *Theology*, II, p. 131; W. Marxsen, *Introduction*, pp. 37-44; G. Bornkamm, *Paul* (New York: Harper & Row, 1971), p. 243. See also J.A. Bailey, 'Who Wrote II Thessalonians?', *NTS* 25 (1978–79), pp. 131-45; G. Krodel, 'The 2 Letter to the Thessalonians', in *Ephesians, Colossians, 2 Thessalonians and The Pastoral Epistles* (Philadelphia: Fortress, 1978), pp. 73-96; W. Trilling, *Untersuchungen zum 2-Thessalonicherbrief* (Leipzig, 1972), p. 27; *idem, Der zweite Brief an die Thessalonicher* (Neukirchen-Vluyn: Neukirchener, 1980), where he reiterates his conclusion from *Untersuchungen* that 'der 2 Thess kann als ein originales Schreiben des Apostles Paulus nicht hinreichend verständlich gemacht werden, wohl aber als pseudepigraphisches Schreiben eines unbekannten Autors späterer Zeit' (p. 23). This view is accepted by K.P. Donfried with the proviso that 2 Thessalonians be regarded as a non-Pauline letter written (perhaps not very much after Paul's letter to the Thessalonians) to a concrete situation in Thessalonica ('The Cults of Thessalonica and the Thessalonian Correspondence', *NTS* 31 [1985], pp. 336-56 [p. 352]). See also G.S. Holland, who also regards 2 Thessalonians as the writing of a Pauline follower (*The Tradition that You Received from Us: 2 Thessalonians in the Pauline Tradition* [Tübingen: Mohr/Siebeck, 1988]).

On the other hand, many scholars would argue that 2 Thessalonians was written by the same author as 1 Thessalonians. So e.g. B. Rigaux, *Saint Paul: Les Epîtres aux Thessaloniciens* (Paris: Gabalda, 1956), pp. 124-52; R. Jewett, 'Enthusiastic Radicalism and the Thessalonian Correspondence', *Proceedings of the 1972 SBL Annual Meeting*, pp. 181-232; Kümmel, *Introduction to the New Testament*, pp. 264-69; E. Best, *A Commentary on the First and Second Epistles to the Thessalonians* (London: Black, 1977), pp. 50-58; J.C. Hurd, 'Concerning the Authenticity of 2 Thess,' (unpublished paper for *SBL* Paul Seminar, Annual Meeting, 1983); I.H. Marshall, *1 & 2 Thessalonians* (Grand Rapids: Eerdmans, 1983), pp. 28-45. This latter opinion commends itself since many of the arguments against its authenticity are based on the difficulty of combining the account in Acts with the existence of these two letters (cf. J.C. Hurd, *The Origin of 1 Corinthians* [New York: Seabury, 1965], p. 14). When the letters are read solely within the framework of the Pauline corpus, however, the arguments against the authenticity of 2 Thessalonians prove far less significant. For instance, by considering that 2 Thessalonians was written prior to 1 Thessalonians, its more primitive apocalyptic teaching proves less problematic and so also does its reference to a previous letter (a reference that obviously does not refer to 1 Thessalonians).

2. *The Integrity of Some of Paul's Letters*
Another preliminary critical issue which must be dealt with is that of
whether the letters in question exhibit original Pauline letter form. 1
and 2 Corinthians, and Philippians are suspected of being compilations
of fragments of Paul's letters. The case of each of these letters will
need to be considered to determine whether they are appropriate for
use in this study.

(1) *1 Corinthians*. There are various theories postulating a composite
character for 1 Corinthians.[1] One piece of evidence put forward to
support a partition theory for 1 Corinthians is the apparent relationship between 2 Cor. 6.14–7.1 and parts of 1 Corinthians. 2 Corinthians 6.14–7.1 is widely recognized as an interpolation into 2 Corinthians, which various scholars identify as an extant portion of the
'Previous Letter' mentioned in 1 Cor. 5.9.[2] Sections of 1 Corinthians
that are similar in tone and content to this fragment (e.g. 6.12-20;
9.24-7; 10.1-22[23]; and 11.2-34)[3] are deemed to be other parts of the
'Previous Letter' that somehow found their way into 1 Corinthians.[4]
W. Schmithals, for example, includes 1 Cor. 15.1-58 and 16.13-24 in
the 'Previous Letter' and conjectures that 'this first epistle has been
preserved for us in its entirety except for the prescript proem and
perhaps some isolated remarks'.[5] E. Dinkler, on the other hand,

---

1. E.g. W. Schenk, who finds four letters combined by a redactor in 1 Corinthians
('Der I Korintherbrief als Briefsammlung', *ZNW* 60 [1969], pp. 219-43 [p. 242]);
J. Harrison argues that 2 Cor. 10.1–13.14, along with 1 Cor. 1.1–4.21, form one
complete letter ('St. Paul's Letters to the Corinthians', *ExpT* 77 [1966], pp. 285-86
[p. 286]); or G. Sellin, who partitions 1 Corinthians into several originally distinct
Pauline communications ('Hauptprobleme des Ersten Korintherbriefes', *ANRW*
Series II.25.4 [1987], pp. 2940-3044). For a good summary of the major partition
theories see H. Merklein, 'Die Einheitlichkeit des ersten Korintherbriefes', *ZNW* 75
(1984), pp. 154-56. For a survey of recent interpolation theories see J. Murphy–
O'Connor, 'Interpolations in 1 Corinthians', *CBQ* 48 (1986), pp. 81-94.
2. See J.C. Hurd for a review and discussion of scholarly opinions (*The Origin of
1 Corinthians*, pp. 235-37).
3. See Hurd, *The Origin of 1 Corinthians*, pp. 44-45.
4. See B. Rigaux for a review of early scholarship on this issue (*The Letters of St
Paul*, p. 109).
5. *Gnosticism in Corinth* (trans. J.E. Steely; Nashville: Abingdon, 1971), pp. 90-
96 (p. 95).

includes chs. 12–14 in the 'Previous Letter', but excludes 2 Cor. 6.14–7.1 since he considers it non-Pauline.[1]

Apportionment of parts of 1 Corinthians to the 'Previous Letter' has the advantage of solving some of the exegetical problems of the letter. For example, the apparent contradiction between Paul's advice concerning idol meat in chs. 8 and 10.23-33 compared with what he says in 10.1-22, is overcome when the latter passage is assigned to an earlier, more legalistic letter. Likewise, the difference between Paul's attitude in chs. 1–4 towards the divisions at Corinth compared with his comment of 11.18 ('I hear that. . . there are divisions among you, and to some extent I believe it') is another case in point. Was Paul less informed about the situation at Corinth in 11.18ff. than in 1.10ff.?[2] A further tension point in 1 Corinthians is at 9.1, which verse bears no apparent logical connection to those preceding. Moreover, ch. 9 is an apology for Paul's apostleship, while chs. 1–4 are characterized by Paul's lack of defensiveness about his apostolic authority. So it has been proposed that Paul wrote these passages at two separate times and that ch. 9 is part of an earlier letter.[3]

On the other hand, the majority of scholars hold that 1 Corinthians is a literary unity. The principal approach within this opinion is to regard the logical breaks in 1 Corinthians as the result either of conscious choice on Paul's part[4] or as the result of Paul experiencing interruptions during the process of composition.[5] It is this latter

1. 'Corinthians, First Letter to the' in *Hastings Dictionary of the Bible* (rev. and ed. F.C. Grant and H.H. Rowley; Edinburgh: T. & T. Clark, 1963), p. 177.

2. S. W. Schmithals claims that 11.2-34 belongs to the 'Previous Letter' (*Gnosticism in Corinth*, pp. 90f.).

3. So J. Héring, *La premier epître de saint Paul aux Corinthiens* (Neuchâtel: Delachaux & Niestlé, 1949), p. 70.

4. So H. Lietzmann, who recognizes the logical break at 9.1 but upholds the literary unity of 1 Corinthians by defining 9.1-18 as an excursus (*An die Korinther I. II* [enlarged by W.G. Kümmel; Tübingen: Mohr/Siebeck, 1969], p. 43).

5. So H. Conzelmann; 'The existing breaks can be explained from the circumstances of its composition. Even the complex that gives the strongest offense, chaps. 8–10, can be understood as a unity' (*I Corinthians* [trans. J.W. Leitch; Philadelphia: Fortress, 1975], p. 4). See also Kümmel, *Introduction*, pp. 275f.; F.W. Grosheide, *Commentary on the First Epistle to the Corinthians* (Grand Rapids: Eerdmans, 1953), pp. 16f.; L. Morris, *The First Epistle of Paul to the Corinthians* (Grand Rapids: Eerdmans, 1963), p. 24; M.E. Thrall, *The First and Second Letters of Paul to the Corinthians* (Cambridge: Cambridge University Press, 1965), pp. 3-5;

solution that is most common. So F.F. Bruce, for example, reasons that some of the difficulties in 1 Corinthians may be solved by recognizing different stages in the composition of the letter: 1 Corinthians may well have been composed over a period of several weeks, beginning with chs. 1–4 and continuing in response to new information from Corinth.[1]

J.C. Hurd's theory is that these problem passages are Paul's response to the fallout from the 'Previous Letter' in which his attitude was markedly different from the one he conveyed in his original mission.[2]

The peculiarities of the form of 1 Corinthians are best explained by its particular function—viz., a letter written largely in response to queries from several sources. It is most readily explained as a single letter of Paul written to correspond with several different concerned groups within Corinth.[3] 1 Corinthians is, then, appropriate for use in analysis of Pauline letter form.[4]

(b) *2 Corinthians.* The literary integrity of 2 Corinthians is also disputed. Even W.G. Kümmel, who regards 2 Corinthians as one letter written with interruptions,[5] admits that 'the difficulty in regarding the text of II Cor. as transmitted as an original unity remains so great that this unity has been called into question in a variety of ways'.[6]

and C.K. Barrett, *The First Epistle to the Corinthians* (London: Black, 1968), pp. 11-17.

1. *1 & 2 Corinthians* (London: Oliphants, 1971), pp. 24f.

2. 'Every section of this letter relates to the group of disputes which resulted from Paul's attempt to obtain the Corinthians' conformity to the Apostolic Decree' (*The Origin of 1 Corinthians*, p. 295). Hurd maintains, further, that what appear to be different occasions for the writing of the letter are, in fact, the result of Paul's response to two different kinds of reports about the situation in Corinth—oral and written—that reached Paul at the same time (*The Origin of 1 Corinthians*, p. 142).

3. Cf. H. Merklein, who also argues for the unity of 1 Corinthians. Chapters 1–4 and 7–16 can be shown to have literary coherence, and chs. 5 and 6 fit appropriately as an introduction to that part of the letter in which Paul largely responds to enquiries from the Corinthian congregation ('Die Einheitlichkeit des ersten Korintherbriefes').

4. See also L.L. Belleville, who argues that 1 Corinthians has a coherent letter structure form which she demonstrates follows a request–command–request structure written in response to the Corinthians' letter ('Continuity or Discontinuity: A Fresh Look at 1 Corinthians in the Light of First-Century Epistolary Forms and Conventions', *EQ* 59 [1987], pp. 15-37).

5. *Introduction*, p. 292.

6. *Introduction*, p. 288.

There are four major points where the integrity of 2 Corinthians can be questioned. The first, as mentioned in our analysis of 1 Corinthians, is the passage 6.14–7.1. The weight of scholarly opinion favours viewing this as an interpolation, either Pauline (perhaps from the 'Previous Letter') or non-Pauline.[1] The major reasons for regarding 6.14–7.1 as an interruption in the text are (1) the ease with which 6.13 and 7.2 flow together when this 'fragment' is removed, and (2) the discrepancy between the context in which this passage is found and the passage itself. In 6.1-13 and 7.2f. Paul commends his ministry and that of his co-workers, for they have opened wide their hearts to the Corinthians. He pleads for the Corinthians also to open wide their hearts (6.13) and to make room for him and his fellows (7.2). Yet 6.14–7.1, which contains an exhortation to separate from unbelievers, is an abrupt shift in subject matter and language. Furthermore, the passage is rife with hapaxlegomena. Some also argue that the chain of quotations in 6.16b-18c is unusual in Paul.[2]

1. See good reviews of both views in Kümmel, *Introduction*, p. 287 n. 15 and n. 16; Hurd, *The Origin of I Corinthians*, p. 236 n. 1; V.P. Furnish, *II Corinthians* (New York: Doubleday, 1984), pp. 371-83.

2. Cf. L. Gaston, *No Stone on Another. Studies in the Significance of the Fall of Jerusalem in the Synoptic Gospels* (Suppl. *NovT* 23; Leiden: Brill, 1970) esp. p. 177. Marxsen calls this passage 'apocalyptic' (*Introduction*, p. 78). J.A. Fitzmyer argues, after an examination of six points of contact between this passage and the Qumran literature, that 'we are faced with. . . a Christian reworking of an Essene paragraph which has been introduced into the Pauline letter' ('Qumran and the Interpolated Paragraph in 2 Cor. 6.14–7.1', *CBQ* 23 [1961], pp. 271-80 [pp. 279f.]). This view is shared by W.K. Grossouw, 'The Dead Sea Scrolls and the New Testament. A Preliminary Survey', *SC* 26 (1951), pp 289-99. Cf. also J. Gnilka, '2 Cor. 6.14–7.1 in the Light of the Qumran Texts and the Testaments of the Twelve Patriarchs', in *Paul and Qumran. Studies in New Testament Exegesis* (ed. J. Murphy–O'Connor [London: Chapman, 1968], pp. 48-68). J.-F. Collange finds this fragment to have been interpolated by Paul in the second edition of his letter (2.14–6.2 and 6.14–7.4) and decides that it was originally 'un document judéo-chrétien pré-existant, aux affinités certaines avec les textes de Qumran et "les Testaments des 12 Patriarchs"' (*Enigmes de la deuxième épître aux Corinthiens* [Cambridge: Cambridge University Press, 1972], pp. 316f.). Also H.D. Betz, '2 Cor. 6.14–7.1: An Anti-Pauline Fragment?', *JBL* 92 (1973), pp. 88-108; J.J. Gunther, '2 Corinthians 6.14–7.1', in *St Paul's Opponents and their Background. A Study of Apocalyptic and Jewish Sectarian Teaching* (Leiden: Brill, 1973), pp. 308-13.

W.G. Kümmel,[1] F.F. Bruce,[2] C.K. Barrett,[3] J. Lambrecht[4] and M.E. Thrall,[5] among others, attempt to refute such arguments for 6.14–7.1 as an interpolation. Yet their responses, on the whole, remain unconvincing, resting largely on the hypothesis that sudden changes in content and language can be explained psychologically—i.e., here Paul is writing at a different time and in a different mood. Furthermore, they rely on the argument that partition theories create more puzzles than they explain.[6]

A second difficult passage is 2.14–7.4. Many of the issues raised concerning this passage are similar to those relating to 6.14–7.1, with the exception that no one has suggested a non-Pauline origin for this possible interpolation. Yet the unconnectedness of thought between 2 Cor. 2.12-13 and 2.14ff., and the ease with which 2.13 flows into 7.5 when this passage is removed, remains a problem for literary unity.

Some have postulated that this discontinuity is due to a different epistolary situation. D. Georgi, for example, believes that his investigation 'hat ergeben dass die Brieffragmente 2.K. 2, 14-7, 4 und 10-13 gegen die Wirksamkeit judenchristlicher Wanderprediger angehen'.[7]

---

1. *Introduction*, pp. 287-88.

2. *1 & 2 Corinthians*, pp. 170-71.

3. *A Commentary on the Second Epistle to the Corinthians* (London: Black, 1973), pp. 23-24.

4. 'The Fragment 2 Cor VI 14–VII 1. A Plea for its Authenticity', in *Miscellanea Neotestamentica* (ed. T. Baarda, *et al.*; Suppl. *NovT* 48; Leiden: Brill, 1978), pp. 143-61.

5. 'A Second Thanksgiving Period in II Corinthians', *JSNT* 16 (1982), pp. 101-24 (p. 121).

6. See Barrett, *2 Corinthians*, p. 23. Cf. N.A. Dahl, who, while seeing how this fragment could reflect a connection between the Qumran community and the early church and so in its context be saying that rejection of Paul is equivalent to siding with the devil, reflects: 'I find it somewhat difficult to imagine a later redactor who was capable of expressing his understanding of Paul's unique apostolic ministry in such an indirect and subtle way, leaving it to the readers to understand the function of the fragment within its context. The possibility that the apostle himself incorporated the fragment may after all have to be reconsidered' ('A Fragment and Its Context: 2 Cor. 6.14–7.1', in *Studies in Paul* [Minneapolis, MN: Augsburg, 1977], pp. 62-69 [p. 69]).

7. *Die Gegner des Paulus im 2. Korintherbrief. Studien zur Religiösen Propaganda in der Spätantike* (Neukirchen–Vluyn: Neukirchener, 1964), p. 301; E. Dinkler, on the other hand, combines 2.14–7.4 with chs. 10–13 ('Corinthians, Second Letter to', p. 180 col. 2).

These Jewish Christian missionaries who came to Corinth after Paul's original letter, Georgi argues, were influenced by Hellenism and so saw themselves as divine men.[1] Thus 2 Cor. 2.14–7.4 is the letter Paul sent in the light of the new situation, and 2 Cor. 10–13 was written after he made another visit.[2] In 2 Cor. 2.14–7.4 and 2 Cor. 10–13, therefore, the opponents are the same, but the two letters were written in response to two different stages in the conflict.

G. Bornkamm shares the view that 2.14–7.4 reflects a distinct letter situation. He takes issue, however, with those who combine this passage with chs. 10–13 to make the 'tearful letter'.[3] Bornkamm contends, rather, that 2.14–7.4 was written at a time when Paul was first aware of opponents at Corinth. Later, after a visit to Corinth that revealed the seriousness of the situation, he wrote 'the letter of tribulation' (chs. 10–13).[4]

On the other hand, scholars such as W.G. Kümmel,[5] C.K. Barrett,[6] F.F. Bruce,[7] P.F. Ellis,[8] N. Hyldahl[9] and V.P. Furnish,[10] to name only a representative lot, explain 2.14–7.4 as a digression. As they see it, this digression was the result of Paul's change of mood as he switched from describing his anxiety to expressing his relief from anxiety.

---

1. *Die Gegner des Paulus*, pp. 220-34. Contra G. Friedrich, who accepts that they were Hellenistic Jews but 'dass sie . . . mit dem Anspruch auftraten, göttliche Sendboten nach Art der griechischen Umwelt zu sein, ist kaum anzunehmen'. Instead, Friedrich suggests that Stephen and his followers were the source of tensions in Corinth ('Die Gegner des Paulus im 2. Korintherbrief', in *Abraham unser Vater. Juden und Christen im Gespräch über die Bibel. Festschrift für Otto Michel* [ed. O. Betz *et al.*; Leiden: Brill, 1963], pp. 181-216 [pp. 196ff.]). Schmithals views 2.14–6.13 as Paul's defence against gnostic opponents (*Gnosticism in Corinth*, pp. 279f.).

2. Georgi, *Die Gegner des Paulus*, pp. 303ff.

3. 'The History of the Origin of the So-Called Second Letter to the Corinthians', in *The Authorship and Integrity of the New Testament* (London: SPCK, 1965), pp. 73-81 (p. 76).

4. 'History of the Origin of. . . Corinthians', pp. 76-77.

5. *Introduction*, p. 291.

6. *A Commentary on the Second Epistle to the Corinthians*, pp. 23, 96ff.

7. *1 & 2 Corinthians*, p. 187.

8. *Seven Pauline Letters* (Collegeville, MN: Liturgical Press, 1982), p. 145.

9. 'Die Frage nach der literarischen Einheit des Zweiten Korintherbriefes', *ZNW* 64 (1973), pp 289-306 (pp. 293, 300). Hydahl, however, excludes 6.14–7.1 from his investigation.

10. *II Corinthians*, p. 35.

M.E. Thrall thinks that the discontinuity between 2.13 and 2.14 is due to a second introductory thanksgiving period occurring at 2 Cor. 2.14–17.[1] She compares this second thanksgiving to similar occurrences in 1 and 2 Thessalonians. So 2 Cor. 2.14-17 serves to introduce the main themes of the next few chapters.

A composite character for 2 Corinthians is also suspected with regard to chs. 8 and 9.[2] Some view these chapters as two distinct letters,[3] while others consider only ch. 9 to be a separate letter—often conceived of as having been written prior to chs. 1–8.[4]

The last four chapters of 2 Corinthians are widely regarded as unconnected to the rest of the canonical letter. This was first proposed by J.S. Semler in his *Paraphrasis II: Epistolae ad Corinthios* of 1776. Semler's thesis was that 10.1–13.10 was a letter written after chs. 1–8 and ch. 9. This theory was revived by A. Hausrath,[5] and later by J.H. Kennedy,[6] K. Lake[7] and H. Windisch.[8] The proposal rests chiefly on the argument that chs. 10–13 reflect a historical situation separate and distinct from that of the earlier chapters of the letter. In chs. 1–9

1. 'A Second Thanksgiving Period in II Corinthians', p. 118.
2. For a history of critical research on these two chapters, see H.D. Betz, *2 Corinthians 8 and 9* (ed. G.W. MacRae; Philadelphia: Fortress, 1985), pp. 3-36.
3. J. Weiss, *Earliest Christianity. A History of the Period AD 30–150* (trans. and ed. F.C. Grant; New York: Harper, 1959), I, pp. 344ff.; Bornkamm, 'The History of the Origin. . . of Corinthians', p. 77; Marxsen, *Introduction*, p. 79; K.F. Nickle, *The Collection. A Study in Paul's Strategy* (London: SCM, 1966), p. 17; Betz, *2 Corinthians 8 and 9*. Bultmann regarded chs. 8 and 9 as originally distinct and attached to two other letters: ch. 8 attached to 1.1–2.13 and 7.5-16; ch. 9 to 2.14–7.14 and chs. 10–13 (*The Second Letter to the Corinthians* [Minneapolis, MN: Augsburg, 1985], p. 18).
4. So J. Héring, *The Second Epistle of Saint Paul to the Corinthians* (trans. A.W. Heathcote and P.J. Allcock; London: Epworth, 1967), p. xv; also Schmithals, *Gnosticism in Corinth*, p. 97. N. Dahl expresses grave doubts about the composite nature of 2 Cor. 1–9, but argues that if it is composite 'the seams should be located between 8 and 9 and/or between ch. 9 and 10 but not between chs. 7 and 8 or between 7.4 and 7.5' ('On the Literary Integrity of 2 Corinthians 1–9', in *Studies in Paul* [Minneapolis, MN: Augsburg, 1977], pp. 38-39 [p. 39]).
5. *Der Vier-Capitel-Brief des Paulus an die Korinther* (Heidelberg: Bassermann, 1870).
6. *The Second and Third Epistles of St Paul to the Corinthians* (London: Methuen, 1900).
7. *The Earlier Epistles of St Paul* (London: Runingtons, 1930).
8. *Der zweite Korintherbrief* (Göttingen: Vandenhoeck & Ruprecht, 1924).

Paul's relationship with the Corinthians appears open and trusting, while in chs. 10–13 he is defensive about his apostolic position, ending the letter in a hostile fashion (13.10). Moreover, in chs. 10–13 there is no mention of the collection (apart from 12.16-18). So on the basis of the abrupt shift of content between 9.15 and 10.1, the perceived change of mood and the lack of mention of the collection, many have been convinced that chs. 10–13 originally comprised a separate letter.[1] Others, however, still consider the literary unit of 2 Cor. 1–13 to be highly defensible.[2]

The issues concerning the literary integrity of 2 Corinthians are, indeed, complex. Frequently, various partition theories are highly convincing. It may be that 6.14–7.1 was part of the Previous Letter, or that 2.14–7.4 represents a distinct epistolary situation, or that chapters 8 and 9 were originally two separate letters, or that chapters 10–13 made up the original 'Letter of Tears'. It may even be that, as Barrett aptly expresses it, 'the letter contained in i–ix has lost its end, that in x–xiii its beginning'.[3]

---

1. So Bultmann, *The Second Letter to the Corinthians,* p. 18; Dinkler, 'Corinthians, Second Letter to', p. 180 col. 2; Schmithals, *Gnosticism in Corinth,* p. 96; T.W. Manson, 'The Corinthian Correspondence (1)', in *Studies in the Gospels and Epistles* (Manchester: Manchester University Press, 1962), pp. 190-91; C.K. Barrett, 'Paul's Opponents in II Corinthians', *NTS* 17 (1971), pp. 236-54 (p. 236); Georgi, *Die Gegner,* p. 24; Héring, *II Corinthians,* p. xiv; Bornkamm, 'History of the Origin of... Corinthians', pp. 73ff.; Furnish, *II Corinthians,* pp. 36ff.; Marxsen, *Introduction,* pp. 77-78; Bruce, *1 & 2 Corinthians,* p. 170; K.H. Schelkle, *Der zweite Brief an die Korinther* (Düsseldorf: Patmos, 1964), p. 24 n. 69. Issues as to whether this is the 'Letter of Tears' and as to the order of this letter relative to the earlier chapters are not pertinent to our discussion. For a helpful discussion on such topics, see R. Batey, 'Paul's Interactions with the Corinthians', *JBL* 84 (1965), pp. 139-46.

2. So J. Munck, *Paul and the Salvation of Mankind* (London: SCM, 1959), p. 171; Kümmel, *Introduction,* p. 290; Lietzmann, *An die Korinther I, II,* p. 139; P. Hughes, *Paul's Second Epistle to the Corinthians* (Grand Rapids: Eerdmans, 1962), p. xxxiv; W.H. Bates, 'The Integrity of II Corinthians', *NTS* 12 (1965–66), pp. 56-69; A.M.G. Stephenson, 'A Defense of the Integrity of 2 Corinthians', in *The Authorship and Integrity of the New Testament,* pp. 82-97; *idem,* 'Partition Theories on II Corinthians', in *Studia Evangelica* Vol. II (ed. F.L. Cross; Berlin: Akademie, 1964), pp. 639-46; Hyldahl, 'Die Frage nach der literarischen Einheit des Zweiten Korintherbriefes', p. 305.

3. *II Corinthians,* p. 244. J. Knox suggests that perhaps the reason 2 Corinthians 10–13 was not published as a separate letter in the second century was because of the absence of both an opening formula and a thanksgiving section at the start of the

The highly doubtful nature of 2 Corinthians' literary integrity means that, while we may use its individual parts as examples of Pauline letter structure, when we find it necessary to make observations about the relationship of the parts of a letter to one another, it proves not to be useful. So when asking questions about the formal features of a Pauline opening formula, for example, we may use the opening formula of 2 Corinthians; however, when asking questions about the relationship of aspects of a Pauline opening formula to the concerns of its respective letter, we must hesitate to use evidence from this letter.

(c) *Philippians*. Two passages in Philippians have caused scholars to question that letter's literary integrity and resulted in various division theories.[1] The first passage is 3.2ff.[2] Many perceive at 3.2 (or thereabouts) 'a shocking change of tone'.[3] Jewett writes that this 'sudden shift in tone' was observed as early as 1685 by Stephanus le Moyne[4], and was subsequently explained as a non-Pauline interpolation by K. Schrader in *Der Apostel Paulus* (1836).[5] This segment has been

---

letter, so its status as a separate letter to the Corinthian church was not recognized ('A Conjecture as to the Original Status of II Corinthians and II Thessalonians in the Pauline Corpus', *JBL* 55 [1936], pp. 145-53 [p. 152 n. 7]).

1. E.g. C.J. Pfeifer, who considers Philippians to be a collection of three letters (Phil. 4.10-20; Phil. 1.1–3.1, 4.2-9, and 4.21-23; and Phil. 3.2–4.1) that Paul wrote to Philippi on separate occasions ('Three Letters in One', *BT* 23 [1985], pp. 363-68).

2. There are various opinions about the extent of the passage in question: e.g. B.J. Rahtjen marks it from 3.1-9 ('The Three Letters of Paul to the Philippians', *NTS* 6 [1959–60], pp. 167-73 [p. 171]); G. Johnston includes 3.2-21 (*Ephesians, Philippians, Colossians and Philemon* [London: Nelson, 1967], p. 31). For surveys of the discussion, see Martin, *Philippians*, p. 16, and J. Gnilka, *Der Philipperbrief* (Freiburg: Herder, 1980), pp. 6-7. As T.E. Pollard says: 'The difference of opinion concerning the beginning of the interpolation is more than matched by difference of opinion concerning where it ends' (p. 57). He then goes on to argue that because of this difference of opinion the very validity of the argument in favour of an interpolation is put into question ('The Integrity of Philippians', *NTS* 13 [1966–67], pp. 57-66 [p. 58]).

3. Johnston, *Ephesians*, p. 31.

4. D. Cook disagrees with Jewett and others, saying that Le Moyne, in fact, did not make much of the change in tone at 3.1 ('Stephanus Le Moyne and the Dissection of Philippians', *JTS* 32 [1981], pp. 138-42).

classified as an interpolation (either Pauline or non-Pauline) largely on the grounds that its excision from the text allows the passage to flow more naturally.[1] So K. Barth writes: 'The half verse 3.1a. . . (finally my brothers, rejoice in the Lord!) has entirely the character of a conclusion, and could very well be followed by 4.21f.'[2]

Others have argued that the content of this section is parallel to that of the earlier part of the letter,[3] which indicates its intimate connection to the central theme of the letter.[4] Gamble maintains that τὸ λοιπόν of 3.1 would be highly unusual in a Pauline conclusion, and that χαίρετε (3.1) is never used as a *final* wish in either ancient letters or the letters of Paul. Thus, according to Gamble, the argument is weak that 3.2–4.1 is an interruption of the flow of thought in 3.1–4.2.[5]

Still others think that these verses reflect a later stage in the life of the Philippian congregation.[6] Yet, as often noted, an abrupt change in tone is not necessarily evidence of a different epistolary situation (cf. Gal. 6.10; 1 Cor. 15.58).[7]

5. R. Jewett, 'The Epistolary Thanksgiving and the Integrity of Philippians', *NovT* 12 (1970), pp. 40-53 (pp. 40-41).

1. Cf. J. Müller–Bardorff, 'Zur Frage der literarischen Einheit des Philipperbriefes', in *Wissenschaftliche Zeitschrift der Universität Jena* (1957–58), pp. 591-604; G. Bornkamm, 'Der Philipperbrief als paulinische Briefsammlung', in *Neotestamentica et Patristica. Eine Freundesgabe, Herrn Professor Dr. Oscar Culmann zu seinem 60. Geburtstag Uberreicht* (Leiden: Brill, 1962), p. 195; Gnilka, *Der Philipperbrief*, pp. 8-9; F.W. Beare, *A Commentary on the Epistle to the Philippians* (London: Black, 1959), pp. 3-4; Schmithals, *Paul and the Gnostics*, p. 80 n. 59. See also V.P. Furnish, who suggests that 3.1bff is an 'extended postscript' that was originally intended to be delivered orally by Epaphroditus and Timothy ('The Place and Purpose of Philippians iii', *NTS* 10 [1963–64], pp. 80-88).

2. *The Epistle to the Philippians* (trans. J.W. Leitch; London: SCM, 1962), p. 91.

3. So Houlden, *Paul's Letters from Prison: Philippians, Colossians, Philemon and Ephesians* (London: SCM, 1977), p. 105; Pollard, 'The Integrity of Philippians', p. 64.

4. See Ellis, *Seven Pauline Letters*, p. 117.

5. *Textual History*, pp. 145f.

6. So Schmithals, *Paul and the Gnostics*, pp. 73f.; also H. Koester, 'Philippians, Letter to the', in *IDB Suppl.*, p. 666.

7. See e.g. E. Lohmeyer, *Die Brief an die Philipper an die Kolosser und an Philemon* (Göttingen: Vandenhoeck & Ruprecht, 1930); Dibelius, *An die Thessalonicher I. II an die Philipper* (Tübingen: Mohr/Siebeck, 1937); R.P. Martin, *Philippians* (London: Oliphants, 1976), pp. 15ff.; G.B. Caird, *Paul's Letters from*

The other passage that has raised the issue of Philippians' unity is 4.10-20 where Paul thanks his readers for the monetary gift they sent via Epaphroditus.[1] For, to quote W. Marxsen: 'It seems very strange that it is not until the end of the letter (iv. 10ff.) that Paul refers to the gift that the Philippians have sent him. We might have expected it to be mentioned in connection with i.5ff.'[2] Since there had been communication between Paul and the Philippians prior to the writing of this letter (2.26), it seems to many inconceivable that Paul should have waited so long to send a written acknowledgment of receipt of their gift.[3]

Others, however, have suggested that in 1.3 Paul thanks the Philippians for their gift in theological language, and that at the end of the letter he only makes his thank you explicit.[4] So F.B. Craddock argues that the position of 4.10-20 in the letter is appropriate.[5] He suggests that the stiffness of Paul's thank-you, together with its relegation to the postscript, might be due to 'some inner conflict between the need to express pleasure over the gift and at the same time witness to his freedom from the victimizing power of material things'.[6]

Furthermore, others have argued that 2.26 may not really indicate any personal exchange. All we know is that Epaphroditus was conscious that the Philippians had heard of his illness. Perhaps, as some suggest, Epaphroditus fell ill on his way to Paul; that information regarding his illness went back to the Philippians; and that subsequently news of the Philippians' worry for Epaphroditus reached Paul

---

Prison (Oxford: Oxford University Press, 1976), p. 100; Pollard, 'The Integrity of Philippians'; B.S. Mackay, 'Further Thoughts on Philippians', *NTS* 7 (1960–61), pp. 161-70. Cf. Jewett, 'Epistolary Thanksgiving', p. 48.

1. Some include vv. 21-23 (e.g. Schmithals, *Paul and the Gnostics*, p. 79), thereby making vv. 21-23 the epistolary conclusion of this brief thank-you letter.

2. *Introduction*, p. 61; see also J.-F. Collange, *L'Epître de Saint Paul aux Philippiens* (Neuchâtel: Delachaux et Niestlé, 1973), pp. 21-23.

3. So Schmithals, *Paul and the Gnostics*, p. 78; also Beare, *A Commentary on the Epistle to the Philippians*, p. 4; G. Barth, *Der Brief an die Philipper* (Zürich: Theologischer Verlag, 1979), p. 11; Bornkamm, 'Der Philipperbrief als paulinische Briefsammlung', p. 195.

4. Cf. Martin, *Philippians*, p. 14.

5. *Philippians* (Atlanta: John Knox, 1985), pp. 75-77.

6. *Philippians*, p. 77. Cf. C.H. Dodd, who saw in Phil. 4.15-19 the awkwardness of a 'well-to-do bourgeois' who felt embarrassed receiving financial assistance ('The Mind of Paul: I', in *New Testament Studies* [Manchester: Manchester University Press, 1953], pp. 67-82 [pp. 71-72]).

even before Epaphroditus himself reached him. Such a theory, as G.B. Caird points out, 'involves no great delay between the receipt and the acknowledgement of the gift'.[1]

Two letter structure arguments, in particular, have served to affirm the integrity of 4.10-20. The first is set out by Jewett, who, following Schubert,[2] argues that the thanksgiving of 1.3-11 contains clear connections with 4.10-20.[3] The second is Gamble's demonstration that 4.10-20 functions naturally as a unit of a Pauline conclusion.[4]

On balance, the arguments in favour of Philippians' literary integrity outweigh those against. As K. Grayston says, 'it is difficult to see why someone at an early time should have combined three letters in this strange order'.[5]

Full use, then, shall be made of Philippians along with 1 Corinthians, but, as noted above, 2 Corinthians shall be used only for those aspects of the investigation where connections are not being made between one letter section and another.

---

1. *Paul's Letters from Prison*, p. 100; cf. Houlden, *Paul's Letters from Prison*, p. 112.

2. Schubert argues that the Philippian thanksgiving introduces at 1.3 the topic of the readers' generosity towards Paul (*Thanksgivings*, p. 74).

3. Jewett, 'The Epistolary Thanksgiving', p. 53.

4. *Textual History*, pp. 145f.

5. *The Letters of Paul to the Philippians and to the Thessalonians* (Cambridge: Cambridge University Press, 1967), p. 4; see also W.J. Dalton, 'The Integrity of Philippians', *Bib* 60 (1979), pp. 97-102 (p. 102). D.F. Watson argues that as Philippians is a rhetorical unity it is best to assume the letter's literary integrity ('A Rhetorical Analysis of Philippians and its Implications for the Unity Question', *NovT* 30 [1988], pp. 57-88).

Chapter 3

THE PAULINE OPENING FORMULAS

The opening formulas of Paul's letters have a threefold formal framework: an 'identification of sender' unit, a 'designation of recipient' unit, and a 'greeting' unit. All of the Pauline opening formulas exhibit this pattern in this order. In fact, the Pauline opening formula is, as we shall see, the most consistent of the formal features of a Pauline letter.

A. *A Comparison of the 'Identification of Sender' Unit in Paul's Letters*

The 'identification of sender' unit invariably begins with Paul's name in the nominative.[1] Paul's placing of his name before that of his recipients is standard for ancient Greek letters of introduction and recommendation, for family letters and for official letters, but not for letters of petition.[2] When Paul wrote his letters, then, he wrote not with an attitude of petition to a superior but with a degree of familiarity.

In both the Thessalonian letters the co-senders Silvanus and Timothy are identified immediately following Paul's name. These are the only letters that contain no description of either Paul or his co-senders. J. Knox has aptly noted the remarkable similarity between the opening

---

1. C.J. Hemer, accepting Luke's representation of Paul as a Roman citizen, describes 'Paulus' as Paul's 'cognomen' and concludes that since Paul does not also give his 'praenomen' and 'nomen', he writes his letters in a familiar tone ('The Name of Paul', *TB* 36 [1985], pp. 179-83). There are, however, substantial reasons to doubt Luke's account that Paul was a Roman citizen (see e.g. W. Stegemann, 'War der Apostel Paulus ein römischer Bürger?', *ZNW* 78 [1987], pp. 200-99). While Paul does write in a relatively familiar voice, we should not use evidence from his non-use of Roman names in support of this.

2. See White, 'Ancient Greek Letters', pp. 88-95. Also, *idem*, 'New Testament Epistolary Literature in the Framework of Ancient Epistolography', *ANRW* Series II.25.2 (1984), p. 1734.

The Pauline Opening Formulas

	1 Thess.	2 Thess.	1 Cor.	2 Cor.	Phil.	Phlm.	Gal.	Rom.
Identification of Sender								
	1.1a	1.1a	1.1	1.1a	1.1a	v. 1a	1.1-2a	1.1-6
Designation of Recipient								
	1.1b	1.1b	1.2	1.1b	1.1b	v. 1b-2	1.2b	1.7a
Greeting								
	1.1c	1.2	1.3	1.2	1.2	v. 3	1.3-5	1.7b

formulas of the Thessalonian letters (and of the Corinthian letters).[1]
He suggested that the original editors and publishers of the Pauline
corpus omitted the opening formula of the second letter to the same
church (i.e. of 2 Thessalonians and of 2 Corinthians) because they
combined the second letter with the first in their editions. When later
editors decided to publish 2 Thessalonians and 2 Corinthians separately
they constructed opening formulas for them on the model of the
opening formulas of 1 Thessalonians and 1 Corinthians respectively. If
Knox's explanation is close to the true scenario its effect on the present
investigation would be to lessen the weight that should be accorded the
evidence from the opening formulas of 2 Thessalonians and 2
Corinthians. A thorough investigation of the originality of these letter
structure sections is not possible at this point. Rather, we need to bear
in mind the possibility that these opening formulas may not be original
and so the importance of evidence from them must be judged accordingly.

Every letter but Romans is sent both by Paul and someone else. The
co-sender(s) are usually described with the designation ἀδελφός. 1
Corinthians 1.1 describes Sosthenes as 'the brother'; Phlm. 1 and 2

---

1. 'A Conjecture as to the Original Status of II Corinthians and II Thessalonians'.

Cor. 1.1 describe Timothy as 'the brother'; and in Galatians Paul says the letter comes from 'all the brothers with me'.[1] The term 'brother' indicates the close kinship that Paul (and his readers) share with the co-sender(s) on the basis of their shared bond in Christ.[2] Also, Paul's use of 'brothers' for his co-senders indicates that 'the emotional tone of his correspondence is friendly and familial'.[3] The use of familial names for people with whom there is no real family tie, but rather for whom the writer bears affectionate feelings, is also found in Aramaic letters.[4] So at the outset of his letters, Paul establishes an attitude of warmth and familiarity between himself, his co-senders and his readers.

Only in Phil. 1.1 does Paul not designate his co-sender (Timothy) as 'brother'. Rather, both Paul and Timothy are described as 'slaves of Jesus Christ', which calls attention to their shared commitment to the service of the gospel—a commitment that extends, as we know from the rest of the letter, even to suffering imprisonment. The unique positioning of Timothy's name in Philippians also draws attention to his equality with Paul in the service of Christ, for in every other letter when Paul includes a description of himself he does so before adding the name of his co-sender(s).

In every letter but those sent to the Thessalonians, as we observed above, Paul describes himself in some way. In Philippians he describes both himself and Timothy as slaves. In Philemon he calls himself a prisoner of Jesus Christ. Paul also designates himself as an 'apostle of Jesus Christ'. In 1 Cor. 1.1 he claims this title and qualifies it with the prepositional phrase 'through the will of God'. The same formula appears in 2 Cor. 1.1, differing from 1 Cor. 1.1 only by the absence of the verbal adjective κλητός. In Galatians Paul designates himself as an 'apostle'. Here, however, rather than using the more common Χριστοῦ Ἰησοῦ, he takes the opportunity to underscore the divine source of his apostleship—that his apostolic identity does not find its

---

1. Betz comments that in Galatians this 'emphatic "all" is unique in Paul and indicates that he wanted to write as the spokesman of a group which is solidly behind him and the letter' (*Galatians. A Commentary on Paul's Letter to the Churches in Galatia* [Philadelphia: Fortress, 1979], p. 40).

2. Cf. Héring, *The First Epistle to the Corinthians* 1.

3. White, 'Ancient Greek Letters', p. 98.

4. See P.E. Dion, 'The Aramaic "Family Letter" and Related Epistolary Forms in Other Oriental Languages and in Hellenistic Greek', *Semeia* 22 (1981), pp. 59-76 (p. 69).

source in the human world, but in Jesus Christ and God the father—with, then, the transcendental power and authority of such a source made clear as Paul reminds his readers that God raised Jesus from the dead.

In two of the four letters in which Paul identifies himself as an 'apostle' (1 and 2 Corinthians, Galatians and Romans) he also speaks of himself as a 'called apostle' (1 Cor. 1.1 and Rom. 1.1). This feature of Paul's apostleship is what sets him apart from the other apostles. For in referring to the Twelve (e.g. 1 Cor. 15.5) or to other apostles contemporaneous with him (2 Cor. 12.11; Phil. 2.25; Rom. 16.7) or to apostles active before him (Gal. 1.17), he does not use the term 'called'.[1] As C. Dorsey puts it: 'The apostles who were known to Paul were "sent out", either by Christ or by a church, to perform a specific function. Paul holds a unique position in that he was "called" by the risen Christ'.[2] Paul, in fact, considered himself to have a special apostolic position that was related to the purpose of his calling, for he was called as an apostle to the Gentiles. Paul saw his distinctiveness in the fact that he was the original apostle to the Gentiles.[3]

The Romans' 'identification of sender' unit stands out because of its comparative length and complexity. Though longer and more complex than Paul's other 'identification of sender' units, Paul here identifies only himself. This is an anomaly among the Pauline opening formulas.

In Romans, Paul begins his self-identification with three nominatival substantives that emphasize his unique and important function in relation to the gospel. The first two, δοῦλος and κλητὸς ἀπόστολος, are found in other Pauline opening formulas. The use of 'slave', of course, stresses the bondage to Christ's service that Paul shares with his readers. This is why in Philippians he can designate both himself and Timothy as slaves.[4] When placed in combination with a reference to his apostolic call (κλητὸς ἀπόστολος), with that combination being

---

1. Cf. C. Dorsey, 'Paul's Use of 'Απόστολος', *RQ* 28 (1986), pp. 193-99 (p. 196).
2. Dorsey, 'Paul's Use of 'Απόστολος' p. 200.
3. So J.A. Kirk: 'Paul's important position lies solely and exclusively in the fact that he was the first person specifically called by the risen Lord to be an apostle to the Gentiles' ('Apostleship since Rengstorf: Towards a Synthesis', *NTS* 21 [1975], pp. 249-64 [p. 263]).
4. Cf. M.V. Abraham: 'As a Christian Paul is a slave of Christ, one who has accepted the mastery of Christ over his life' ('Paul: The Unique Apostle', *IJT* 26 [1977], pp. 62-72 [p. 68]).

found only in Romans, it gives a deeper sense to Paul's apostolic understanding. For he is one whose bondage to Christ requires him to exercise a specific apostolic role—that of an apostle to the Gentiles.[1]

The third nominatival substantive is a participial phrase (ἀφωρισμένος εἰς εὐαγγέλιον θεοῦ) and is unique to the 'identification of sender' unit of the Romans opening formula. 'Set apart for the gospel of God' indicates most clearly the unique position Paul considered he had been called to. This phrase has invited suggestions that Paul saw himself in the tradition of Jeremiah, and so 'integrates himself into the world plan of God as a significant and indispensable member'.[2] Paul's conviction of the unique nature of his apostleship has also been taken by some to mean that he claimed for himself a particularly pivotal role in God's plan in bringing about the last days through the conversion of the Gentiles.[3]

J. Knox, however, argues that this latter proposal regarding Paul's apostolic self-consciousness is too 'exalted'. If this were the case, Knox asks, why would Paul stay at least ten years in the eastern Roman empire attending not just to evangelism but also to the care and nurture of Christian communities. Furthermore, if Paul believed that the consummation of the plan of God depended on his preaching of the gospel to all nations, why do we not read some reference to this in his imprisonment letters. Surely Paul would allude to this during that period of time when such a mission was being thwarted. Knox sees Paul's apostolic self-understanding to be that he was the one 'who had been sent *primarily* and *expressly* to the Gentiles or the nations'.[4] Paul considered himself to have a particular responsibility for the defence of the preaching to the Gentiles and for the rightful place of the Gentiles within God's purposes.[5]

---

1. So C.K. Barrett, *The Signs of an Apostle* (London: Epworth, 1970), pp. 45-46.
2. K.H. Rengstorf, 'ἀπόστολος', in *Theological Dictionary of the New Testament* (ed. G. Kittel, trans. and ed. by G.W. Bromiley; Grand Rapids: Eerdmans, 1964), I, p. 438. See also J.D.G. Dunn, *Romans 1–8* (Dallas, TX: Word, 1988), p. 22.
3. So O. Cullmann, 'Le caractère eschatologique de devoir missionaire et de la conscience apostolique de S. Paul', *Revue d'Histoire et de Philosophie religieuses* 16 (1936), pp. 210-45; A. Fridrichsen, 'The Apostle and His Message', p. 3; Munck, *Paul and the Salvation of Mankind*, p. 43; Barrett, *The Signs of an Apostle*, p. 42.
4. 'Romans 15.14-33 and Paul's Conception of His Apostolic Mission' *JBL* 83 (1964), pp. 1-11 (pp. 5-6).
5. Knox, 'Romans 15.14-33', p. 6.

After these three descriptive phrases the focus shifts in v. 2 to a description of the gospel. There is a balance of descriptive ideas on either side of ὃ προεπηγγείλατο. On the one side, Paul describes himself as an apostle who has been set apart for the gospel. On the other, he describes that gospel as being the fulfilment of God's promises. So Paul's authority is underscored by the fact that his apostleship is on behalf of a gospel that is the fulfilment of God's purposes. Paul's authority is the direct result of the authority of the gospel.[1]

The focus of the prepositional phrase περὶ τοῦ υἱοῦ αὐτοῦ of v. 3 remains on the gospel of God, for it concerns the content and object of the gospel. The description of 'his son' in vv. 3-4 is a carefully crafted chiastic form:

ἐκ σπέρματος. . .
    κατὰ σάρκα
    κατὰ πνεῦμα. . .
ἐξ ἀναστάσεως νεκρῶν

Worked into the chiasmus is a counterpoint of attributive participial phrases τοῦ γενομένου and τοῦ ὁρισθέντος υἱοῦ θεοῦ.

There are, however, two features of vv. 3-4 that unbalance the otherwise symmetrical structure of these verses—the appearance of the expression ἐν δυνάμει and the use of ἁγιωσύνης. These two features are particularly noteworthy, for if, as many have argued, Paul has in these verses incorporated an early Christian credal formula,[2] then the inclusion of words that disrupt the balance of that credal formulation might signal Paul's own personal emphases.[3]

---

1. Cf. J.-N. Aletti, 'L'authorité apostolique de Paul. Théorie et pratique' in *L'Apôtre Paul. Personnalité, style et conception du ministère* (ed. A. Vanhoye; Leuven: Leuven University Press, 1986), pp. 229-46 (p. 246). See also J.H. Schütz, *Paul and the Anatomy of Apostolic Authority* (Cambridge: Cambridge University Press, 1975), p. 248.

2. See e.g. A.M. Hunter, *Paul and His Predecessors* (London: Nicholson and Watson, 1940), pp. 25-30; Käsemann, *Romans*, p. 10; C.K. Barrett, *The Epistle to the Romans* (New York: Harper, 1957), pp. 3, 18; C.E.B. Cranfield, *The Epistle to the Romans* (Edinburgh: T. & T. Clark, 1975, 1979), I, p. 57 n. 5; R.N. Longenecker, *The Christology of Early Jewish Christianity* (London: SCM, 1970), p. 96; Bornkamm, *Paul*, p. 248.

3. See R. Jewett's suggestion that there are several levels of redactional activity visible in this confession ('The Redaction and Use of an Early Christian Confession in Romans 1.3-4' in *The Living Text; Essays in Honor of Ernest W. Saunders* [ed. R. Jewett and D.E. Groh; Washington: University Press of America, 1985], pp. 99-122). Jewett suggests that the Pauline redactional level includes the insertion of the

The opening formula of Romans continues in v. 4b, being still governed by the περί of v. 3a. So the second occurrence of the name of God's son, viz. ' Ιησοῦ Χριστοῦ. This identification is the climax of a string of descriptive units used to delineate εὐαγγέλιον θεοῦ (v. 1b) and then τοῦ υἱοῦ αὐτοῦ (v. 3a). The good news of God is Jesus Christ. Paul, however, does not expect the gospel of Jesus Christ to be news to his readers, since he affirms that both he and they acknowledge Christ's lordship.[1]

Here in vv. 1-3 we begin to see something of the dynamic of (1) Paul's identification with his readers, yet (2) his separation from them. For while Paul affirms that both he and his readers are under the lordship of Christ (with, of course, a κύριος implying a δοῦλος), he reserves the special designation δοῦλος Χριστοῦ 'Ιησοῦ (v. 1) for himself. This characteristic balance between equality and authority is common to all of Paul's letters because, as J.L. White observes, 'though Paul and his congregations were familially related by God's grace, Paul had been assigned the responsibility of securing his brethren's spiritual maturation'.[2] This dual feature of Paul's relationship with his readers is especially clear in Romans.

After identifying Jesus Christ as the content of the gospel, Paul then places his apostleship in relation to Christ in saying δι' οὗ ἐλάβομεν χάριν καὶ ἀποστολήν (v. 5a), which sets out a direct line of authority from Christ to Paul. The plural ἐλάβομεν has been variously understood. It is usually seen as a literary plural, largely because Paul in other contexts never shares the apostolic role. Yet χάρις is a gift to all Christians (e.g. Rom. 5.2). So *BDF* interprets ἐλάβομεν here as a literary plural with the proviso that 'ἀποστολήν evidently applies to Paul himself, but the addressees and all Christians (4. τοῦ κυρίου ἡμῶν) are included in χάρις, so that he could not have written ἔλαβον χάριν'.[3]

---

phrase ἐν δυνάμει and the qualifying genitive ἁγιωσύνης (p. 113). Jewett also proposes that Paul's redaction accords with the prominent themes of his letter. The phrase ἐν δυνάμει corresponds with his interest in showing the power of the gospel (1.16; 15.13; 15.19) (p. 118). The qualifying of the spirit with the phrase 'of holiness' 'made clear that the divine power celebrated in the confession entailed moral obligations' (p. 117). This theme is developed, according to Jewett, in Romans 5–8 and in 12.1.

1. Cf. V.H. Neufeld, *The Earliest Christian Confessions* (Grand Rapids: Eerdmans, 1963), p. 51; O. Kuss, *Der Römerbrief* (Regensburg: Pustet, 1963), p. 8.
2. 'Ancient Greek Letters', p. 98.
3. *BDF*, para. 280.

It is possible, however, to avoid such an awkward interpretation by
regarding ἐλάβομεν as an authentic literary plural[1] and the καί of
χάριν καὶ ἀποστολήν as either (1) epexegetical (we received grace,
i.e. apostleship)[2] or (2) the coordinate of an hendiadys.[3] The sense in
this latter case would then be: (the) grace of apostleship, with apostleship seen as dependent on grace. E.A. Nida argues that the καί of v. 5
does not join two co-ordinate ideas (grace and apostleship) but rather
two ideas, one of which is semantically subordinate, with the result
that apostleship defines a particular aspect of the grace that Paul has
received.[4] Understood in this way, Paul is here describing, by means
of an epistolary plural, the direct relationship between the gift of his
apostleship[5] and the Lord whom the Roman Christians acknowledge,
and so drawing their attention to his special role in relation to their
faith.

So the descriptive process has come full circle, with Paul returning
in v. 5 to a description of his own identity. In a style contiguous with
what has already been seen, Paul uses in vv. 5b-6 four prepositional
phrases: εἰς ὑπακοὴν πίστεως; ἐν πᾶσιν τοῖς ἔθνεσιν; ὑπὲρ τοῦ
ὀνόματος αὐτοῦ; and ἐν οἷς ἐστε καὶ ὑμεῖς κλητοὶ Ἰησοῦ
Χριστοῦ.

The first phrase describes the purpose of Paul's gift of apostleship,
viz. 'the obedience of faith'.[6] Whether πίστεως is a subjective genitive
('obedience that results from faith'),[7] an objective genitive ('obedience

1. The function of a literary plural is 'to bring the reader (or hearer) into associa-
tion with his own action' (*BDF*, para. 280).
2. Grace and apostleship being in apposition.
3. Cf. *BDF*, para. 442 [16], where Rom. 1.5 is cited as an example of καί used
for an hendiadys (thereby implicitly contradicting the interpretation given for the literary plural in ἐλάβομεν [*BDF*, para. 280], where the καί was evidently not understood to be used for an hendiadys).
4. 'Implications of Contemporary Linguistics for Biblical Scholarship', *JBL* 91
(1972), pp. 73-89 (p. 81).
5. See also H. von Lips, who argues that χάρις is semantically connected
throughout Paul's letters to χάρισμα, so that Paul understood his apostleship to be a
divine gift to the Christian community comparable to the other spiritual gifts ('Der
Apostolat des Paulus—ein Charisma? Semantische Aspekte zu *charis-charisma* und
anderen Wortpaaren im Sprachgebrauch des Paulus', *Bib* 66 [1985], pp. 305-43).
6. Note the parallelism to the εἰς phrase in v. 1b, which also concerns the purpose
of Paul's apostleship.
7. So Robertson, 'obedience that comes from faith' (*A Grammar of the Greek
New Testament in the Light of Historical Research* [New York: Hodder &
Stoughton, 1914], p. 500).

to faith'), or epexegetical ('obedience that equals faith'),[1] the fact is that Paul's commission is to bring about faith in the gospel, the content of which he has just delineated, and that faith involves obedience. As Nida puts it, 'an examination of the semantic structures shows clearly that between Paul's activity as an apostle and the people's believing and obeying there is a causative relationship. Paul is thus the causative agent.'[2]

The second prepositional phrase of the description, ἐν πᾶσιν τοῖς ἔθνεσιν, casts a line, as it were, to the audience. The group to whom Paul has been sent, τὰ ἔθνη, is the group to which the Romans belong (cf. ἐν οἷς ἐστε καὶ ὑμεῖς of v. 6). Here Paul makes a direct connection between his apostleship and his readers, for at this point the Roman readers would know that he considers that they are among his apostolic charges.[3]

His description continues in the third prepositional phrase, ὑπὲρ τοῦ ὀνόματος αὐτοῦ. The antecedent for the possessive pronoun is Ἰησοῦ Χριστοῦ of 4b, which also describes the purpose and manner of Paul's apostleship. His work is on behalf of the name of Christ Jesus. This is a reinforcement of what he said at the beginning, just as was the εἰς phrase earlier in this verse.

In the final prepositional phrase, which fills out all of v. 6, Paul carefully and tactfully places his readers in relation to himself. For they are part of his mission, not because Paul has chosen them but because God has chosen them for Paul. However, the syntactical relation between κλητοὶ Ἰησοῦ Χριστοῦ and the first part of v. 6 is, at best, rather distant. The force of the first part of v. 6 comes from the relative pronoun οἷς, the antecedent obviously being ἔθνεσιν. The second part of the verse, κλητοὶ Ἰησοῦ Χριστοῦ, is not, however, related to the first part—i.e. κλητοὶ Ἰησοῦ Χριστοῦ is not the object of ἐστε. A comma needs to be understood after ὑμεῖς. Such an understanding would set up a pattern for vv. 5-6 analogous to that of vv. 3-4 where a series of descriptive prepositional phrases culminate in an

---

1. So Nida, 'Implications of Contemporary Linguistics', p. 82.
2. Nida, 'Implications of Contemporary Linguistics', p. 82. Cf. Rengstorf who writes that Paul sees 'in his apostolate (ἀποστολή) a proof of divine grace (χάρις). . . which leads man to obedient subjection to God' ('ἀπόστολος', p. 439).
3. Cf. Dahl: 'They too are included among the nations to whom the Lord has sent Paul, giving him grace to carry out his apostolic task' ('The Missionary Theology in the Epistle to the Romans', p. 75).

identifying substantive phrase. So whereas in v. 4b the phrase was Ἰησοῦ Χριστοῦ τοῦ κυρίου ἡμῶν, in v. 6 it is κλητοὶ Ἰησοῦ Χριστοῦ—with these words of v. 6 identifying the subject of ἐστε just as the phrase at the end of v. 4 identified the subject of the participles γενομένου and ὁρισθέντος.

In v. 6 Paul finally identifies his readers. They are those 'called of Jesus Christ'. The genitive here is generally understood to be a genitive of possession,[1] thereby meaning 'called to belong to Jesus Christ'. And this is almost certainly the sense, since a subjective genitive would be contradictory to Paul's general understanding that it is God (not Jesus Christ) who does the calling (e.g. 1 Cor. 1.9; 1 Thess. 5.23-24).

It is to be noted, however, that here in Romans is the only instance in all of Paul's letters where addressees are identified within an 'identification of sender' unit of an opening formula. κλητοὶ Ἰησοῦ Χριστοῦ is not the beginning of the 'designation of recipient' unit because it is not in the dative; rather it is the conclusion of Paul's self-introduction. It should be understood in comparison to the substantive phrase κλητὸς ἀπόστολος of v. 1, which functions in apposition to Παῦλος. This latter phrase is a straightforward statement of identity—Paul is a called apostle. What is stressed in the substantive phrase of v. 6, however, is not identity but relationship. The Roman Christians are in a called relationship to Jesus Christ. Paul obviously shares this relationship to Christ but he, unlike them, has been called to a specific role in relation to Christ.

The most noteworthy feature of the 'identification of sender' unit of the opening of Romans is its comparative length. That Paul includes so much information at this point suggests how little information he and his readers had shared with each other. It suggests, in other words, that in this letter Paul is presenting himself to his readers and giving them as full and as positive a picture of himself and what he stands for as he can. Generally a communication will not go into detail on matters that the author and the readers share in common, since that can be a hindrance to real communication.[2] Where authors are seeking to establish credibility with an audience, however, they will point out

1. See *BDF*, para. 183; also Sanday and Headlam, *Romans*, p. 12.
2. Cf. Nida: 'Going into detail about common information immediately creates a barrier to real communication, since it suggests to the receptor that the source and he do not have much in common after all or that the message is really being directed to someone else' ('Implications of Contemporary Linguistics', p. 80).

those things that are a bond between them and present the credentials on which acceptance of the communication rests.

Another remarkable feature is that this letter, alone among all the Pauline letters, is sent only by Paul. When noted in combination with Paul's underscoring of his apostolic stature (1.1), the issue of his apostolic relationship with his readers seems to be signalled right at the beginning of the letter. This is seen even more clearly in contrast to the Thessalonian letters and Philippians, where Paul identifies himself and his co-senders as if they were all equally important. In these letters Paul does not stress his apostolicity. It may be that, in Romans, the combination of an emphasis on his apostolic role, along with Paul's sending the letter from himself alone, indicates a special concern that the readers accept his understanding of his unique position. E. Best observes that it is in those letters written to churches where Paul's apostolic position was being questioned that he asserts his apostleship at the letter-opening.[1] By analogy with the Corinthian letters and Galatians, Best argues that Paul's use of 'apostle' in the opening of Romans is one of the indications that Paul is also writing to Rome in a self-defensive manner.[2] Whether or not evidence from the rest of the opening and closing sections of Romans corroborates the hypothesis that Paul wrote in a self-defensive stance remains to be seen.

In Romans, Paul's self-identification progresses from (1) an affirmation of his special role in relation to the gospel, to (2) highlighting the fact that the gospel for which he was commissioned is the very one the Romans have believed in, since it concerns τοῦ κυρίου ἡμῶν, to (3) a direct reference to his apostleship as a commission from Christ, which immediately concerns his readers because they are his apostolic charges. It is possible that κλητοὶ Ἰησοῦ Χριστοῦ of v. 6b, coming as it does at the end of this elaborate development that details the basis for Paul's authority with his readers, sounds an exhortative note. Perhaps Paul is concerned that the Roman believers were not living in accordance with their called position. On the other hand, this peculiar identification of his readers may signal that Paul was concerned to affirm his respect for the Christian integrity of his readers, while at the same time expressing his opinion that he is called to exercise his apostolic office among them.

1. 'Paul's Apostolic Authority—?', *JSNT* 27 (1986), p. 7.
2. 'Paul's Apostolic Authority—?', p. 8.

B. *The 'Designation of Recipient' Unit*

The 'designation of recipient' unit of the Pauline opening formulas invariably uses the dative case. The designation typically includes the word ἐκκλησία along with the name of the city or region where the church is found. So the Thessalonian letters are addressed to 'the church of the Thessalonians'. Both the Corinthian letters have 'to the church of God which is at Corinth'. The address of 1 Corinthians also includes 'everyone everywhere who calls on the name of the Lord Jesus Christ in every place, theirs and ours'. T.W. Manson suggests that here τόπος refers to churches (i.e. places of worship) analogous to the Jewish use of the term.[1] He takes the meaning to be that the letter is addressed both to churches that Paul founded and to those founded by other Christian missionaries: 'The force of the whole pre-script is thus to stress the unity of the Church as a whole, and at the same time to insist on the equality of the different communities comprised in the unity. The Corinthian Christians are Saints by calling along with all the others and on precisely the same footing as others.'[2] The address of 2 Corinthians incorporates all the saints in all of Achaia. The letter to the Galatians begins in a similar fashion: 'to the churches in Galatia'. Philippians does not use the word 'church' in this unit, but its address to all the saints at Philippi, including the bishops and deacons, conveys the same sense.

The peculiarities of the 'designation of recipient' unit of Philemon result from that letter being a personal letter to Philemon.[3] The singular possessive σου in the phrase τῇ κατ' οἶκον σου ἐκκλησίᾳ suggests that the church met in the house of Philemon, since he is the first mentioned, and therefore that the letter is primarily addressed to him.[4] Paul wanted to ensure his letter was heard by both specific individuals (Archippus and Apphia) and the house church to which Philemon belonged.[5]

---

1. 'The Corinthian Correspondence (1)', pp. 192 and 208-209.
2. 'The Corinthian Correspondence (1)', p. 192.
3. For another opinion, see C.S. Winter, who argues that Philemon is not a personal letter but is addressed primarily to a church, within which the individual addressed is a member ('Paul's Letter to Philemon', *NTS* 33 [1987], p. 1).
4. Knox, on the other hand, argues that since Archippus is the person nearest this phrase he must be the person to whom the letter is addressed (*Philemon*, p. 62).
5. Cf. E. Lohse, *A Commentary on the Epistles to the Colossians and to Philemon* (trans. W.R. Poehlmann and R.J. Karris; ed. H. Koester; Philadelphia: Fortress, 1971), p. 191.

The 'designation of recipient' unit of Romans lacks the word ἐκκλησία. Romans' address appears more inclusive—'to all those in Rome who are beloved of God and who are called to be saints'.[1]

The phrase ἐν θεῷ πατρί or ἐν Χριστῷ is a common description of the church to which Paul is writing. In the Thessalonian letters, 1 Corinthians and Philippians Paul describes the recipient church using one or other of these prepositional phrases. It would appear that in so doing he affirms their good standing in the faith[2], for the letters in which Paul does not so speak of the recipient church are 2 Corinthians and Galatians. We know from the letter-body of both of these letters that Paul did not consider these churches to be living in accordance with the gospel as he had taught it to them. We may, then, surmise that the absence of this phrase from 2 Corinthians and Galatians could be the result of Paul's concern over the present faith and practice of these churches.

The phrase also does not occur in Philemon and Romans. As noted above, in these letters alone Paul does not address his recipients as a church. In the case of Philemon the reason for this is obvious. In the case of Romans the reason is less clear. Neither ἐκκλησία nor ἐν Χριστῷ/ἐν θεῷ πατρί appear in the 'designation of recipient' unit of Romans. The absence of the latter description is no doubt the result of the absence of the former. And the absence of both is noteworthy. Such an omission might signal Paul's concern over some feature or features of his recipients' faith and practice. Such a functional reason

---

1. I consider ἐν 'Ρώμῃ at Rom. 1.7 and 15 to be original. Cranfield's assessment of the probable explanations for the textual variants is convincing (*The Epistle to the Romans* I, pp. 6-11). Cf. B. Metzger, *A Textual Commentary on the Greek New Testament* (London: United Bible Societies, 1975), p. 505. See also Dahl: 'It is as a letter to Rome that the epistle has an integral function in Paul's apostolic ministry. The deletion of the concrete address, as well as of the last sections of the Epistle, will have to be explained as the result of editorial activity which must have occurred between the times of Paul and Marcion' ('The Particularity of the Pauline Epistles as a Problem in the Ancient Church', p. 269).

2. Cf. J.A. Ziesler who points to the ethical sense conveyed by 'in Christ': 'Christ in believers means that Christ's life is in them, that he is working in them, which produces fruit. . . for moral renewal' (*The Meaning of Righteousness in Paul. A Linguistic and Theological Inquiry* [Cambridge: Cambridge University Press, 1972], p. 168).

for the absence of 'church' from the address is suggested, for example, by J.C. Beker[1] and F. Watson.[2]

Rather than affirming that his Roman readers are an ἐκκλησία, perhaps even a church ἐν Χριστῷ/ἐν θεῷ πατρί, Paul might be addressing them in an hortatory manner. He may be reminding them pointedly of their call, rather than affirming them in their faith.

It is to be noted further that only in Romans and 1 Corinthians does Paul describe his readers as 'called to be holy'. In 1 Corinthians this might signal Paul's concerns for the faith and practice of his readership which are indicated fully in the letter-body. On the other hand, in 1 Corinthians the phrase 'called to be holy', and its accompanying 'beloved in Christ Jesus', may serve to affirm Paul's relationship with the individuals who comprise 'the church of God at Corinth'. If this were the case, then by analogy, the occurrence of the plural description for his readers in the Roman letter apart from the word 'church', suggests that Paul is reaching out and affirming the individuals within his readership, rather than only addressing a group. Paul explicitly directs his letter to the many believing persons at Rome ('to all who are in Rome'). These different believers were both Gentile[3] and Jewish Christians.[4] It would seem most probable that Paul does not address his readers as a 'church' because he wants his letter to communicate with the many different individual Christians in Rome, even if they are not part of one Christian group. It would be wise not to enlarge

1. Beker suggests that 'Paul's dialogue with Jews in Romans compels him to forego the term *ekklesia* because he intends to show that the true *ekklesia* is a future eschatological reality that will only be realized when it comprises the whole people of Israel (*Paul the Apostle*, p. 316).

2. Watson considers that the absence of 'church' from the address of Romans is one of the pieces of evidence that at Rome there is not one Roman congregation, but two opposing groups of Christians (*Paul, Judaism and the Gentiles*, p. 104). Paul writes in order to reconcile them to each other under the Pauline gospel.

3. Most scholars hold that Romans is addressed to a predominantly Gentile readership. Cf. Sanday and Headlam: 'there were Jews in the Church. . . but it is further clear that St Paul regards the church as broadly and in the main a Gentile church' (*Romans*, p. xxxiii). Also, Gaston writes: 'As in his other letters, he is writing to Gentile Christians (1.5, 13-15; 11.13; 15.15-21), dealing presumably with a Gentile–Christian situation' (*Paul and the Torah*, p. 116); see also, Kümmel: 'the letter characterizes its readers unambiguously as *Gentile Christians*' (*Introduction*, p. 309); and Klein, 'Paul's Purpose in Writing the Epistle to the Romans', p. 40.

4. Cranfield states: 'That the church in Rome included some Jews may be taken as certain' (*The Epistle to the Romans* I, p. 18).

this observation to a hypothesis that the absence of 'church' indicates an admonitory attitude on Paul's part towards his readers.

The 'designation of recipient' unit of Romans, then, is distinctive in the general character of its address. It is unique also in not describing the addressed group as ἐν Χριστῷ/ἐν θεῷ πατρί. It is similar to 1 Corinthians, however, in stressing that the readers are called to be holy.

C. *The 'Greeting' Unit*

The 'greeting' unit of the Pauline opening formula invariably begins with χάρις ὑμῖν καὶ εἰρήνη. As noted in the previous chapter, 'grace to you and peace' as an opening greeting breaks with Greek epistolary convention, which generally used simply χαίρειν. Some have suggested that the origin of Paul's distinctive greeting is Semitic rather than Greek, for the most commonly used word in a Semitic epistolary greeting was 'peace'. This proposal, however, does not fully account for the Pauline formula. As J.M. Lieu writes, Paul's formula 'to both Greeks and Jews. . . must have sounded very distinctive'.[1] So Paul's combination of grace and peace in his opening greeting must be seen as an expression of the apostolic goal he has for his readers. Lieu puts it: 'If the letters were read to the gathered congregation at worship, they would declare that Paul, as an "apostle of Jesus Christ by the will of God", willed for and proclaimed to that congregation the gifts of salvation made available by God through Jesus Christ. Thus, the letters manifest in his absence the role Paul assumed when present.'[2] Paul's transformation of the conventional epistolary greeting formula, then, functions to remind his readers both of his apostolic authority and of the gifts of grace and peace which they have received.[3]

In all Paul's letters but 1 Thessalonians χάρις ὑμῖν καὶ εἰρήνη is supplemented by the prepositional phrase ἀπὸ θεοῦ πατρὸς ἡμῶν καὶ κυρίου Ἰησοῦ Χριστοῦ.

1. J.M. Lieu, ' "Grace to you and Peace": The Apostolic Greeting', *BJRL* 68 (1985), pp. 161-78 (p. 167).
2. Lieu, 'Grace to You and Peace', p. 179.
3. Cf. White, who writes: 'Though Paul never cites the conventional wish for health, he does express his concern for his recipients' welfare; his concern is not with ordinary well-being, but with his recipients' spiritual conformity to the standards of a new spiritual age' (*Light from Ancient Letters*, p. 20).

In Galatians Paul goes on to describe the work of Christ and then closes his 'greeting' unit with a doxology ascribing glory to Christ forever, ending with 'amen'. This addition signals Paul's concern over his Galatian addressees' interpretation of the gospel and underlines Paul's conviction that he has apostolic authority to convey the power of that salvation offered in Christ. The opening formula of Galatians, then, serves less to re-establish a common bond than to set Paul apart as the authoritative apostle.

The Romans 'greeting' unit, however, is entirely standard. It functions, as do comparable units in all the other Pauline letters apart from Galatians, to affirm the faith Paul shares in common with his readers, to (re)establish the common bond they have in Christ, and to remind them of his apostolic hopes for them.

D. *Comparative Observations*

The relationships between the units in the opening formulas of 1 and 2 Thessalonians, 2 Corinthians, and Philemon are straightforward—each fulfilling its function with nothing untoward calling for attention. The opening formula of Philippians is likewise straightforward, although its 'designation of recipient' unit is a little more descriptive than the others just mentioned. The opening formula of 1 Corinthians affirms Paul's apostolic role in the 'identification of sender' unit, while at the same time affirming his regard for his readers in the 'designation of recipient' unit where Paul describes his readers as beloved in Christ Jesus and called to be holy.

The opening formulas that exhibit the greatest number of irregularities are those of Galatians and Romans. Galatians has an exceptionally brief and sparse 'designation of recipient' unit, reflecting, no doubt, the stern manner with which Paul approaches his readers in this letter. Both the 'identification of sender' and the 'greetings' units take every opportunity to stress the essentials of Paul's gospel: God raised Christ from the dead (1.2); Christ gave himself for our sins and believers are now freed from the grip of the present evil age (1.4); and glory is to be ascribed to God (1.5). The fact that so much doctrinal material appears in the opening formula of Galatians suggests that Paul is primarily concerned with correcting the Galatian churches' understanding of the gospel. The fact that the doctrinal material appears in both the first and the third units (the first being the one where Paul usually says most about himself; the third being the one where he customarily expresses his prayer for his readers) suggests that Paul considered it vitally important to present a correct picture of his role as apostle and to try to reshape his readers' understanding of the good news.

The opening formula of Romans is quite ill-proportioned in comparison with that of Paul's other letters, with the preponderance of its abnormal length occurring in the 'identification of sender' unit. Here Paul defines his apostolic role by emphasizing that he is both a slave of Christ Jesus and that he is set apart for the gospel of God. Paul evidently considers that such a self-identification is insufficient of itself and so incorporates a credal statement (1.3-4) that is placed in direct relationship to his commissioning on behalf of the gospel. He gives an apologetic, as it were, for his apostolic credibility by affirming the creed that he shares with his readers.[1] In so doing he creates a bond between himself and his readers. Then he returns to a description of his apostolic commission (v. 5), in the process making it clear that he considers his addressees to be among his charges.

---

1. Cf. S. Brown, who considers that the pre-Pauline confessional hymn in 1.3-4, along with Paul's expression of his personal experience of the righteousness of God in Christ (1.16-17), suggest Paul's 'purpose. . . to be to recommend himself to a community which he does not know personally. Before he expounds to the Romans his own personal gospel, he shows himself prepared to accept a traditional formulation' (*The Origins of Christianity*, p. 127).

Chapter 4

THE PAULINE THANKSGIVINGS

A. *Paul Schubert's Work on the Structure of the Pauline Thanksgivings and a Proposal*

The Pauline thanksgivings, as noted in Chapter 2, were subjected to a rigorous literary analysis earlier in this century by Paul Schubert.[1] Schubert maintained that there are two types of thanksgiving periods and that the differences between them have to do chiefly with how each proceeds to its 'final' clause. Schubert's Type Ia begins with a principal verb (εὐχαριστῶ) which is followed by participle constructions and a final clause(s). The participle constructions—either one, two or three participle constructions—modify the principal verb. The constructions include a temporal participle plus a temporal adverb phrase (e.g. μνείαν ποιούμενοι ἐπὶ τῶν προσευχῶν ἡμῶν, 1 Thess. 1.2ff.). This temporal construction is then followed by another participle construction that functions causally, with the final participle(s) being invariably built on verbs of hearing or of learning—i.e. ἀκούειν, μνημονεύειν, εἰδέναι and πείθεσθαι.[2] A Type Ia thanksgiving generally terminates with a purpose clause(s) introduced by ἵνα or εἰς with the articular infinitive.

Schubert argued that both the temporal and the causal participle constructions of Type Ia modify the thanksgiving's principal verb.[3] The first participle construction (generally μνείαν ποιούμενοι ἐπὶ τῶν προσευχῶν ἡμῶν), having temporal force, modifies both εὐχαριστῶ τῷ θεῷ πάντοτε as a whole and the adverb πάντοτε on its own.[4] The causal participle construction does not modify the preceding participle but the principal verb εὐχαριστῶ: 'I thank

---

1. *Thanksgivings.*
2. *Thanksgivings*, p. 62.
3. *Thanksgivings*, p. 66.
4. *Thanksgivings*, p. 66.

God... because I have heard (remember, know, trust)'.[1] The terminal clauses of Type Ia, however, modify the first participle construction, since they record Paul's prayer, as well as all the preceding material, since for Paul petitionary prayer is always given in a spirit of thanksgiving.[2]

A Type Ib thanksgiving also begins with the principal verb εὐχαριστῶ. This is followed by a causal ὅτι clause that is subordinate to the principal verb clause. Then follows a consecutive clause introduced by ὥστε that is subordinate to the ὅτι clause.[3]

The major differences between Type Ia and Ib, according to Schubert, are: (1) the absence in Type Ib of a temporal participle clause with a temporal adverb phrase and a causal participle clause or adverb phrase, which separate the initial εὐχαριστῶ formula from its terminal clauses; (2) the way the thanksgiving concludes, either with a final ἵνα clause for Type Ia or a causal ὅτι clause for Type Ib; and (3) the relationship between the temporal adverb and the pronominal object phrase in each type of thanksgiving. In Type Ia the pronominal object phrase, περὶ ὑμῶν, modifies the following temporal participle clause where Paul tells how he daily intercedes for them, resulting in the meaning 'as often as we think about you in our (daily) prayers'.[4] In Type Ib both the pronominal object phrase and the temporal adverb modify the principal verb.

Of those letters that concern us here, Schubert identifies Type Ia thanksgivings in 1 Thessalonians, Philippians and Philemon, and Type Ib thanksgivings in 2 Thessalonians and 1 Corinthians. Schubert considers the Romans thanksgiving to be a 'mixed type': 1.8ff. is Type Ib; 1.10ff. is Type Ia. Schubert's comments concerning any functional distinction between the two types of thanksgivings consist in saying that Type Ia thanksgivings are 'structurally more elaborate', and so they are appropriate to 'the more elaborate, intimate and personal letters of Paul', whereas Type Ib, 'the simpler thanksgivings', tend to 'characterize the structurally less elaborate and less intimate, less personal letters'.[5]

Schubert has contributed much to an understanding of syntactical relations among the units of a Pauline thanksgiving. Also of impor-

---

1. *Thanksgivings*, p. 67.
2. *Thanksgivings*, p. 67.
3. *Thanksgivings*, p. 35.
4. *Thanksgivings*, p. 70.
5. *Thanksgivings*, p. 183.

The Pauline Thanksgivings

Key	1 Thess. 1.2-10	2 Thess. 1.3-12	1 Cor. 1.4-9	Phil. 1.3-11	Phlm. 4-6	Rom. 1.8-15
A. Ἐυχαριστῶ...	A 1.2a	A 1.3a	A 1.4a	A 1.3a	A v. 4a	A 1.8a
B. Manner of Thanksgiving	B 1.2b	B 1.3b	B 1.4b	C 1.3b	B v. 4b	B 1.8b
				B 1.4		C 1.8c
C. Cause	C 1.2c-5a	C 1.3c	C 1.4c-5	C 1.5-6	C v. 5	B 1.9
D. Explanation	D 1.5b-10	D 1.4-10	D 1.6-9	D 1.7-8		E 1.10
E. Concerns for Readers/Prayer Report		E 1.11-12		E 1.9-11	E v. 6	D 1.11-12
						E 1.13a
						D 1.13b-15

tance is Schubert's observation that 'each thanksgiving not only announces clearly the subject matter of the letter, but also foreshadows unmistakably its stylistic qualities, the degree of intimacy and other important characteristics'.[1] And this insight with regard to the introductory function of the Pauline thanksgivings has been largely confirmed by recent comparisons of the language of the thanksgivings with similar language in parts of the various letter-bodies.

The Pauline thanksgivings contain warm, encouraging and affirmative statements. This type of statement has been labelled by A.C. Sundberg as 'enabling language'.[2] Sundberg noted that such 'encouraging, supportive, complimentary language'[3] also appears in Paul's various letter-bodies. That enabling language occurs both in the thanksgivings and the letter-bodies suggests (1) that what Paul says in his thanksgiving is not formal but rather an expression of his real feelings for his readers[4] and (2) that such statements reveal something of his relationship with his readers.[5]

Schubert's analysis of Paul's thanksgiving periods concentrates almost exclusively on the initial part of the thanksgivings (i.e. on εὐχαριστῶ τῷ θεῷ πάντοτε περὶ πάντων ὑμῶν) and, where applicable, on the temporal constructions that follow. He does not, however, analyse in comparable detail the structure and function of the terminal clauses. Nor does he give much attention to the function of καθώς clauses or similar consecutive clauses, which are standard features of a Pauline thanksgiving.

Our proposal is that there is only one type of Pauline thanksgiving within which there may occur five distinct functional units. The first unit (A) contains the principal verb εὐχαριστῶ and its personal object τῷ θεῷ (μου). The second unit (B) has adverbial and/or participial constructions that serve to indicate the manner in which Paul gives thanks. The pronominal object phrase περὶ (ὑπὲρ) πάντων ὑμῶν occurs in this unit in every letter except Philemon.

---

1. *Thanksgivings*, p. 77.
2. 'Enabling Language in Paul', *HTR* 79 (1986), pp. 270-77.
3. 'Enabling Language in Paul', p. 271.
4. Cf. Sundberg: 'The enabling statements in Paul are not repeated phrases to which Paul had become habituated' ('Enabling Language in Paul', p. 275).
5. Cf. Sundberg: 'These statements are fresh, spontaneous statements, rich in their variety. They are an intimate insight into the mind of Paul' ('Enabling Language in Paul', pp. 275-76).

The third functional unit (C) of a typical Pauline thanksgiving has causal constructions in the form of phrases using ἐπί[1] or ὅτι and/or participial clauses that function to indicate the reason for Paul's thanksgiving. The participles in this unit are usually built on verbs of learning or hearing.[2]

A fourth function unit (D) is explanatory in function and begins either with καθώς[3] (1 Thessalonians, 1 Corinthians and Philippians) or some other consecutive explanatory conjunction such as ὥστε (2 Thessalonians) or γάρ (Romans). This unit usually modifies the preceding causal unit and so functions to elaborate on the cause for Paul's thanksgiving. Schubert recognized that the 'regular occurrence of the καθώς clauses in the Pauline thanksgivings is not accidental, but that a very definite formal functional significance within the thanksgiving pattern attaches to it'.[4] He did not, however, work with the καθώς clauses as a separate functional unit within the thanksgiving.

A fifth functional unit (E) reports what Paul prays for regarding his addressees. The unit often begins by calling attention to Paul's prayer by using the verb προσεύχομαι. The content of Paul's prayer is introduced by some such construction as ἵνα with the subjunctive (2 Thess. 1.11; Phil. 1.9), or ὅπως with the subjunctive (Phlm. 6) or εἴ πως with the infinitive (Rom. 1.10). This unit can contain more than one final clause (e.g. 2 Thessalonians has two: ἵνα, ὅπως; Philippians three: ἵνα, εἰς τό, ἵνα). The two Pauline thanksgivings that do not contain such a final section, as can be seen from the chart, are 1 Thessalonians and 1 Corinthians. Both of these letters end rather with an explanatory section, which section is then rounded off with a faith statement.

It is, in fact, in this final section of his thanksgivings that Paul reveals his real concerns for his addressees.[5] This is in line with

---

1. Schubert's comparative study of thanksgiving periods in biblical materials (both Pauline and non-Pauline), as well as in extra-biblical Hellenistic sources, shows that εὐχαριστῶ ἐπί with the dative is typical of causal adverb phrases (*Thanksgivings*, p. 75).

2. Cf. Schubert, *Thanksgivings*, p. 62.

3. See G.B. Winer, who considers that καθώς is correlative and so gives an explanation for what has preceded rather than a reason (*A Treatise of the Grammar of New Testament Greek Regarded as the Basis of New Testament Exegesis* [Edinburgh: T. & T. Clark, 1870], pp. 555, 561).

4. *Thanksgivings*, p. 31.

5. Cf. Schubert, who claims that at the purpose clause introduced by ἵνα or εἰς with the articular infinitive 'the specific epistolary situation begins to influence form

Schubert's observation that the ἵνα clauses often indicate a paraenetic function.[1]

Schubert recognized that structural differences among the thanksgivings reflected various epistolary situations. He wrote: 'When a Pauline thanksgiving period contains a prominent, structurally significant feature, real or apparent, the first step is to seek its explanation in the epistolary situation which produced the specific letter'.[2] In accordance with the work of Schubert, therefore, I propose that the presence or absence of these five functional units in a Pauline thanksgiving is fundamental in determining the function of any particular Pauline letter.

B. *Analyses of the Respective Thanksgivings*

In the previous chapter the individual units of the Pauline opening formulas were compared with one another. This was possible because of the uniformity in order of the functional units in the Pauline opening formulas. This same regularity, however, does not exist within the various thanksgivings. Furthermore, individual functional units are much more dependent on one another in a thanksgiving than in an opening formula. For these reasons, it is necessary to look at the whole of each letter's thanksgiving in turn. This approach will be maintained, for similar reasons, throughout the remainder of the investigation.

1. *The Thanksgiving of 1 Thessalonians*
The thanksgiving of 1 Thessalonians begins with a principal verb phrase (unit A), with the principal verb here being in the plural. This is in keeping with the opening formula where three senders are identified. Paul then characterizes the manner of his thanksgiving (unit B) with his customary πάντοτε modifying περὶ πάντων ὑμῶν. Following that, he goes on to stress his ceaseless prayer for his converts in two causal constructions. There are two participles in this causal

and content more strongly, a fact which accounts for the greater variety of form and content observable in the thanksgivings from this point on' (*Thanksgivings*, p. 62).

1. *Thanksgivings*, p. 89.
2. *Thanksgivings*, p. 75. Also: 'Our entire study of the form and function of the εὐχαριστῶ-period suggests that there are quite definite motivations (in the epistolary situation) which account for the presence of each structural unit, peculiar or normal' (Schubert, *Thanksgivings*, p. 79; see also p. 64).

unit (unit C), μνημονεύοντες and εἰδότες. The occurrence of two participles in a Pauline thanksgiving is unusual.[1] The result is that this thanksgiving, with its repetition of verbs of knowing, stresses Paul's confident knowledge of the vibrant faith of the Thessalonians, based on his awareness of both their past and their present responses to the gospel.

The explanatory clauses of the thanksgiving (unit D) serve to review the history of the relationship between Paul and his readers, and so to elaborate on the cause of Paul's thanksgiving given in the previous unit. This section further acknowledges the healthy life of faith that the Thessalonians display. The body of 1 Thessalonians is then introduced at 2.1 with a formulaic expression of direct address (αὐτοὶ γὰρ οἴδατε, ἀδελφοί).[2]

Schubert regarded all of 1.2–3.13 as the thanksgiving of 1 Thessalonians, with that thanksgiving having two repetitions of the basic thanksgiving formula (2.13 and 3.9) and closing with εἰς with the articular infinitive at 3.13.[3] Due to its length, Schubert maintained that the thanksgiving period of 1 Thessalonians functions as the body of that letter[4] and not as a typical thanksgiving.[5]

There are, however, several difficulties with Schubert's understanding. The first is that by regarding the thanksgiving of 1 Thessalonians as 'the full development of the contents' of that letter, Schubert radically alters the function of a Pauline thanksgiving for one letter. A second difficulty is that Schubert does not account for the presence of the optative mood in the verbs of his proposed thanksgiving's final clause, i.e. κατευθύναι in 3.11 and πλεονάσαι in 3.12. Nowhere else does the optative mood occur in a final section of a Pauline thanksgiving. And here it changes the character of 3.9-13 from expressing purpose to that of a wish.

---

1. Though Philippians has more causal constructions (a causal participle clause and two causal adverb phrases), only 1 Thessalonians has two causal participle constructions.

2. Cf. White, who considers that the 'disclosure formula at 2.1 is a clear indication that the letter-body is opening' (*Body*, pp. 70f.).

3. *Thanksgivings*, p. 22.

4. Schubert: 'The thanksgiving is the letter, i.e., "the main body" of the letter' (*Thanksgivings*, p. 26).

5. Schubert: 'Generally speaking, it may be said that the Pauline thanksgivings, with the exception of I Thess., serve as a rather formal introduction to the body of the letter' (*Thanksgivings*, p. 24).

A further difficulty with Schubert's view is that 3.9-13, in terms of content and function, fits into the schema of a typical Pauline apostolic parousia. It concerns a visit[1] and includes prayers—either those by Paul for his readers or a request by Paul for prayer on his behalf.[2]

Furthermore, the thanksgiving of 1.2-10 adequately introduces the body of 1 Thessalonians. Thus the original preaching of the gospel by Paul and Paul's defence of his integrity (1.5) are taken up in 2.1-12; the Thessalonians' original reception of that gospel (1.5) and their suffering (1.6) are discussed in 2.13-20; and Paul's concern over the Thessalonians' suffering and his joy at their steadfast faith (1.6-7) are repeated in 3.1-13. Also to be noted is the fact that both the thanksgiving and the letter-body end on an eschatological note.[3] In my view, then, the thanksgiving period of 1 Thessalonians ends at 1.10 with the body of the letter opening at 2.1.

The character of the thanksgiving of 1.2-10 is one of gratitude to God for the Thessalonians' example of Christian faith and work. Their example has made Paul's work easier, for those who know them already know something about the content of the gospel (1.8-10). It is probable, therefore, that it is because of Paul's attitude of gratitude that this thanksgiving does not end with the customary purpose constructions (unit E). The genuine encouragement that Paul feels from the Thessalonians' faith is all that he wants to express in this thanksgiving. And this note of gratitude sounds throughout the letter-body as well.[4]

The function of 1 Thessalonians, therefore, at least as far as it can be gleaned from the thanksgiving period of the letter, seems to be primarily to express Paul's gratitude for the Thessalonians' steadfast faith in the face of persecution. The fact that there is in the thanksgiving no mention of things for which Paul prays (unit E) more than likely results from the fact that the letter-body itself almost exclusively

1. Cf. 1 Cor. 4.19; Phlm 21; Gal. 4.20 (even though this is only a wish to be present); and Rom. 15.22-23, all of which concern a visit and all of which, as we shall see, fall within the apostolic parousia section of a letter.

2. Cf. these passages that also fall within the apostolic parousia sections: 2 Thess. 3.1; Phlm 22; see also Rom. 15.30.

3. Cf. 1.10: καὶ ἀναμένειν τὸν υἱὸν αὐτοῦ. . . τῆς ἐρχομένης; 3.13: ἐν τῇ παρουσίᾳ τοῦ κυρίου. . . ἀγίων αὐτοῦ.

4. Cf. 2.19-20: 'For what is our hope or joy or crown of boasting before our Lord Jesus at his coming? Is it not you? For you are our glory and joy.' Also 3.7: 'In all our distress and affliction we have been comforted by your faith'.

concerns Paul's *cause* for thanksgiving—Paul's profound gratitude for the church at Thessalonica.

2. *The Thanksgiving of 2 Thessalonians*

The thanksgiving period of 2 Thessalonians begins with a εὐχαριστῶ formula (unit A), with the principal verb occurring as an infinitive modified by ὀφείλομεν. The plural subject corresponds to the plural senders of the opening formula. This is followed by a manner unit (unit B) where the pronominal object phrase is modified by καθὼς ἄξιόν ἐστιν. The unusual inclusion of ἀδελφοί highlights Paul's warm relationship with his readers. Then there is a causal construction (unit C) where Paul gives the reason for his thanksgiving, viz. that the Thessalonians have exhibited a growing faith and love for each other. A lengthy explanatory section (unit D) then follows, which extends from ὥστε with the infinitive at v. 4 to the end of v. 10. This explanatory section consists of two main semantic constructions.

The first main construction of the explanatory unit of the thanksgiving of 2 Thessalonians is in v. 4. The result of the Thessalonians' exemplary life of faith is that Paul and his fellow-workers are able to boast in all the churches about the Thessalonians' ὑπομονή and πίστις, which exist even in the face of past and present persecution. The next main construction begins at v. 5, where ἔνδειγμα refers to the steadfastness and faith exhibited by the Thessalonians in their sufferings—which sufferings are evidence of the righteous judgment of God.[1] This statement is explained in three subordinate constructions that follow: εἰς with the articular infinitive in v. 5b; the εἴπερ construction in vv. 6 and 7a; and the temporal construction ἐν τῇ ἀποκαλύψει... φλογός ... ἐν τῇ ἡμέρᾳ ἐκείνῃ of vv. 7b-10.[2] Thus (1) their sufferings have a purpose, for they allow them to be considered worthy of the kingdom of God (v. 5b); (2) their sufferings are not the last act of the play, but there is a further scene in which God's righteous judgment will be shown, and those who now afflict the Thessalonians will be afflicted while the Thessalonians shall have rest (vv. 6-7a);[3] and (3) they will be vindicated when the Lord Jesus is revealed and executes God's righteous judgment on both those who do

---

1. See *BDF*, para. 480 (6), which suggests that ὅ ἐστιν can be understood either as preceding ἔνδειγμα or as a loose 'accusative in apposition to a clause'. The sense, in either case, is 'which is evidence'.
2. 'Εν here with the dative is taken temporally to mean 'when'.
3. Εἴπερ refers to a further condition (or fact) (so *BDF*, para. 454 [2]).

not know God and those who are not in obedience to the gospel (vv. 7b-10).[1]

These explanatory statements of vv. 4-10 are bound together by a ὅτι clause found in the final explanatory construction: ὅτι ἐπιστεύθη τὸ μαρτύριον ἡμῶν ἐφ᾽ ὑμᾶς (v. 10). This clause ties in with the first explanatory construction of v. 4 where Paul exhibits pride in and reliance on the exemplary faith of the Thessalonians. The faith of the Thessalonians and their faithful sufferings, therefore, are proleptic signs of the righteous judgment of God, as well as the ground on which Paul bases his hopes in such a judgment. Paul explains how the Thessalonians' abounding faith and love, which is the cause of his thanksgiving, is also a sign of God's faithfulness and evidence that God will indeed set all things right.

The thanksgiving of 2 Thessalonians continues with a unit (unit E) which reports on what Paul prays for concerning his readers. Its structure is comparable with the beginning of the thanksgiving: a principal verb (προσευχόμεθα), a temporal adverb (πάντοτε) and a pronominal object phrase (περὶ ὑμῶν). This construction relates the purpose of Paul's prayers directly to his cause for thanksgiving (εἰς ὃ καὶ προσευχόμεθα) in a manner not found elsewhere in the Pauline thanksgivings. The repetition of the εὐχαριστῶ type formula stresses both (1) the relationship between Paul's prayer for his readers and his thankfulness for them and (2) the importance of the prayer that follows.

Paul's prayer, which is contained in subjunctive constructions with ἵνα (v. 11b) and ὅπως (v. 12), is that God would strengthen the Thessalonians to remain faithful—that they would continue to have the spiritual resolve that he has affirmed they have in abundance. The prayer that the Thessalonians might remain faithful so that Christ's name would be glorified echoes the earlier part of the thanksgiving where Paul affirmed that this process had already begun.[2]

That the thanksgiving period of 2 Thessalonians ends at 1.12 is indicated by the fact that at 2.1 Paul uses a formula of direct address in which he focuses his remarks on an issue evidently of immediate concern to his readers—the parousia. With this sentence Paul opens the

---

1. The two articles of v. 8, τοῖς μὴ εἰδόσιν and τοῖς μὴ ὑπακούουσιν, suggest two differing groups of people.
2. Cf. v. 4: ὥστε αὐτοὺς ἡμᾶς ἐν ὑμῖν ἐγκαυχᾶσθαι. . . ὑπὲρ τῆς ὑπομονῆς ὑμῶν; v. 10b: ὅτι ἐπιστεύθη τὸ μαρτύριον.

body of his letter with a matter of mutual concern—a matter introduced in vv. 7b-10 of the thanksgiving.

P.T. O'Brien considers that in 2 Thessalonians there are two thanksgiving periods, 1.3-12 and 2.13-14.[1] G. Krodel also identifies these two passages as two thanksgivings,[2] arguing that the author of 2 Thessalonians attempted to duplicate the form of Paul's original letter to the Thessalonians—and in so doing gives himself away as a copyist.[3] J.T. Sanders regards 2.13–3.5 as a second *eucharisto* period.[4] Schubert, on the other hand, argues that there is only one thanksgiving period in 2 Thessalonians; he acknowledges that there is an *eucharisto* formula at 2 Thess. 2.13ff., but concludes that 'this is not a complete thanksgiving' but an inseparable unit whose structure and style are paraenetic.[5]

I, too, regard the second occurrence of the 'eucharisto' formula at 2 Thess. 2.13 as an expression of thanksgiving embedded in the body-middle of the letter, analogous to the second such occurrence in 1 Thessalonians (2.13); for the passage does not fulfil the function of 'eucharisto' periods, which is to indicate 'the occasion for and the contents of the letters which they introduce'.[6]

The function of 2 Thessalonians suggested by its thanksgiving period is the encouragement of steadfastness during persecution through a firm hope in God's imminent righteous judgment. The causal unit expresses Paul's gratitude for the state of his readers' faith. The lengthy explanatory unit affirms his respect for them while also setting their present suffering in an eschatological frame of reference. The glue that keeps them on the right side of the picture is the fact that they have believed (1.10b). Paul prays that what has begun with such promise among the Thessalonians may bear its fruit.

1. *Introductory Thanksgivings*, pp. 167-69.
2. 'The 2 Letter to the Thessalonians', pp. 77-78.
3. 'The 2 Letter to the Thessalonians', p. 79.
4. 'The Transition from Opening Epistolary Thanksgiving to Body', p. 356. Cf. L. Morris, who calls 2.13-15 a 'thanksgiving' (*The First and Second Epistles to the Thessalonians* [Grand Rapids: Eerdmans, 1959], p. 236). It is doubtful, however, that he is using this term in its technical sense.
5. *Thanksgivings*, p. 30.
6. *Thanksgivings*, p. 25. Cf. O'Brien, who says that the thanksgiving at 2 Thess. 2.13 'does not have an epistolary function' (*Introductory Thanksgivings*, p. 184).

3. *The Thanksgiving of 1 Corinthians*

The thanksgiving period of 1 Corinthians is brief and straightforward. The εὐχαριστῶ formula (unit A) is standard. On the other hand, the manner unit (unit B) is exceptional because the customary πάντων in the pronominal object phrase (περὶ κ.τ.λ.) is absent and the only construction Paul uses to express his manner of thanksgiving is the adverb πάντοτε. This may signal Paul's displeasure with some among the Corinthian church.

The reasons for Paul's thankfulness (unit C) are found in the causal constructions ἐπί with the dative and the ὅτι clause. Paul's gratitude to God regarding the Corinthians is distinctly focused on the gifts of God to the Corinthians. Compared to the causal constructions in Paul's other thanksgivings, where some aspect of a healthy life of faith in the community is the reason for thanksgiving (e.g. 1 Thess. 1.3; 2 Thess. 1.3b; Phil. 1.5; Phlm. 5; Rom. 1.8b), the distinctive nature of the Corinthian causal construction is clearly seen. For in 1 Corinthians Paul speaks of the wonderful spiritual endowments God has given to the Corinthians (note that both verbs are in the passive voice), but makes no mention of their good use of these gifts.

The explanatory unit (unit D) of the thanksgiving fills out what has been alluded to in the causal constructions. The Corinthians have been given much by way of spiritual gifts, with such gifts being a result of the establishment of the gospel among them.[1] Because of God the Corinthians have all they need to be guaranteed safety ἐν τῇ ἡμέρᾳ τοῦ κυρίου ἡμῶν Ἰησοῦ (v. 8). The thanksgiving ends with a faith statement (v. 9) that proclaims the faithfulness and call of God, with this final statement serving to remind the Corinthians that the root of their hope is in the steadfastness of God and that the intention of God for them is κοινωνία.

That the thanksgiving period of 1 Corinthians ends at 1.9 is indicated by the fact that at 1.10 Paul plunges into the first of many concerns he will address in the body of the letter.[2] The character of what is to follow is signalled by the words of the body-opening (παρακαλῶ δὲ ὑμᾶς, ἀδελφοί, διὰ τοῦ ὀνόματος τοῦ κυρίου ἡμῶν Ἰησοῦ Χριστοῦ). Paul's apostolic petitions and advice, written

---

1. The expression μαρτύριον τοῦ Χριστοῦ (v. 6) is an objective genitive, 'witness concerning Christ' (see Robertson, *Grammar*, p. 500).
2. Cf. Funk, *Language*, p. 264; Doty, *Letters*, p. 43.

in response to current issues of which he has been informed in
Corinth, will make up most of the letter-body of 1 Corinthians.

The thanksgiving period of 1 Cor. 1.4-9 is distinctive vis-à-vis
Paul's other letters because of its lack of mention of any cause for
thanks originating in the Corinthian community itself. Rather, Paul's
cause for thanks is exclusively rooted in God's grace to the Corinthians (v. 4) and his assurance of their salvation is rooted in the fact that
πιστὸς ὁ θεός (v. 9). The final faith statement of the thanksgiving
period (1.9) is both a fitting conclusion for a thanksgiving focused
entirely on God and a fitting transition into the body of the letter, for
its reminder of God's call to fellowship highlights an issue that is basic
to the concerns Paul wants to address at Corinth.

The lack of a prayer report unit (unit E) is noteworthy. It may be,
as was the case with 1 Thessalonians, that such a lack functions to
focus attention on the causal unit. In 1 Thessalonians that resulted in an
expression of Paul's overwhelming gratitude for his converts in Thessalonica. In 1 Corinthians, since the causal unit concerns the graciousness of God towards the Corinthian believers, the thanksgiving functions to remind the Corinthians of the privilege and responsibility that
the gift of their salvation has brought them.

There is no thanksgiving in 2 Corinthians.[1] Rather, after the opening formula there follows a doxological passage (εὐλογητὸς ὁ θεός)
in the course of which Paul expresses his care for the Corinthians.[2]

4. *The Thanksgiving of Philippians*

The thanksgiving period of Philippians contains all of the units of a
typical Pauline thanksgiving period. The εὐχαριστῶ formula (unit A)
is standard, although, as in 1 Corinthians, thanks is expressed in the
first person singular even though the letter is sent by more than one
person. The manner construction (unit B) uses the standard πάντοτε.
It also uses the prepositional phrase ἐν πάσῃ δεήσει μου and the
participle clause μετὰ χαρᾶς τὴν δέησιν ποιούμενος. The pronomi-

---

1. Schubert cites 2 Cor. 1.10-11 as a compact Pauline thanksgiving period
(*Thanksgivings*, p. 46). Yet, even though parts of this passage bear some similarity
to typical εὐχαριστῶ-periods (e.g. ἐκ πολλῶν προσώπων διὰ πολλῶν
εὐχαριστηθῇ may be seen as a variation on the principal verb unit), there is not
sufficient comparative material to warrant its use in this study

2. Cf. A.C. Sundberg who says that rather than a thanksgiving period '2 Corinthians has a *berakah* (a praise-giving or eulogy)' ('Enabling Language in Paul', p. 271
n. 6). So also J.H. Roberts, 'The Eschatological Transitions to the Pauline Letter
Body', *Neotestamentica* 20 (1986), p. 29.

nal object phrase ὑπὲρ πάντων ὑμῶν is separated from its usual position following πάντοτε. There does not appear to be any significance in the use of ὑπέρ rather than περί. The repetition of πᾶς in this section stresses the inclusiveness (πάντων ὑμῶν) and the constancy of Paul's prayers for the Philippians (πάντοτε; πάσῃ δεήσει). With πᾶς in the first causal section of the Philippian thanksgiving and κοινωνία in the second causal section, the prevalent κοινωνία theme of the body of the letter is introduced in the εὐχαριστῶ period.

The causal unit (unit C) is divided into two parts, the first being ἐπὶ πάσῃ τῇ μνείᾳ ὑμῶν that occurs between unit A and unit B. The syntactical function of this prepositional clause is causal rather than temporal, and so the meaning is not 'whenever I think of you' but 'for every expression of your remembrance of me'.[1] The second part of the causal unit occurs in vv. 5 and 6 with two constructions (ἐπὶ τῇ κοινωνίᾳ ὑμῶν... νῦν and πεποιθὼς αὐτὸ τοῦτο). The last construction contains a characteristic verb of knowing.

Paul, then, gives three reasons for thanksgiving: (1) because of the Philippians' remembrance of him (ἐπὶ πάσῃ τῇ μνείᾳ ὑμῶν), which probably alludes to the monetary gift directly referred to in 4.10-20;[2] (2) because of their past and continuing partnership in the gospel; and (3) because he knows that their perfection will be completed.

The explanatory section (unit D) consists of a καθώς clause with a pronominal object clause (καθώς ἐστιν δίκαιον ἐμοὶ τοῦτο φρονεῖν ὑπὲρ πάντων ὑμῶν), which is followed by a causal clause introduced by διά with the articular infinitive, then a temporal participle clause (ἔν τε τοῖς... ὄντας), and finally another causal clause introduced by γάρ (v. 8).

The καθώς clause is correlative and functions to give an explanation for the preceding unit. The construction διά with the articular infinitive is the only example of such a construction in a Pauline thanksgiving. As it functions in parallelism to the καθώς clause[3] it furnishes an explanation as to why it is appropriate for Paul to give thanks as he does. So the καθώς and διά constructions serve to underscore the basis of intimacy that undergirds Paul's thanksgiving.

The temporal participle clause should probably be translated as 'since' (you are all sharers with me), for it modifies the preceding two

---

1. The genitive here is subjective. So Schubert, *Thanksgivings*, pp. 73f.
2. Cf. Martin, *Philippians*, p. 47.
3. So Robertson, *Grammar*, p. 966.

constructions; i.e. Paul's love for the Philippians is the consequence of their partnership with him in his sufferings. The final unit of the explanation, which is introduced by γάρ (v. 8), affirms that Paul loves the Philippians deeply, as he has just said. The thanksgiving period of Philippians closes in vv. 9-11 with Paul's intercession (unit E). Paul prays three things for the Philippians: (1) that (ἵνα) their love would increase in knowledge and discernment; (2) that (εἰς with the articular infinitive) they would be able to approve the things that really matter; and (3) that (ἵνα) at the eschatological day they would be pure and blameless and filled with those fruits of righteousness that come through Jesus Christ. The body of Philippians then opens at 1.12 with a direct address to Paul's readers (γινώσκειν δὲ ὑμᾶς βούλομαι, ἀδελφοί).[1]

The most noteworthy feature of the Philippian thanksgiving period is its abundance of causal constructions. Paul evidently considers that he has ample reason for thanksgiving. As in 1 Thessalonians, what is primary for Paul as he writes is the cause his readers have given him for thanksgiving. His gratitude for the Philippians' remembrance of him, for their steadfast fellowship in the gospel, and for the assurance he has of their ultimate perfection, is what he chiefly wants to express to his readers.

5. *The Thanksgiving of Philemon*

The thanksgiving of Philemon exhibits four of the five units of a typical Pauline thanksgiving period. The principal verb formula (unit A) is normal. The manner unit (unit B), however, is unusual in that it lacks a pronominal object phrase, which phrase is replaced by the singular genitive pronoun σου connected to the temporal participle clause. This is fitting, of course, in a letter sent to an individual. The manner in which Paul gives thanks is described simply as 'always' and 'in my prayers'. The impression given is that Paul does not need or want to waste time assuring his reader of his constancy in prayer beyond the mere use of πάντοτε.

The thanksgiving then proceeds directly to a causal construction (unit C) using a participial clause where the grounds for Paul's thanks are given: the love and faith that his addressee has toward the Lord and the saints. There is no explanatory unit, which may be due to

---

1. White also considers that this disclosure formula opens the body (*Body*, p. 73). Cf. Doty, *Letters*, p. 43.

Paul's confidence in the relationship he has with his addressee—or, more likely, to his desire to proceed directly to the purpose construction where he will allude to the reason for which he writes this letter.

The content of Paul's prayer is given in unit E. Here the real concern of the letter is raised: 'in order that the sharing of your faith (or, 'the fellowship inspired by your faith') may become effective (operative) in a realization of our full capacity for good in the cause of Christ'. Here, in fact, the function of a thanksgiving as an introduction to the concerns that follow in the body of a letter can be plainly seen.

Verse 7 is a direct address (ἀδελφέ) to Philemon in which Paul reestablishes the relationship he shares with his addressee. This verse functions as the basis on which he will make the request that follows in v. 8.[1] At v. 7, then, Paul begins the body of his brief letter to Philemon.[2]

The primary function of the thanksgiving section in Philemon is to introduce the request of the letter by affirming Paul's respect for Philemon and praying for his continued spiritual growth.

6. *The Thanksgiving of Romans*

The structure of the thanksgiving period of Romans is more complex than that of any other Pauline thanksgiving. While it contains all five components of a typical Pauline thanksgiving, the units are arranged in a somewhat complicated fashion. Schubert thought Romans was of the 'mixed type' and gave the impression that 'the thanksgiving is broken up into a large number of comparatively short periods'.[3] My analysis, however, reveals that there is here only one thanksgiving period in which, as is demonstrated below, the five functional units are broken apart.[4]

---

1. Schubert (*Thanksgivings*, p. 5) and O'Brien (*Introductory Thanksgivings*, p. 49) see v. 7 as a 'transition' verse that links the thanksgiving to the body of the letter. Cf. Lohse, who calls v. 7 'the transition to the content proper of the body' (*A Commentary on the Epistles to the Colossians and to Philemon*, p. 192) and White, who calls v. 7 the 'background' for the letter-opening request formula of v. 8 (*Body*, p. 48).

2. See White, 'The Structural Analysis of Philemon', p. 34. White concludes that the 'joy' expression of v. 7 opens the letter-body of Philemon.

3. *Thanksgivings*, p. 33.

4. Funk considers 1.8ff. to be a secondary or 'parallel' apostolic parousia ('Apostolic "Parousia"', p. 250). As our analysis of Pauline apostolic parousias will show, however, if this were an apostolic parousia it would be inexplicably unique as

The Romans thanksgiving begins at 1.8 with the usual principal verb formula (unit A). The principal verb is modified by the exceptional occurrence of πρῶτον μέν. The manner unit (unit B) occurs in two parts. The first, διὰ Ἰησοῦ Χριστοῦ, occurs after the principal verb. This first part of the manner unit is unusual in two ways: (1) because of its grammatical make-up, being a prepositional phrase rather than an adverb or participle, and (2) because it serves to focus on Paul's relationship to Christ rather than on Paul's action of praying. The standard pronominal object phrase περὶ πάντων ὑμῶν occurs in this manner unit. The thanksgiving period proceeds to a ὅτι clause that constitutes unit C. The cause for Paul's thanksgiving is the faith of the Romans which is proclaimed everywhere.

Then occurs the second part of the manner unit beginning with μάρτυς γάρ and functioning with the ὡς ἀδιαλείπτως clause to declare the manner in which Paul prays.[1] Paul declares the constancy and fervency of his prayers. This second part of the manner unit functions in relationship not to the preceding causal construction, as is the case with the other thanksgivings, but rather in relation to the following purpose construction. The content of this second part of the manner unit is also exceptional. In the context of affirming his devoted prayer, Paul underscores his role as preacher of the gospel. This accords with his use of the first part of the manner unit in Romans, but not with the function of manner units elsewhere.

The thanksgiving of Romans continues with a twofold repetitive form: unit E; unit D; unit E; unit D. The first of the prayer report units (unit E) begins by stressing the action of praying (cf. Phil. 1.9; 2 Thess. 1.11) and continues with εἴ πως ἤδη ποτὲ εὐοδωθή-σομαι. . . ἐλθεῖν πρὸς ὑμᾶς (v. 10b), which is an unusual final clause.[2] The content of Paul's prayer is a wish that he could come to the Christians at Rome.[3] This is an exceptional prayer for a

it would contain only the 'visit' unit. The material in 1.8-15 is better viewed as a thanksgiving.

1. The correlative pronoun ὡς with the idea of testifying (μάρτυς) functions in a declaratory fashion to mean 'how' (so Robertson, *Grammar*, p. 1032).

2. See E.D. Burton, who remarks that an omitted apodosis is sometimes virtually contained in a protasis—with the protasis expressing a possibility that is an object of hope or desire—and so has nearly the force of a final clause (as here where εἰ means 'to see if') (*Moods and Tenses of New Testament Greek* [Edinburgh: T. & T. Clark, 1898], p. 276).

3. See M. Zerwick, who comments that εἰ can be used 'in virtual questions expressing, as here, an uncertain expectation associated with an effort to attain

thanksgiving period. Paul evidently felt the need to explain himself on this point for he repeats and clarifies his wish in the next unit, which is an explanatory unit (unit D). It begins with ἐπιποθῶ γὰρ ἰδεῖν ὑμᾶς and then follows with ἵνα... μεταδῶ, which gives the purpose of Paul's hoped-for visit. Paul explains that the purpose of his coming is to impart a spiritual gift. He qualifies this statement by explaining that the intended purpose of such an impartation is that they might be strengthened. Then Paul states that his visit will, in fact, result in a mutual strengthening. At this point, despite the vague and careful character of Paul's language, it is clear that Paul considers himself to have a responsibility for his Roman readers.[1]

This use of an explanatory unit is unusual, for in all of the other Pauline thanksgivings such a unit is syntactically connected to a causal unit and so explains why Paul is thankful. In Romans, however, Paul explains and clarifies not his cause for thanksgiving but the content of his prayer. Furthermore, whereas ἵνα is normally used in the purpose units of Paul's other thanksgivings to *introduce* Paul's thankful prayers, in Romans the ἵνα clause is used to *clarify* or *explain* the content of his prayer.

The second occurrence of the prayer report unit (unit E) is in v. 13a with οὐ θέλω δὲ ὑμᾶς ἀγνοεῖν, ἀδελφοί. In the ὅτι clause Paul repeats what he said in the εἴ πως clause of v. 10,[2] which commenced the first prayer report unit. That the Roman Christians should understand his heartfelt desire to visit them and the fact that he has tried to come many times was evidently most important to Paul. So his use of the emphatic formulaic οὐ θέλω ὑμᾶς ἀγνοεῖν, ἀδελφοί underlines this fact.

Then there follows another ἵνα clause that functions as the beginning of the second part of the explanation unit (unit D) in which Paul again explains his intentions for the visit, i.e. ἵνα τινὰ καρπὸν σχῶ.[3] Paul clarifies his intentions by saying that what he wishes to achieve among the Romans is what he has already achieved among other Gen-

---

something' (*Biblical Greek* [Rome: Scripta Pontificii Instituti Biblici, 1963], para. 403).

1. Cf. Wedderburn: 'It is clear from 1.11 that Paul feels himself responsible to further the Romans' faith' (*The Reasons for Romans*, p. 98).

2. Note also the occurrence of ἐλθεῖν πρὸς ὑμᾶς in both v. 10b and v. 13a.

3. Note that both ἵνα clauses (at v. 11 and v. 13) contain indefinite pronouns.

tiles.[1] In this second part of the explanation unit Paul implies that his visit to the Roman believers will be in line with his apostolic commission to the Gentiles (cf. vv. 5 and 6)[2] and so he has a definite concern also for them.

This second part of the explanation unit ends with more explanatory clauses in which Paul describes himself as a debtor to Greeks and to barbarians, to the wise and to the ignorant (v. 14). This is an expansion of what he has already said—that his apostleship is to all the Gentiles and so in writing to the Romans he is pursuing his apostolic task.[3]

In the explanatory and prayer report units of the Romans thanksgiving, then, Paul says that the content of his prayer for Roman believers is that he could be with them, and further tells them that he has often tried to come but has been hindered (the two E units). He explains this desire to visit, moving cautiously from the vague to the straightforward[4]—i.e. from alluding to a spiritual gift (first unit D, v. 11), to a clarification of his apostolic obligations (second unit D, v. 14), to a declaration that he very much wishes[5] to preach the gospel to the Roman believers (second unit D, v. 15). The thanksgiving builds towards its final statement where Paul makes clear the intention for his visit—the preaching of the gospel to the Roman believers.

There is some difficulty in identifying the close of the Romans thanksgiving. Schubert considered that a typical Pauline thanksgiving closed with what he called an 'eschatological climax'. He recognized

1. The double καί means 'also' (so Robertson, *Grammar*, p. 1181), with καθώς indicating that what Paul seeks to impart to the Romans is that which he also imparts to other Gentiles.

2. So Abraham: 'By virtue of his divine commission to be the apostle to the Gentiles (Rom 1.13f.; 11.13; 15.15; Gal. 1.16; 2.7f.) Paul considers himself to have authority over all Gentiles. This explains Paul's writing to the churches in Rome and Colossae, churches which he had not founded nor visited before he wrote to them' ('Paul: The Unique Apostle', p. 72).

3. Cf. Dahl: In writing to the Roman Christians Paul was 'hoping to reap some harvest in the world capital by his missionary work as he had among the rest of the Gentiles' ('The Missionary Theology in the Epistle to the Romans', p. 78).

4. Note his use of opaque language in the earlier parts of this final unit when talking about his visit: χάρισμα, στηριχθῆναι, καρπόν.

5. The construction τὸ κατ' ἐμὲ πρόθυμον stresses Paul's desire, for the use of κατά with the accusative personal pronoun emphasizes Paul's readiness. And the fact that there is an article further stresses his eagerness—'as far as I am concerned'; 'for my part'. So C.F.D. Moule, *An Idiom-Book of New Testament Greek* (Cambridge: Cambridge University Press, 1977), p. 58.

that such a standard climax did not occur in Romans, but argued that vv. 16-17 were an appropriate substitute since the terms σωτηρία, εὐαγγέλιον and the phrase δικαιοσύνη τοῦ. . . ἀποκαλύπτεται have 'eschatological significance'.[1] And many have agreed with him.[2] The fact that there is a structural parallel between 1.8-17 and 15.14-33[3] might also suggest that 1.8-17 is an indivisible structural unit.

Another element in identifying the close of the Romans thanksgiving period is of course the determination of the letter body-opening. The only recognizable body-opening formula is that of v. 13a (οὐ θέλω δὲ ὑμᾶς ἀγνοεῖν, ἀδελφοί). J.T. Sanders,[4] R.W. Funk,[5] J.L. White[6] and R. Jewett[7] argue that the 'disclosure formula' at v. 13a marks the transition from the thanksgiving to the letter-body in Romans. Yet this disclosure formula does not serve the function of opening the letter-body. It only introduces the issue of Paul's long-standing desire to visit the Romans. The function of a body-opening, however, is: 'To introduce the information in such a way, either by disclosing new information or by recalling previous communications of which both parties are cognizant, that a basis of mutality is founded. Once this matter of mutual concern has been introduced, the body-middle may carry the relevant details forward.'[8]

As there is no entirely satisfying option either for the ending of the thanksgiving or for the opening of the body, the merits of several alternatives should be weighed. These alternatives are:

1. *End of thanksgiving, 1.11-12*: 'For I long to see you, that I may impart to you some spiritual gift to strengthen you, that is, that

---

1. *Thanksgivings*, p. 33.
2. E.g. O'Brien, *Introductory Thanksgivings*, pp. 200-202; Käsemann, *Romans*, p. 10; Gamble, *Textual History*, p. 90. See also the second edition of *Pauline Parallels* (ed. F.O. Francis and J.P. Sampley; Philadelphia: Fortress, 1984), p. 326.
3. As noted by O. Michel: 'Es kann also kein Zweifel sein, dass Röm. 15.14-33 also Briefschluss sich an den Eingang Röm 1.8-17 Punkt für Punkt anschliest. Vielleicht liegt in dieser Verklammerung eine bestimmte literarische Gewohnheit die allerdings dem Römerbrief ein eigenese Gepräge gibt' (*Der Brief an die Römer* [Göttingen: Vandenhoeck & Ruprecht, 1963], p. 325). Funk agrees with Michel ('Saying and Seeing', p. 210). Cf. Bjerkelund, *Parakalo*, p. 157.
4. 'Transition', *JBL* 81 (1962), p. 360.
5. *Language*, p. 264.
6. *Body*, pp. 52f.
7. 'Ambassadorial Letter', pp. 12ff.
8. White, *Body*, p. 95.

we may be mutually encouraged by each other's faith, both yours and mine.'

Body-opening, 1.13: 'I want you to know, brethren, that I have often intended to come to you (but thus far have been prevented), in order that I may reap some harvest among you as also among the rest of the Gentiles.'

2. *End of thanksgiving, 1.14-15*: 'I am under obligation both to Greeks and to barbarians, both to the wise and to the foolish: so I am eager to preach the gospel to you also who are in Rome.'

Body-opening, 1.16-17: 'For I am not ashamed of the gospel: it is the power of God for salvation to everyone who has faith, to the Jew first and also to the Greek. For in it the righteousness of God is revealed through faith for faith; as it is written, "He who through faith is righteous shall live".'

3. *End of thanksgiving, 1.16-17*: 'For I am not ashamed of the gospel: it is the power of God for salvation to every one who has faith, to the Jew first and also to the Greek. For in it the righteousness of God is revealed through faith for faith; as it is written, "He who through faith is righteous shall live".'

Body-opening 1.18: 'For the wrath of God is revealed from heaven against all ungodliness and wickedness of men who by their wickedness suppress the truth.'

The first option must use the transitional formula of 1.13 for the body-opening. As noted above, this is functionally inappropriate as the opening of a letter-body, for it does not introduce matters with which the body-middle is concerned. There is little else to commend this option since 1.11-12 is not a typical conclusion for a thanksgiving. The third option is largely supported by Schubert's contention that 1.16-17 functions as an eschatological conclusion for the thanksgiving. This contention, however, rests solely on highlighting significant theological terms in these verses. It also requires that 1.18 function as the opening for the body of the letter, even though the verse does not open up a matter of mutual concern. Furthermore, 1.18 is grammatically dependent on the preceding verses.

In the second option, 1.16-17 provides a relatively appropriate letter-body opening. Here we have a statement in the first person singular (cf. the letter body openings at 1 Cor. 1.10; Phil. 1.12) that opens up that which Paul will make central in the body of his letter. J.M. Bassler provides an interesting literary observation of relevance here, for she notes that Rom. 1.16–2.10 exhibits several features of a *Ringkomposition*[1]—which would further suggest that 1.16 belongs with the passage that it heads, rather than as the close of the thanksgiving. So I conclude that the thanksgiving of Romans is 1.8-15.[2]

C. *Comparative Observations*

The thanksgiving of Romans is distinctive in several ways. We observe first of all that the causal unit (unit C) is exceptionally brief and formal, in contrast to the other Pauline thanksgivings where this unit is generally longer and always conveys a sense of personal relationship with the readers. In 2 Thessalonians, for example, Paul is thankful because the church exhibits a growing faith and he knows that their love for each other is growing (2 Thess. 1.3); likewise, in 1 Corinthians Paul expresses thankfulness because of all that God has given that church in Christ Jesus. The feature of Paul's personal knowledge of his readers is normally emphasized in a causal unit by the use of verbs of knowing or hearing (see e.g. 1 Thess. 1.3-5; Phlm. 5). In the Romans causal unit, however, there is no hint of a personal relationship (note the lack of verbs of knowing). Rather, Paul's cause for thanksgiving rests on the same knowledge that everyone has of the Roman believers, for their faith is being reported all over the world.

The manner unit of the Romans thanksgiving is also unusual. The content of this two-part unit is largely concerned with emphasizing Paul's apostolic role (διὰ ᾽Ιησοῦ Χριστοῦ)[3] and his commission to preach the gospel (v. 9b). It would appear that Paul wants to communicate that it is as their apostle that he gives thanks for them. Furthermore, the second part of the manner unit of Romans modifies not the causal construction but rather the following prayer report unit. This effects a shift from the normal pattern of a Pauline thanksgiving. It turns the focus away from the causal unit, thereby making the thanksgiving function primarily to tell the readers what Paul's prayer con-

---

1. *Divine Impartiality. Paul and a Theological Axiom* (SBLDS 59; Chico, CA: Scholars, 1982), pp. 123-28.

2. Cf. Roberts, 'The Eschatological Transitions to the Pauline Letter Body', p. 29; S.N. Olson, 'Epistolary Uses of Expressions of Self-Confidence', *JBL* 103 (1984), p. 590; Dunn, *Romans 1–8*, p. 27; Ziesler, *Paul's Letter to the Romans*, p. 35.

3. This διά phrase echoes the διά phrase in v. 5 where Paul affirmed his apostleship.

cerns are, rather than to reaffirm and restore a relationship of apostolic love.

The explanatory constructions also modify not the causal construction, as is normal, but rather the prayer report unit. This suggests that whereas in the other Pauline thanksgivings the communicative thrust concerned Paul's relations with his readers and his thankfulness for certain aspects of their Christian life (the causal unit), in Romans the communicative thrust of the thanksgiving concerns the content of his prayer that is communicated in the prayer report unit. Whereas the prayers in Paul's other thanksgivings refer to Paul's hope that his readers would continue to grow on the continuum he has described in his cause for thanksgiving, in Romans Paul's prayers centre entirely around his hopes for a visit.

The ending of the Romans thanksgiving is, as we have seen, arranged in a twofold repetitive pattern. This pattern appears to function so as to build towards a climax at v. 15. Paul says first that the content of his prayer is that he could come and visit the faithful in Rome, assuring them that this desire is a longstanding one (v. 10b, the first part of the prayer report unit). He then gives his agenda for such a visit, saying that he hopes that mutual encouragement will come from such a visit (vv. 11-12, the first part of the explanation unit). After that he repeats his long-held wish to come to Rome, using the emphatic formula at v. 13a (the second part of the prayer report unit). Again he feels it is necessary to explain the agenda he envisions for his visit (the second part of the explanation unit). This explanation begins as vaguely as the other explanation had. Paul talks about 'achieving some result' among the Romans and he makes an implied reference to his apostolic commission. He wants to achieve among the Romans what he has achieved among the rest of the Gentiles (v. 13b). He then goes on to underscore once again his apostolic obligation to all Gentiles (v. 14).[1] At the end of this explanation unit, however, Paul states plainly the intention he has for his visit: that he is very eager to preach the gospel to his Roman readers (1.15).

This finely tuned structure is so constructed as to make the words of 1.15 take on a particular vibrancy. Paul's desire to preach the gospel to the Roman believers is at the heart of his prayer. A visit to them is vital for him because he longs to be able to exercise his apostolic obli-

---

1. Cf. this concern in 1.5-6 and what has been seen to be Paul's stress on his apostolic call in 1.8-9.

gation by preaching to them as he has preached to 'the rest of the
Gentiles' (v. 13b). That Paul expresses a desire to preach to the
Roman believers does not imply that he thought he would be preaching
to the unconverted. Rather, in the context of having affirmed his
respect for their faith, he is expressing a desire that these Roman
believers would hear *his* preaching of the gospel.[1]

The prayer report units in the other Pauline thanksgivings give the
content of Paul's prayers for the spiritual health of his readers. In the
Romans thanksgiving it appears that Paul's concern for the spiritual
health of his readers involves their hearing his presentation of the
good news.[2]

---

1. M.A. Kruger argues that 'some fruit' in 1.13 must refer to the collection of
money for the poor in Judea (cf. Rom. 15.28) because 'to tell them that he would like
to make converts among them. . . would have been so great a blunder that we cannot think of attributing such an intention to Paul' ('*Tina Karpon*, "Some Fruit" in
Romans 1.13', *WTJ* 49 [1987], pp. 167-73 [pp. 170-71]). Kruger, however, sees
only two options: that Paul is speaking either of converting his readers or of something else entirely.

2. Cf. P. Bowers, who writes that Paul is here referring 'not to the prospect of a
future evangelistic mission to win converts in Rome but to a ministry of edification
within the Roman church of just the sort embodied in the letter' ('Fulfilling the
Gospel: The Scope of the Pauline Mission', *JETS* 30 [1987], pp. 185-98 [p. 196]).

Chapter 5

THE PAULINE APOSTOLIC PAROUSIAS

The term 'apostolic parousia' was coined by R.W. Funk to designate a section of a Pauline letter that was particularly concerned with Paul's apostolic presence.[1] Here Paul sought to make his presence felt either by means of the letter itself, reference to an emissary, or mention of a hoped-for visit.[2] Funk considers that the most complete example of the form and content of an apostolic parousia is to be found in Rom. 15.14-33.[3]

A. *The Boundaries of the Pauline Apostolic Parousias*

The apostolic parousia section of 1 Thessalonians begins with a direct address (2.17) in which Paul expresses his longing to see the Thessalonians. It extends right to the opening of the paraenetic section at 4.1.[4]

There is no proper apostolic parousia in 2 Thessalonians. While Paul requests the prayers of the Thessalonians (3.1-5), which is one of the functions of an apostolic parousia (cf. Phlm. 22b, Rom. 15.30-32), this passage offers very little by way of comparative material with other Pauline apostolic parousias.

The apostolic parousia section of 1 Corinthians is contained in 4.14-21. It occurs at the end of the theological section of the body[5] and before the part of the letter where Paul responds to specific queries from the Corinthians (5.1–15.58). Funk considers that 16.1-11 is also an apostolic parousia, albeit a 'secondary' one.[6] While this passage

---

1. 'Apostolic "Parousia"'.
2. 'Apostolic "Parousia"', p. 266.
3. 'Apostolic "Parousia"', p. 250.
4. So Funk, 'Apostolic "Parousia"', p. 254; cf. H. Boers, 'Form Critical Study of Paul's Letters', *NTS* 22 (1975–76), pp. 140-58 (p. 158).
5. Cf. White, *Body*, p. 140.
6. 'Apostolic "Parousia"', p. 250.

The Pauline Apostolic Parousias

Key	1 Thess. 2.17-3.13	1 Cor. 4.14-21	Phil. 2.19-24	Phlm. 21-22	Gal. 4.11-20	Rom. 15.14-32
F. Letter Writing				F.1/F.2		F.1 15.14-15a
1. Manner	H.4 2.17-18	F.1 4.14		v. 21a		F.2 15.15b
2. Authority	H.5 2.19-20	F.2 4.15		F.3 v. 21b		F.s 15.16
3. Appeal		F.3 4.16				F.2 15.17-21
S. Special						
G. Sending of Emissary.	G.1 3.1-2a	G.1 4.17a	G.1 2.19a			
1. Reference to Sending	G.2 3.2b	G.2 4.17b	G.3 2.19b			
2. Credentials	G.3 3.2c-5	G.3 4.17c	G.2 2.20-22			
3. Expectation						
S. Special Unit	G.s 3.6-8		G.1 2.23			
H. Apostolic Visit	H.5 3.9	H.1 4.18-19a	H.2 2.24a	H.1 v. 22	H.5 4.11-19	H.4 15.22
1. Intention		H.2 4.19b	H.1 2.24b		H.3 4.20	H.3 15.23-28a
2. Submission						
3. Desire	H.3 3.10a					H.1 15.28b
4. Hindrances	H.6 3.10b	H.6 4.19c-21				
5. Love/Concern						H.2 15.29
6. Purpose						
S. Special Unit	H.s 3.11-13					H.s 15.30-32

does refer to a visit and an emissary, the section is chiefly concerned not with making Paul's apostolic presence felt, but rather with instructions for the collection. It will not, then, be included in this analysis. Likewise the section in 2 Corinthians that concerns a visit for the sake of the collection (2 Cor. 8.16-24; 9.1-5) will not be included in the study.

In Philippians the apostolic parousia begins at 2.19, where Paul tells his readers that he hopes to send Timothy to them soon, and ends at v. 24. Funk considers 2.25-30 to be a 'secondary' apostolic parousia.[1] The material in 2.25-30, however, concerns a messenger (Epaphroditus) whom the Philippians had originally sent to Paul. Furthermore, unlike a typical apostolic parousia, the reason Paul gives for sending his 'brother' back home entirely concerns the relationship that exists between Epaphroditus and the Philippians. Phil. 2.25-30, therefore, is not relevant for this comparative analysis.

Paul's letter to Philemon contains a brief apostolic parousia in vv. 21-22 where Paul both speaks of the manner of his writing of the letter and of a proposed visit.

In Galatians the portion of the letter that concerns a visit is 4.11-20. While the mention of a visit in this passage is really just a wish to be present, it is nevertheless that part of the letter where Paul makes direct reference to the authority of his apostolic presence. Funk does not include v. 11 in his delineation of the apostolic parousia of Galatians,[2] but, for reasons that will be clear below, v. 11 should be considered an integral part of that letter's apostolic parousia.

The apostolic parousia of Romans begins at 15.14 and extends to 15.32. Funk regards 15.33 as part of the apostolic parousia of Romans,[3] but, as we shall see in our next chapter on the Pauline conclusions, this verse fits better into the conclusion section of the letter.

B. *An Expansion of Funk's Structural Analysis*

With Rom. 15.14-33 as his model, Funk divides up the Pauline apostolic parousias into five major units: (1) the fact of Paul's writing, his disposition and purpose; (2) the basis of Paul's apostolic relation to the

---

1. 'Apostolic "Parousia"', p. 250. White, on the other hand, treats all of 2.19-30 as the body-closing/apostolic parousia section of Philippians (*Body*, p. 140).
2. 'Apostolic "Parousia"', p. 254.
3. 'Apostolic "Parousia"', p. 250.

recipients; (3) implementation of the apostolic parousia, which concerns both his hope to come and the dispatch of an emissary; (4) an invocation of divine approval and support for the apostolic parousia; and (5) benefits from the apostolic parousia.[1]

By means of an analysis based on the wider screen of all of Paul's apostolic parousias, however, it can be seen that there are only three such major functional units and that they concern: (1) Paul's writing of the letter (unit F); (2) Paul's dispatch of an emissary (unit G); and (3) Paul's visit (unit H). Funk, of course, acknowledges all three of these items to be present in a functional way in a Pauline apostolic parousia,[2] but by relying on the apostolic parousia of Romans alone he fails to recognize these as the major structural units. So, for example, because Romans does not mention an emissary, Funk treats the dispatch of an emissary merely as an occasional occurrence under his third section. This analysis shows, on the other hand, that the emissary unit is a more standard feature of an apostolic parousia.

The first functional unit, that of Paul's 'writing of the letter' (unit F), occurs with a verb phrase using γράφω and speaks of the manner in which Paul is writing the letter (F. 1). There is also another construction that modifies γράφω in which there is some explicit or implied reference to Paul's apostolic authority to write (F. 2). Another construction that appears in unit F is an appeal to fall into line with Paul's apostolic teaching (e.g. 1 Cor. 4.16 παρακαλῶ οὖν ὑμᾶς μιμηταί μου γίνεσθε). This sub-unit will be termed F. 3. We will see that the Romans apostolic parousia has a unique sub-unit (F.s.).

The second major functional unit of Paul's apostolic parousia sections deals with the sending of an emissary (unit G). The emissary unit contains a sub-unit (G. 1) in which the principal verb is πέμπω. In the case of Philippians, which concerns the future dispatch of an emissary, the word ἐλπίζω appears in this sub-unit (Phil. 2.19a, 23). In other cases this sub-unit makes reference to an emissary who was dispatched prior to the writing of the letter (1 Thess. 3.1-2a) or who is being dispatched with the letter (1 Cor. 4.17). In every case the emissary's credentials are given (sub-unit G. 2: 1 Thess. 3.2b; 1 Cor. 4.17b; Phil. 2.20-22). Also in every case Paul explains what he expects the emissary to do for him (or, in the case of 1 Thessalonians, to have done for him) while with the congregation (sub-unit G. 3: 1 Thess. 3.2c-5; 1

---

1 'Apostolic "Parousia"', pp. 252-53.
2. 'Apostolic "Parousia"', p. 266.

Cor. 4.17c; Phil. 2.19b). In the 'emissary' unit of 1 Thessalonians
there is a special sub-unit in which Paul tells his readers of the emissary's report and of how this report affected him (G.s.).

The third type of unit of a Pauline apostolic parousia, the 'visit' unit
(unit H), occurs in one of two forms. One form is an 'announcement
of a visit'; the other is an expression of a 'desire to visit'.

In a typical 'announcement of a visit' (found in 1 Corinthians,
Philippians, Philemon and Romans), Paul states his intention to come.
The principal verb sub-unit (H. 1) uses ἔρχομαι (except for Phlm. 22,
which speaks euphemistically). This type of 'visit' unit may contain a
construction (sub-unit H. 2) which indicates Paul's submission to God's
will in the matter of his coming (e.g. 1 Cor. 4.19b, ἐὰν ὁ κύριος
θελήσῃ).

A 'desire to visit' unit (found in 1 Thessalonians, Galatians and
Romans) contains a principal verb sub-unit (H. 3) in which Paul speaks
of his desire to come and see his readers. Sometimes he stresses how
he is praying for this to come about (1 Thess. 3.10a). The 'desire to
visit' unit also often contains reference to the fact that Paul has so far
been hindered from coming (sub-unit H. 4). It can also contain an
expression of love or concern for the readers (sub-unit H. 5).

Both types of visit units may make some sort of reference to the
purpose of the visit (sub-unit H. 6). We see that the visit unit of
Romans combines aspects from the two types of visit units.

In 1 Thessalonians and Romans there is also a special sub-unit that
we have labelled H.s. We will discuss these special cases later.

C. *Analyses of the Respective Pauline Apostolic Parousias*

1. *The Apostolic Parousia of 1 Thessalonians*
The apostolic parousia of 1 Thessalonians (2.17–3.13) contains a 'visit'
unit (unit H: 'desire to visit') and an 'emissary' unit (unit G). The
'visit' unit dominates this apostolic parousia, occurring in two parts,
being divided by the 'emissary' unit.

In the first part of the 'visit' unit Paul declares how earnestly he
tried to visit the Thessalonians and yet how he was hindered by Satan
(sub-unit H. 4; 2.17-18). He then goes on to affirm his love for the
Thessalonians (sub-unit H. 5; 2.19-20). The other part of the visit unit
begins with another assertion of his love for the Thessalonians (sub-
unit H. 5; 3.9) and continues with Paul's statement of his desire to see
his Thessalonian converts (sub-unit H. 3; 3.10a). He describes how he

prays constantly, and then says that he hopes the visit will result in his being able to supply what their faith lacks (sub-unit H. 6; 3.10b). This part of the visit unit closes with a benediction (sub-unit H.s.; 3.11-13) which uses three verbs in the operative—a grammatical feature which reappears in the letter's concluding benediction (5.23a). Beyond this grammatical similarity between the benediction of the apostolic parousia and that which closes the letter there is also a similarity of content, since both benedictions refer to 'the coming of our Lord Jesus Christ' and pray for blamelessness (ἀμέμπτος—3.13 and 5.23). The benedictory nature of the closing of the apostolic parousia of 1 Thessalonians is unique in the Pauline letters.

The 'emissary' unit occurs between the two parts of the 'visit' unit. Paul explains that he and his co-workers sent Timothy because they so much wanted to know how things were with the Thessalonians (sub-unit G. 1; 3.1-2a). Timothy's credentials are then given (G. 2; 3.2b) and Paul gives the purpose for which Timothy was sent (G. 3; 3.2c-5). There were three reasons for having sent Timothy: to strengthen and encourage their faith; to help them not to be agitated in their tribulations; and so that Paul would know the state of their faith. This part of the 'emissary' unit includes an explanatory parenthesis on suffering (vv. 3b-4) that reminds the Thessalonians (οἴδατε) that Paul had previously warned them that they would suffer. Paul has heard from Timothy concerning the Thessalonians and he tells them about his encouraging report (G.s.; 3.6-8).

While the 'visit' unit dominates the apostolic parousia of 1 Thessalonians, Paul's desire to visit plays a subordinate role to that of expressing his love and gratitude for the faith of the Thessalonians, which has remained intact even during persecution. In fact, Paul's expression of love in the second part of his 'visit' unit (3.9-10a) is patterned, at least in part, on a εὐχαριστῶ period:

Principal Clause:	τίνα γὰρ εὐχαριστίαν
	δυνάμεθα τῷ θεῷ
	ἀνταποδοῦναι
Pronoun object phrase:	περὶ ὑμῶν
Cause:	ἐπὶ πάσῃ τῇ χαρᾷ. . .

And this suggests that a desire to express his love and gratitude, and so to encourage the Thessalonians, is the primary function of the 'desire to visit' unit in 1 Thessalonians. The closing of the 'visit' unit with a benediction, which prays that the Thessalonians would remain steadfast and blameless at the return of the Lord, underscores the encouraging function of this unit. The 'emissary' unit is largely concerned with Timothy's happy report of the Thessalonians' steadfast faith, and so it too serves to express Paul's love for his readers.

Thus the dominant function of the apostolic parousia of 1 Thessalonians is to express Paul's love for his Thessalonian converts and to encourage them in their faith. Both the two-part 'visit' unit and the 'emissary' unit function primarily to reinforce the apostolic trust that Paul has placed in the Thessalonians. The first part of the 'visit' unit concludes with an expression of apostolic dependence, ὑμεῖς γάρ ἐστε ἡ δόξα ἡμῶν καὶ ἡ χαρά (2.20), as does also the 'emissary' unit, ὅτι νῦν ζῶμεν ἐὰν στήκετε ἐν κυρίῳ (3.8).

Reference to the emissary and a statement regarding a hoped-for visit are the means Paul uses to make his apostolic presence felt among his Thessalonian readers. The apostolic parousia of 1 Thessalonians, in fact, establishes Paul's apostolic presence in the community by articulating his love and gratitude and concern for the spiritual health of his readers.

2. *The Apostolic Parousia of 1 Corinthians*
The apostolic parousia in 1 Cor. 4.14-21 contains all three functional units: (1) a 'writing' unit (vv. 14-16), (2) an 'emissary' unit (v. 17), and (3) a 'visit' unit (vv. 18-21). Paul first describes the manner in which he writes (sub-unit F. 1; 4.14), saying that he writes to warn and not to shame them. In the apostolic authority sub-unit (F. 2; 4.15) Paul claims that he is their spiritual father. On this basis a general appeal is made (sub-unit F. 3; 4.16).

The 'emissary' unit (4.17) contains three sub-units. The first (G. 1) begins with διὰ τοῦτο and so refers back to the general appeal in 4.16. It then explains why Paul sent Timothy—because Paul does not think that the Corinthians are imitating him. The second sub-unit (G. 2; 4.17b) gives Timothy's credentials. The third (G. 3; 4.17c) states the purpose of Timothy's visit as being to remind the Corinthians of Paul's teaching. In this sub-unit we hear echoes from the opening formula, particularly 1.2 where Paul identifies the Corinthian church as one among the churches of God. For in v. 17c Paul reminds the Corinthians that what he taught them is the same as what he taught all the churches. In both 1.2 and 4.17c, therefore, there seems to be a desire on Paul's part to help the Corinthians see that they are part of a larger Christian community. This final sub-unit also clarifies the appeal in 4.16: that imitating Paul is accepting his apostolic authority and so following his apostolic teaching.[1]

The 'visit' unit (4.18-21) is an 'announcement of a visit' type. Paul uses the announcement of his visit as an opportunity to warn both his readers (H. 1; 4.: 18-19a) and his arrogant opponents at Corinth (H. 6; 4.21). He also states that his visit is under God's control (H. 2; 4.19b) and that its purpose will be to demonstrate the superiority of the power of the kingdom of God, which he possesses (H. 6; 4.19c-21).

So both the 'writing' unit and the 'visit' unit of the apostolic parousia of 1 Corinthians function to assert Paul's apostolic authority. The 'emissary' unit functions in a similar way by expressing Paul's concern that the church at Corinth remember and obey his ways, which are the ways of Christ Jesus.

The function of the apostolic parousia of 1 Corinthians is, then, to remind Paul's readers of his authority as their spiritual father. This authority will be made more immediate to his readers through Timothy's presence with them. The apostolic parousia of 1 Corinthians also functions to warn Paul's readers of the importance of following his teaching, for his coming visit will clearly demonstrate the superior power of the gospel he preaches and so will silence his Corinthian opponents. So the apostolic parousia of 1 Corinthians seeks, through the letter itself, reference to the emissary and mention of a coming visit, to re-establish the power of Paul's presence among his readers.

3. *The Apostolic Parousia of Philippians*

The apostolic parousia of Philippians is comprised of an 'emissary' unit (2.19-23) and a 'visit' unit (2.24). The 'emissary' unit begins with a statement about how Paul hopes to send Timothy soon (G. 1; 2.19a), with that theme being further explained at its close (G. 1; 2.23) where Paul states that he will send Timothy as soon as he has a better idea of what is in store for himself. Between these two statements there is a brief purpose sub-unit (G. 3; 2.19b) in which Paul says that he wants to send Timothy so that he might know how things are with the Philippians. Likewise, a lengthy credentials unit occurs in this middle portion (G. 2; 2.20-22) that recommends Timothy as one who, like Paul, will be genuinely concerned about the Philippians' welfare.

---

1. Cf. A. Reinhartz, 'On the Meaning of the Pauline Exhortation: "*mimetai mou ginesthe*—Become Imitators of Me"', *SR* 16 (1987), pp. 393-403 (p. 397).

The 'visit' unit (2.24) is an 'announcement' type. It is brief and straightforward, comparable, as we shall see, with the one in Philemon. Paul claims that his coming to them will be in accordance with God's will (H. 2; 2.24a) and that he will come to his readers quickly (H. 1; 2.24b).

The function of this apostolic parousia appears to centre chiefly around commending an emissary to the Philippians, for the most extended part of this letter section is sub-unit G. 2 which concerns the emissary's credentials. Paul evidently wants to prepare his readers to accept without reservation Timothy's apostolic authorization. Since there is no 'writing' unit, we may assume that in Philippians, as in his first letter to the Thessalonians (though unlike 1 Corinthians), Paul felt no need to explain or justify his letter. This suggests that his relationship with his readers at the time of writing is open and trusting and that he does not expect the contents of his letter to cause any difficulty between them.

Furthermore, the fact that Paul does no more than announce a hoped-for visit to them, without stating a purpose for his stay, again suggests how comfortable he is with the spiritual state of his readers. He does not find it necessary to underline the authoritative aspect of his presence (cf. 1 Cor. 4.18-21).

The function of Philippians' apostolic parousia is, then, primarily to establish Timothy as Paul's apostolic surrogate. So Philippians is the one letter of the Pauline corpus where in the opening formula Paul names his co-sender before describing himself (Phil. 1.1).

4. The Apostolic Parousia of Philemon

The apostolic parousia of Philemon contains a 'writing' unit (F; v. 21) and a 'visit' unit (H; v. 22). The 'writing' unit differs from other Pauline 'writing' units in that here Paul combines a manner sub-unit (F. 1) with an assertion of his apostolic authority to write (F. 2). The manner in which Paul writes is based on his assurance of Philemon's obedience to his apostleship. The general appeal (F. 3) is also based on his apostleship, with the participle εἰδώς qualifying the principal verb ἔγραψα as does the participle πεποιθώς at the beginning of the unit. So Paul seeks graciously to persuade his reader(s)[1] to do as he asks.

---

1. Paul is writing to Philemon, but he wants both specific (Archippus and Apphia) and general (the house church) witnesses to his communication. Cf. Lohse, *A Commentary on the Epistles to the Colossians and to Philemon*, p. 191.

Paul's expression of confidence here functions to underline the request he has made in the letter.[1] The appearance of a 'writing' unit suggests that Paul felt the need to explain or justify his writing of the letter. Clearly Paul wants to remind his reader(s) that he writes on the basis of his apostolic authority. His letter, then, is to function as a means of conveying his apostolic presence.

The 'visit' unit (H) is of the 'announcement' type. Paul indicates his reliance on God with regard to his visit (διὰ τῶν προσευχῶν ὑμῶν). As with the comparable unit in Philippians, there is no articulation of the apostolic authority that will accompany such a visit. This suggests that Paul is on good and intimate terms with his reader(s).

The function of the apostolic parousia of Philemon is to establish that through this letter Paul's apostolic authority is being conveyed.

5. *The Apostolic Parousia of Galatians*

The apostolic parousia of Galatians contains only a 'visit' unit that functions like a 'desire to visit' unit. We noted earlier that in other 'desire to visit' units there occurs an expression of love (cf. 1 Thessalonians, sub-unit H. 5). In Galatians, however, rather than an expression of love we find an expression of concern (H. 5; 4.11-19). Paul begins this sub-unit with φοβοῦμαι (v. 11). He is fearful that he has laboured in vain and is concerned about the enemies of the gospel in his converts' midst (v. 17). Paul indicates the seriousness of his concern by stating that he fears that his readers have all but lost their understanding of the gospel (v. 11). Paul then declares that he wishes he could be present with them since he is so concerned over the state of their salvation (H. 3; 4.20).

Throughout the 'visit' unit Paul interleaves expressions of concern with the mention of his presence, which he uses as a reminder of how genuinely he is concerned about their spiritual well-being. So the 'visit' unit of Galatians' apostolic parousia functions almost exclusively to emphasize Paul's concern over the state of his Galatian churches. This unit also functions to remind the Galatians of how things used to be (4.14-15). It is a poignant appeal for obedience to Paul's apostolic authority.

---

1. Cf. S.N. Olson: In 'Phlm 21 the confidence of compliance functions to reinforce the appeal of the whole letter' ('Pauline Expressions of Confidence in His Addresses', *CBQ* 47 [1985], pp. 282-95 [p. 288]).

The absence of a 'writing' unit in Galatians should probably be seen in a different light from the absence of such a unit in 1 Thessalonians and Philippians. For in 1 Thessalonians and Philippians, as suggested earlier, Paul did not justify or explain his letter because he assumed his authority was accepted among his addressees and because he did not expect his letter to cause offence. In Galatians, of course, Paul was sorely aware that the apostolic authority of his letter might not be accepted (1.1; 1.6-7) and that what he says in the letter may cause offence (4.16). Furthermore, not only is there no 'writing' unit in Galatians, but there is also no 'emissary' unit. The letter, then, is the one vehicle Paul has of re-establishing his authority among the Galatian churches. Even his mention of a coming visit is vague, which, again, underscores the weight that the letter itself must bear in conveying Paul's apostolic presence.

The absence of any justification for having written (a 'writing' unit) stems from the same source as the absence of a thanksgiving in this letter. For to justify or explain his letter implies both an attitude of respect for his readers (cf. Phlm. 21) and/or a working relationship (cf. 1 Cor. 4.14). The absence of a thanksgiving in Galatians indicates that neither of these factors existed between Paul and his Galatian churches. So, even though his letter must be the sole means of establishing his apostolic presence, Paul probably omits any reference to the manner in which he writes because he reserved this custom for communications to those with whom he had less strained relationships.

The function of the apostolic parousia of Galatians, therefore, is to remind Paul's readers of their former obedience and of his love and concern for them. In short, its function is (1) to appeal to a lost love and compliance, and thereby (2) to indicate that, through this letter, Paul is seeking to re-establish his apostolic credibility and leadership among them.

6. *The Apostolic Parousia of Romans*

The apostolic parousia of Romans (15.14-32) consists of two parts: a 'writing' unit (unit F; 15.14-21) and a 'visit' unit (unit H; 15.22-32). The 'writing' unit begins with a sub-unit expressing the manner in which Paul has written (F. 1; vv. 14-15a). Convinced of his readers' goodness, knowledge and ability to manage their own affairs, he says that he considers his writing them to be a somewhat bold act. So he begins the 'writing' unit of Romans by assuring his readers that he considers them to be spiritually healthy and responsible. This particular note of graciousness is distinctive to the apostolic parousia of Romans vis-à-vis those of Paul's other letters. This sub-unit, then, functions as an apology for the writing of the letter.[1]

Paul then goes on, as is customary (cf. 1 Corinthians and Philemon), to remind his readers of his apostolic authority (F. 2). This sub-unit occurs in two parts, being intersected by another sub-unit (F.s.; 15.16) in which the purpose for writing is given. In the first part of the sub-unit that deals with his authority to write (F. 2; v. 15b), Paul says διὰ τὴν χάριν τὴν δοθεῖσάν μοι ὑπὸ τοῦ θεοῦ, which echoes his assertion of apostleship in the letter's opening formula at 1.5, δι' οὖ ἐλάβομεν χάριν καὶ ἀποστολήν.[2] The following purpose sub-unit (F.s.) consists of two balanced purpose clauses:

εἰς τὸ εἶναί με
    λειτουργὸν Χριστοῦ 'Ἰησοῦ εἰς τὰ ἔθνη,
    ἱερουργοῦντα τὸ εὐαγγέλιον τοῦ θεοῦ,

ἵνα γένηται
    ἡ προσφορὰ τῶν ἐθνῶν εὐπρόσδεκτος,
    ἡγιασμένη ἐν πνεύματι ἁγίῳ.

In the first of these purpose clauses, Paul says that he writes so that he might be a priest of Christ Jesus to the Gentiles (v. 16a). This does not indicate, as some scholars hold, that Paul had a cultic understanding of his role.[3] The term 'priest' is metaphorical, just as are Paul's descriptions of himself as a planter (1 Cor. 3.6), as God's fellow worker (1 Cor. 3.9), or as a masterbuilder (1 Cor. 3.10).[4] Paul describes his role further in the following participial phrase: as Jesus Christ's priest to the Gentiles. He is the one who ministers the gospel

1. So Olson, 'Pauline Expressions of Confidence', p. 292.
2. Cf. Wedderburn: This passage 'confirms the impression given implicitly in Paul's opening greetings to the Romans that he was claiming that his apostolic commission had made him responsible for the Roman Christians too' (*The Reasons for Romans*, p. 98).
3. E.g. K. Weiss, 'Paulus—Priester der christlichen Kultgemeinde', *ThLZ* (1954), pp. 355-64.
4. See J. Ponthot, 'L'expression cultuelle du ministère paulinien selon Rom. 15, 16', in *L'Apôtre Paul. Personnalité, style et conception du ministère* (ed. A. Vanhoye; Leuven: Leuven University Press, 1986), pp. 254-62 (p. 261). Cf. Ziesler who notes that while Paul is clearly using cultic language the wisest course is not to understand him literally at this point (*Paul's Letter to the Romans*, pp. 341f.).

of God (v. 16b). As Deissmann put it, Paul considers his preaching of the gospel to Gentiles to be 'his holy duty'.[1]

The second purpose clause also stands in relation to γράφω. Here Paul says that he writes so that the offering of the Gentiles might become acceptable. While some think Rom. 15.16 refers to the collection project,[2] the context suggests that the 'offering of the Gentiles' refers to Paul's Gentile converts.[3] For the parallelism of these two purpose constructions requires that 'the offering' be understood in relation to Paul's ministry of the gospel to Gentiles. Furthermore, when Paul has cause to speak of the collection he does so plainly (cf. Rom. 15.25-28).

Paul clarifies what he means in a second participial phrase: acceptability means being sanctified by the Holy Spirit (v. 16d). The final lines of both of the two purpose clauses use a participle to describe more fully the subject of each's previous phrase: first ἱερουργοῦντα, describing what it means to be λειτουργόν, then ἡγιασμένη, describing what it means that ἡ προσφορά is εὐπρόσδεκτος. In both constructions τὰ ἔθνη occurs in the middle phrase.

These two purpose clauses remind the reader of what Paul claims about himself in the letter's opening formula and thanksgiving—that he is the apostle to the Gentiles (1.5) whose commission is to bring about the 'obedience of faith' (1.5) and also to preach the gospel to those at Rome (1.15).[4] In the 'writing' unit of the apostolic parousia we learn more about Paul's commission regarding the Gentiles: that they might be ἡγιασμένη by the Holy Spirit (15.16).

The following sub-unit (15.17-21) is a continuation of the apostolic authority to write sub-unit (F. 2). The οὖν of v. 17 is emphatic rather than inferential, meaning 'I have indeed cause for boasting'. Paul is here commending himself to his readers.[5] The usual treatment of τὰ

---

1. *The Religion of Jesus and the Faith of Paul* (trans. W.E. Wilson; London: Hodder & Stoughton, 1923), p. 262.

2. E.g. Nickle, *The Collection*, p. 134 n. 259.

3. So Cranfield writes: 'The sacrifice offered to God by Christ, which Paul has here in mind, consists of the Gentile Christians who have been sanctified by the gift of the Spirit' (*Romans. A Shorter Commentary*, p. 365). Cf. K. Barth, *The Epistle to the Romans*, p. 530; Käsemann, *Romans*, p. 393; Wedderburn, *The Reasons for Romans*, p. 98.

4. Cf. Cranfield, who suggests that in this passage Paul, as well as at the opening of the letter, states that the Roman church falls 'within the sphere of his apostolic commission' (*Romans* I, p. 20).

5. So Olson, 'Epistolary Uses of Expressions of Self-Confidence', p. 596.

πρὸς τὸν θεόν (15.17) is as an adverbial accusative, meaning 'the things for God' or 'my work for God'.[1] The neuter plural article is better understood, however, to refer to the σημεῖα and τεράτα of which Paul subsequently speaks (v. 19), with πρὸς τὸν θεόν being a standard prepositional phrase. On this understanding, Paul sees his authority to write as based on the fact that his apostleship has been validated by the power of signs and wonders (ἐν δυνάμει σημείων καὶ τεράτων) that Christ has worked through him (κατειργάσατο Χριστὸς δι' ἐμοῦ, v. 18).[2] So Paul claims authority because (1) he has been the agent of the dynamic Spirit of God and (2) his Gentile converts have entered into obedience as a result of witnessing the power of both word and deed through him (δι' ἐμοῦ). Paul regards himself as having an authority which is based on the fact that Christ called him and made use of him to demonstrate the power of the gospel. And he considers that the obedience of Gentiles is achieved through his service as Christ's spiritual agent.

The consecutive construction ὥστε. . . τοῦ Χριστοῦ of v. 19b lays stress on the fact that all the area from Jerusalem to Illyricum has been so evangelized. The fulfilling (πεπληρωκέναι, v. 19b) of the gospel of Christ is achieved when Gentile converts have witnessed the power of the Spirit (the δύναμις πνεύματος θεοῦ, v. 19a) through his ministry. J. Knox takes πληρόω in its geographical sense to mean that the gospel has been preached, whether by Paul or others, throughout the whole northeastern portion of the Mediterranean world.[3] Yet the consecutive conjunction ὥστε suggests that what is described in v. 19b is the consequence of what is described in vv. 18-19a. So Paul's statement about the fulfilling of the gospel from Jerusalem to Illyricum is another statement about the manner in which the gospel has been preached in these places.[4] Paul says that the gospel has been fully preached, in the power of signs and wonders, in an arc around the northeastern Mediterranean. This information serves to qualify further the manner in which he writes this letter. For Paul is here stress-

1. So *BDF*, para. 160.
2. Cf. Schütz, *Paul and the Anatomy of Apostolic Authority*, pp. 239f.
3. 'Romans 15.14-33', pp. 9-10.
4. Cf. Schütz, who derives a similar meaning from πεπληρωκέναι: 'The term fulfill does not describe the end of that labor, but rather the way in which Paul has executed his task: fully, in word and deed, with signs and wonders, etc.' (*Paul and the Anatomy of Apostolic Authority*, p. 47).

ing his apostolic credentials. It is on the basis of his proven apostolic mandate that he is writing to the Roman believers.

Paul's stated purpose for writing in the previous sub-unit now takes on a new meaning. It would appear that Paul is saying that he writes to the believers at Rome in order to exercise his apostolic commission also among them. Yet he evidently feels that he is treading on thin ice in saying this. He makes a point of stressing that his practice has been not to build on another's foundation (15.20). This verse functions as a signal to his readers, comparable to what we heard in the opening formula and thanksgiving, that Paul considers them already Christians and his responsibility for them not their salvation, but rather only their understanding of his gospel.

It is clear from the very nature of Paul's letters that Paul felt a responsibility not just to evangelize as many areas as he could but also to nurture and firmly establish the churches that he had founded.[1] In Romans, Paul is writing to nurture a church that was founded by someone else.[2] Yet this anomaly fits within a certain understanding of Paul's self-perception. He saw himself as the divinely authorized apostle to the Gentiles with a responsibility even to the Roman believers. It was therefore his responsibility to strengthen and enrich their faith.[3]

The 'visit' unit of the Romans apostolic parousia is distinctive in several ways. First, as noted earlier, it is a combination of both a 'desire to visit' type and an 'announcement' type. The 'desire to visit' lacks the customary expression of love and/or concern (cf. 1 Thessalonians and Galatians). Second, the 'announcement' is unique in that the proposed visit is always referred to in a way that sets it off as subordinate either to his trip to Spain (15.24, 28-29) or his trip to Jerusalem (15.32).

---

1. Noted by Knox, 'Romans 15.14-33', p. 6.

2. Cf. Dahl, who writes, 'Paul wrote to the Christians in Rome in order to exhort and strengthen them without intruding upon them and without doubting the genuineness of their Christian faith' ('The Missionary Theology in the Epistle to the Romans', p. 77).

3. Cf. Bowers, who writes that Romans is a 'letter of reinforcement to the Roman congregation' (p. 198) the function of which is edification and nurture ('Fulfilling the Gospel: The Scope of the Pauline Mission', p. 196); and Schütz, who argues that Paul regards both missionary preaching and the 'obedience', or ongoing Christian responsibility of Gentile Christians, as his apostolic commission. It is his self-perception as one who has a special responsibility for the 'obedience' of Gentiles that 'enables Paul to assume the responsibility to remind the Romans of those things he mentions' (*Paul and the Anatomy of Apostolic Authority*, p. 213).

The secondary importance of a visit to Rome is further suggested in the appeal section (H.s.; 15.30-32). In other Pauline apostolic parousias appeals are either functionally connected to the 'writing' unit (cf. 1 Cor. 4.16; Phlm. 21b) or to a direct expression of concern for his readers in the 'visit' unit (Gal. 4.12a). These appeals are all brief general appeals calling for compliance with Paul's apostolic teaching. In Romans, however, the appeal is much more extensive. It is not a direct appeal to his apostolic authority but is rather a means of drawing his readers into a sympathetic relationship with him as he heads towards Jerusalem. Paul makes it clear that his visit to Rome cannot take precedence at the moment, for he must first go to Jerusalem with the collection. Yet he pleads for their support in his endeavour and this appeal is a significant feature of the apostolic parousia of Romans.[1]

The 'visit' unit of this apostolic parousia both expresses Paul's desire to come and announces that he will come. In expressing his desire to come Paul begins by saying that he has often been prevented from coming (H. 4; 15.22). Unlike a similar statement in 1 Thess. 2.17-18 where Paul blames Satan for not being able to come sooner, in Romans Paul says that the reason he has not come is due to his service in the East. Now, however, his eastern mission is over, and he declares that he has wished to see them for a very long time (H. 3; 15.23). N. Dahl's suggestion that the meaning of Rom. 15.23 is that Paul now considers his churches in the eastern part of the empire to be well enough established that they could carry on without his supervision makes good sense of this statement.[2] In this 'desire to visit' unit (H. 3) Paul makes it clear that, while he wants to see his readers, Rome is neither his immediate nor his long term goal. He will seem them on his way to Spain (15.24), after he has gone to Jerusalem (15.25, 28). Paul's mention of these two other destinations has, as we saw in Chapter 1, provoked various theories about Paul's intentions as he writes to Rome: either (1) Paul is writing to Rome in order to establish sympathetic support for his Spanish mission, or (2) Paul writes as a practice run of some sort for his presentation in Jerusalem.

Yet Paul's references to Spain and Jerusalem can also be understood as explanations as to why he is not present with the Romans at the

---

1. Cf. Bassler: 'Our analysis of the letter suggests strongly that whatever other factors were present, one important aspect of the occasion for writing this letter was the request for intercessory help in the matter of the collection' (*Divine Impartiality*, p. 169).

2. 'The Missionary Theology in the Epistle to the Romans', p. 76.

moment.[1] It may also be that Paul knows that the letter's content would be far more appropriately presented in person. The letter as a substitute for personal presence in this case needs to be explained, for what Paul has written is really beyond the scope of a letter.[2] So Paul describes the predicament he is in (he must go to Jerusalem) and affirms that his intention is to come to them as quickly as he can—and, in fact, to go on to Spain with their help.

More than that, Paul's explanation about the nature of the collection (15.25-27) suggests that he wanted to underscore his representative role with the Jerusalem church on behalf of Gentiles,[3] and thereby to draw his readers into a closer relationship with both himself and the other Gentile churches.[4] It suggests furthermore that he wanted to involve the Roman believers in his missionary vision.[5]

By telling his readers about his long range plan to evangelize Spain, and by mentioning that he hopes the Romans will help him, Paul is stating the seriousness of his intention to get to Rome and also reasserting his respect for his readers. He wants to see the Romans and furthermore he wants to be helped by them in his journey further west. So Paul announces that he will come to them on his way to Spain

1. Cf. K.P. Donfried, who considers that this passage 'must be understood as an apology as to why Paul has *not yet* been in Rome' ('A Short Note on Romans 16', in *The Romans Debate*, p. 51).

2. Cf. Bassler, who writes that in Romans Paul moves 'beyond the normal limits of a letter' (*Divine Impartiality*, p. 169).

3. The significance that the collection had for Paul is generally taken to reside in its symbolism as an expression of the validity of the salvation of the Gentiles (Nickle, *The Collection*, p. 127). Paul is the one who manages the collection project (1 Cor. 16.1-4; 2 Cor. 8 and 9) and who was charged with its execution in connection with being given responsibility for the Gentile mission (Gal. 2.10). The charge in Gal. 2.10 is best seen as referring to the collection project that Paul subsequently undertook and that is recorded in 1 and 2 Corinthians and Romans (so Knox, *Chapters in a Life of Paul* [Nashville: Abingdon–Cokesbury], pp. 57-58). In heading the collection project Paul took the position of representative on behalf of the Gentiles before the Jerusalem church. That Paul was willing to risk his life to deliver the collection (Rom. 15.31) indicates how seriously he took his role and how crucial he felt it to be for the survival of Gentile churches that they receive legitimation from Jerusalem. See also F. Watson, *Paul, Judaism and the Gentiles*, pp. 174-76.

4. Cf. Dahl, who considers that this appeal for intercession is in part an appeal for 'the Christians in Rome. . . to ally themselves with other Pauline churches' ('The Missionary Theology in the Epistle to the Romans', p. 77).

5. Cf. H. Koester, who suggests that Paul is here seeking to 'include the Roman Christians in the universal event of the progress of the gospel' (*History and Literature of Early Christianity* [Philadelphia: Fortress, 1983], p. 142).

(H. 1; 15.28b). Then follows a typical construction in which the visit is spoken of as in accordance with God's good pleasure (H. 2; 15.29). Significantly, this sub-unit speaks of the visit as one characterized by the fullness of the blessing of Christ. This reminds the reader of 15.19b, where Paul describes the manner of his work in the East (πεπληρωκέναι τὸ εὐαγγέλιον τοῦ Χριστοῦ), and so of Paul's missionary responsibilities and accomplishments.

Paul has told his readers that he is on his way to Jerusalem but wants to evangelize Spain with their help. He has shared with them his anticipation that many in Jerusalem will not accept his efforts and has asked them to support him. It would appear that Paul may be seeking to encourage the Roman Christian community to regard him as their apostolic leader.

D. *Comparative Observations*

There are, as we have seen, three functional elements in a typical Pauline apostolic parousia: one that concerns the writing of the letter; another that concerns the emissary; and a third that concerns a visit. Only 1 Cor. 4.14-21 contains all three units. 1 Thess. 2.17–3.13 and Phil. 2.19-24 contain a 'visit' unit and an 'emissary' unit; Phlm. 21-22, Gal. 4.11-20 and Rom. 15.14-32 contain a 'writing' unit and a 'visit' unit. The only unit that occurs in every letter of Paul is the 'visit' unit—a fact that reinforces contemporary scholarship's understanding of a letter as a substitute for personal contact and of an apostolic parousia as the letter section that attempts to remind his readers of the power of his presence.[1] Furthermore, except for 1 Cor. 4.14-21, in every case where there is a 'writing' unit an 'emissary' unit does not occur.

Set out in chart form, the data appears as follows:

1 Thess.		emissary	visit (desire)
1 Cor.	writing	emissary	visit (announcement)
Phil.		emissary	visit (desire)
Phlm.	writing		visit (announcement)

---

1. So R.W. Funk: 'In his letters Paul speaks regularly of forthcoming visits to his churches. . . These remarks are gathered, as a rule, into a section which may be termed "apostolic *parousia*". . . This section indicates the strong oral orientation of the apostle's ministry, for which he regarded the letter as a weak substitute' (*Parables and Presence. Forms of the New Testament Tradition* [Philadelphia: Fortress, 1982], p. x).

Gal.	writing	[visit (desire)]
Rom.	writing	visit (desire & announcement)

In letters that have an 'emissary' unit and not a 'writing' unit, it appears that the importance of the letter as a means of personal contact is secondary to that of the emissary.[1] So in 1 Thessalonians and Philippians, a 'writing' unit is absent because his written communication is of less significance to their relationship than the contact established by the emissary. In Philemon, Galatians and Romans, on the other hand, where an 'emissary' unit is missing, it is the letter that alone substitutes for his presence.[2] Therefore in those letters where an 'emissary' unit is absent, the letter itself carries greater significance.[3] For a letter in these cases is the only replacement Paul has at the moment for his personal presence.[4]

The absence of an 'emissary' unit from the apostolic parousia of Romans indicates that Paul considered this letter would have to convey his message in full. So, as with his letters to Philemon and the Galatians, Paul wrote in the knowledge that his letter alone would have to speak for him.

The 'writing' unit of the Romans apostolic parousia is distinctive in that there is no general appeal, based on Paul's apostolic authority, to obey his teaching. This fact undoubtedly reflects Paul's relationship with his readers; for since his addressees had not previously acknowledged his apostolic authority, it would be inappropriate for Paul to include here his usual appeal. At the same time, as we have seen, pre-

1. So White: 'When [Paul] was unable to send an emissary and the correspondence itself had to play a major role, he moved directly from his appeal to the letter to the prospect of a visit. Correlatively, when he could send a messenger to represent him, actual reference to the letter was suppressed' ('Saint Paul and the Apostolic Letter Tradition', p. 440).

2. The explanation of why 1 Corinthians has both an 'emissary' unit and a 'writing' unit may be that, even though Paul has an emissary to send with the letter, he considers that this particular situation requires that the believers attend both to the words of the emissary and of the letter.

3. Cf. White: 'When [Paul] could not send an apostolic courier, nor pay an immediate visit, he emphasized the importance of attending to his written instruction' ('Ancient Greek Letters', p. 100).

4. So White writes: 'The letter is the written equivalent of the oral presentation which Paul would have delivered to the congregation, if he had actually been present' ('New Testament Epistolary Literature', p. 1743). In this regard it is instructive to note that, in Romans, what Paul says he would do were he present is preach the gospel (1.15).

sent throughout this apostolic parousia is Paul's implicit defence of his apostolic credibility (15.15b-21; 15.25-27).

The 'writing' unit of the Romans apostolic parousia is also unique because of Paul's inclusion of a 'purpose for writing' sub-unit (F.s.; 15.16), which suggests that Paul felt an explanation was in order regarding the nature of his letter. Paul acknowledges that the Roman Christians are to be commended for their faith (ὡς ἐπαναμιμνῄσκων ὑμᾶς, v. 15). Yet Paul explains in this 'writing' unit that the reason he writes as he does is out of his conviction that his commission to preach the gospel involves the Roman Christians. It would appear that Paul thinks his readers should know the Pauline gospel for his sake as well as for theirs—for his sake because God has given him responsibility for the 'offering of the Gentiles'; for theirs because as his divinely appointed charges they need to hear the gospel from him.[1]

So while Paul begins the apostolic parousia section by acknowledging his respect for his readers and indeed by calling his letter a 'reminder', he claims, nevertheless, that he writes in accordance with his apostolic mandate. His readers then must understand that he writes because of his commission to present an acceptable Gentile offering, one sanctified in the Holy Spirit. Accordingly, the apostolic parousia section of Romans stresses the importance Paul attached to preaching the gospel to Gentiles (15.16).

The lack of an 'emissary' unit shows that Paul regarded this letter as his only vehicle for communicating with the believers at Rome. We have suggested that Paul considered that what he has written goes beyond the normal bounds of a letter, for he is careful to explain how impossible it is for him to be present and yet how important he considers presence with them to be (15.32). We may then surmise that since the purpose Paul expresses for his visit in the letter's thanksgiving is to preach the gospel to the Roman Christians (1.15), and since Paul cannot now be present and so must use the letter as his surrogate, in Romans Paul is preaching the gospel.[2] This is very probably why he

1. This proposal is of a piece with Dahl's suggestion, based on an analysis of Paul's paraenesis in Galatians, that Paul's perception of his apostolic responsibility involved the 'necessity of preparing pure and blameless Gentile congregations for the day of Christ' (White, 'Saint Paul and the Apostolic Letter Tradition', p. 439, who cites with approval Dahl's conclusion ['Paul's Letter to the Galatians: Epistolary Genre, Content, Structure'], p. 73).

2. Cf. Dahl: 'What Paul does in his letter is what he had for a long time hoped to do in person: he preached the gospel to those in Rome (see 1.15)' ('The Missionary

stresses that he writes in accordance with his apostolic obligation to preach the gospel (15.16). Paul's concern to explain his inability to be present, yet his desire to be present with his readers (a concern evident both in the thanksgiving and the apostolic parousia), seem then to function in part as justifications for the unusual nature of his letter.

The significance of this suggestion is not, as has been emphasized above, that Paul regarded his readers as only partially converted, or more importantly as 'still lacking the fundamental kergyma',[1] i.e. as in need of conversion,[2] but rather that Paul knew himself to stand under obligation to preach the gospel to Gentiles, which obligation included the Romans. Paul was required to preach to the believers in Rome because of his role as representative apostle to the Gentiles. And perhaps partly in order to underline his important representative role Paul emphasized his commitment to taking the collection to Jerusalem.

The 'visit' unit of the apostolic parousia of Romans is unusual on two levels. First, it is a combination of a 'desire to visit' and an 'announcement of a visit'. This fact alone suggests that Paul is ambiguous about the prospect of visiting Rome in the immediate future. Second, both types of 'visit' units in the Roman letter are peculiar. The 'desire to visit', as we might expect, does not express any personal feelings for his readers. The 'announcement' is curiously focused, being concerned primarily with Paul's imminent trip to Jerusalem and only secondarily with a visit to Rome, and then only in connection with his journey onward to Spain.

Paul uses the 'visit' unit of Romans, then, to affirm his long-standing regard for his readers (ἐπιποθίαν δὲ ἔχων τοῦ ἐλθεῖν πρὸς ὑμᾶς ἀπὸ πολλῶν ἐτῶν, v. 23), to acknowledge that personal contact with them is what he really desires (v. 32), and to explain that his priority at the moment must be to deliver the collection at Jerusalem (vv. 25-28). Paul's lengthy explanation of the necessity and value of his trip to Jerusalem (vv. 25-28) and his appeal for his readers to pray for the trip (vv. 30-31) suggest that he wanted (1) to remind his readers of his representative role on behalf of the Gentiles and (2) to involve

Theology in the Epistle to the Romans', p. 77). Also *idem*, 'Paul addressed an apostolic letter to the Christians in Rome, preaching the gospel in writing' (*ibid.*, p. 75).

1. Klein, 'Paul's Purpose in Writing the Epistle to the Romans', p. 48.

2. As Aune writes: 'Paul's letter is written 'to demonstrate the truth of the Christian gospel and to convince the hearers to commit themselves to it and become Christian converts' (*The New Testament in Its Literary Environment*, p. 219).

them in his responsibilities. Paul's mention of his trip to Spain further suggests that he wanted his readers to know he regarded them highly enough to want them to be partners in his evangelistic work.

Chapter 6

THE PAULINE CONCLUSIONS

A. *The Functional Units of a Pauline Conclusion*

There are five possible units within a Pauline letter conclusion: (1) a peace-benediction (unit J); (2) a grace-benediction (unit K); (3) a unit that either exhorts or commands (unit L); (4) a unit that rejoices, using the word χαίρω (unit M); and (5) a greetings unit (unit N). As we shall see, on two occasions a unit with a unique function occurs (unit S). There is no standard order for these functional units, with the exception that unit K invariably ends the conclusion. The two units that always occur in a Pauline conclusion are the greetings (unit N) and the grace-benediction (unit K). This suggests that the basic function of a Pauline conclusion is to reinforce personal aspects of that relationship shared by Paul and his readers and testify to the faith they share in common.

The peace-benediction (unit J), when it occurs, often begins the letter conclusion. Romans, as we shall see, has two peace-benedictions. God is the subject of the benediction in all cases except 2 Thessalonians, which uses 'Lord', and Galatians, which does not use a subject. God is described with the genitive case as a 'God of peace'. Generally, the peace-benediction then progresses to a statement expressing Paul's prayer that the presence of the 'God of peace' might be with all of his readers. As we shall see, the Thessalonian letters differ in this regard, as do also Galatians and the second peace-benediction of Romans. A Pauline peace-benediction functions, as White states, to provide 'a kind of eschatological climax to the entire message'.[1]

The grace-benediction (unit K) has as its subject ἡ χάρις, which is qualified as being that of 'the Lord Jesus Christ'. Paul then generally indicates that his prayer is that this grace would be with all of his

---

1. 'Saint Paul and the Apostolic Letter Tradition', p. 442.

The Pauline Conclusions

Key	1 Thess. 5	2 Thess. 3	1 Cor. 16	2 Cor. 13	Phil. 4	Phlm.	Gal. 6	Rom. 15-16
J Peace	J 5.23-24	J 3.16		J 13.11b	J 4.9b		J 6.16	J 15.33; J 16.20a
L Command/Exortation	L 5.25; L 5.27		L 16.13-16; L 16.22	L 13.11a	L 4.8-9a		L 6.17	L 16.17-18; L 16.19b
M Rejoicing			M 16.17-18		M 4.10-20			M 16.19a
N Greeting	N 5.26	N 3.17	N 16.19-21	N 13.12	N 4.21-22	N v. 23-24	N 6.11	N 16.3-16; N 16.21-23
S Special							S 6.12-15	S 16.1-2
K Grace	K 5.28	K 3.18	K 16.23-24	K 13.13	K 4.23	K v. 25	K 6.18	K 16.20b; K 16.24

readers. Some peace-benedictions pray that Christ's peace would be with everyone's spirit. H. Gamble has observed that Paul's prayers for grace and peace in letter conclusions echo the greetings of Paul's opening formulas, thereby forming an enclosing structure for the letters. 'The prescriptive greeting of his letters χάρις ὑμῖν καὶ εἰρήνη, is clearly echoed in the conclusions by the prayer-wish for peace and the grace-benediction. We might say that the letters are bracketed by a chiastic repetition of corresponding wishes.'[1]

The hortatory unit (unit L) occurs in every letter but 2 Thessalonians and Philemon. In several cases this unit occurs twice in one letter conclusion. It uses the imperative mood and the readers are generally addressed directly as 'brethren'.

The χαίρω unit (unit M) occurs in 1 Corinthians, Philippians and Romans. It is the least frequent of any of the letter conclusion units. In every case, as has been noted, it uses the verb χαίρω, which generally occurs in conjunction with a causal construction using ἐπί with the dative and/or ὅτι.

The greetings unit (unit N) is a standard feature of every Pauline letter conclusion. This unit serves four functions. In it Paul may exhort his readers to greet people in their midst on his behalf; he may convey greetings to his readers on behalf of others; he may exhort his readers to greet one another with a 'holy kiss'; or he may give his autograph.

B. *The Boundaries of the Pauline Conclusions*

Paul begins his conclusion of 1 Thessalonians with a peace-benediction at 5.23 immediately following the end of the letter's paraenetic section (4.1–5.22). The conclusion of 1 Thessalonians then is 5.23-28. Likewise, the conclusion of 2 Thessalonians begins with a peace-benediction (3.16) following the paraenetic section (3.6-15). The conclusion of 2 Thessalonians is 3.16-18.

There is no peace-benediction at the close of 1 Corinthians. After the letter-body concludes with instructions about the contribution for the saints (16.1-11) and information about why Apollos has not come (16.12), there follows a hortatory unit (16.13-16) that opens the conclusion of 1 Corinthians. The conclusion of 1 Corinthians then is 16.13-24.

---

1. *Textual History*, p. 73.

At the conclusion of 2 Corinthians Paul signals that he has reached the close of his letter by the use of λοιπόν, ἀδελφοί and by saying good-bye (χαίρετε). Like that of 1 Corinthians, this letter's conclusion begins with a hortatory unit. The conclusion of 2 Corinthians is then 13.11-13.

Paul also opens the conclusion of Philippians with τὸ λοιπόν, ἀδελφοί (4.8) and so this letter's concluding section too begins with a hortatory unit. Gamble argues that the conclusion of Philippians begins at 4.9b with the peace-benediction.[1] But this peace-benediction, like the one in 2 Corinthians, begins with καί and so is to be understood in conjunction with what precedes it. The conclusion of Philippians therefore begins with the hortatory unit of 4.8-9a. The boundaries of the conclusion of Philippians then are 4.8-23.

Philemon's conclusion begins at v. 23 immediately following the apostolic parousia section (vv. 21-22). The autograph at v. 19 functions to close the body rather than as part of the letter conclusion. White suggests that the autograph occurs here in Philemon in order to convey a sense of Paul's apostolic authority so that the reader may resolve to comply with the message of the letter.[2] This letter's conclusion is found then in vv. 23-25.

Paul opens the conclusion of Galatians at 6.11 right after the close of the paraenetic section at 6.10. The conclusion of Galatians then extends from 6.11 to the close of the letter at 6.18.

Determination of the boundaries of the conclusion of Romans involves a decision regarding various aspects of the literary integrity of ch. 16. There are three issues involved here: the authenticity of 16.25-27; the authenticity of 16.1-23; and the authenticity of 16.24.

In the textual tradition the doxology has been variously placed either after 14.23, 15.33, or 16.23.[3] Largely because of this 16.25-27 is widely considered to be secondary[4] and often suggested to have originated with Marcion.[5] The highly questionable origin of this passage

---

1. *Textual History*, pp. 145f.; see also p. 88.
2. 'New Testament Epistolary Literature', p. 1741.
3. In some MSS, it also occurs either twice or in different forms.
4. See Cranfield, *Romans*, p. 808; Wiles, *Intercessory Prayers*, p. 72; Barrett, *Romans*, p. 286; Gamble, *Textual History*, p. 124. For more literature, see Kümmel, *Introduction*, p. 316 n. 39.
5. First suggested by Corssen, 'Zur Überlieferungsgeschichte des Römerbriefes', *ZNW* 10 (1909), pp. 1-45, 32-34. See also A. von Harnack, 'Uber I Kor. 14, 32 ff. und Röm. 16.25ff. nach der ältesten Überlieferung und der marcionitischen Bibel',

renders it inappropriate for inclusion in an investigation of Pauline letter conclusions.

The fact that in the textual tradition the doxology occurs both after ch. 14 and after ch. 15 brings also the originality of 16.1-23 into question.[1] Even before textual evidence was a factor, however, the seemingly inappropriate content of ch. 16—especially the extensive greetings in a letter to Christians whom Paul did not know, and the apparently urgent command in 16.17-20 that seems out of character with the rest of the letter—raised doubts about the chapter. The 'Ephesian hypothesis', first proposed by D. Schülz and later accepted by T.W. Manson, among others,[2] interprets the evidence as follows: (1) that the greetings of 16.3-16 are unlikely in a letter to a church Paul had never visited; (2) that other New Testament references to Prisca and Aquila place them in Ephesus, after expulsion from Rome (Acts 18.18f., 26; 1 Cor. 16.19), and also the mention of the 'first convert in Asia' (Rom. 16.5) suggests an Ephesian destination; (3) that the content and tone of the hortatory segment in 16.17-20 is incongruous with the exceptionally diplomatic and general tone Paul takes in chs. 12–15.13; (4) that 15.33 could serve as an epistolary conclusion; and (5) that 16.1-2 may introduce a separate letter of recommendation for Phoebe, a letter in conformity with the form of the Hellenistic ἐπιστολὴ συστατική.[3] On the basis of such evidence the 'Ephesian

Studien zur Geschichte des Neuen Testaments und der Alten Kirche, I, *Zur neutestamentlichen Textkritik* (Berlin, 1931), pp. 180-90; G. Zuntz, *The Text of the Epistles. A Disquisition upon the Corpus Paulinum* (London: Oxford University Press, 1953), pp. 227-28; Kümmel *Introduction*, p. 317; Donfried, 'A Short Note on Romans 16', p. 57. Some have also noted its literary and theological relationship to the Pastoral epistles; so, e.g. Barrett, *Romans*, p. 286.

1. So E.J. Goodspeed, 'Phoebe's Letter of Introduction', *HTR* 44 (1951), pp. 55-57 (p. 55).

2. Manson, 'St Paul's Letter to the Romans—and Others'. See also Deissmann, *Light from the Ancient East*, pp. 234-36; Marxsen, *Introduction to the New Testament* 108; M.J. Suggs, '"The Word is Near You": Rom. 10.6-10 Within the Purpose of the Letter', in *Christian History and Interpretation* (ed. W.R. Farmer, *et al.*; Cambridge: Cambridge University Press, 1967), pp. 289-312; Bornkamm, *Paul*, pp. 79f., 247; Kinoshita, 'Romans—Two Writings Combined'; J. Fitzmyer, 'The Letter to the Romans', in *The Jerome Biblical Commentary* (Englewood Cliffs, NJ; Prentice–Hall, 1968), pp. 292-93.

3. See especially Deissmann, *Light from the Ancient East*, p. 235; and J.I.H. McDonald, 'Was Romans XVI a Separate Letter', *NTS* 16 (1969–70), pp. 369-72.

hypothesis' argues that ch. 16 of Romans is a fragment of a letter originally addressed to the church at Ephesus.[1]

Such objections to the integrity of 16.1-23 are not, however, without reasonable responses. (1) As Gamble has suggested, the extensive greetings in 16.3-16 may be especially appropriate at the end of a letter written to a church to which Paul is introducing himself and from which he is encouraging openness.[2] Furthermore, the descriptions Paul adds to many of the names serve the function of conveying his personal knowledge of individuals within the Roman Christian community, thereby bolstering his credibility with his readers. It would be difficult to suggest a function for such descriptions in a letter to the community at Ephesus, since a great degree of familiarity existed between Paul and his readers there.[3] (2) It is entirely possible that those who left Rome because of the Edict of Claudius returned after the emperor's death in 54 CE.[4] (3) The passage in 16.17-20 is not as much at odds with Paul's tone in the rest of Romans as some would argue. Paul's use of παρακαλῶ indicates that his approach here is polite rather than demanding.[5] And the content of the passage has parallels within the body of the letter, such as σκάναλον and διδαχή.[6] Furthermore, the danger that Paul warns of is general and so this passage does not point towards Paul having any more specific knowledge of events at Rome here than he does in the rest of the letter.[7]

(4) The suggestion that 15.33 could have been the original conclusion of Romans does not bear much weight since, as a comparative

---

1. So e.g. Bornkamm, *Paul*, p. 247. Goodspeed suggests, on the other hand, that all that has been lost is the letter's opening salutation. Paul's letter to Ephesus contained only canonical Rom. 16 (along with the missing salutation). The function of Paul's letter was to introduce and recommend Phoebe to the Ephesian church and assure this woman a favourable and safe reception within that community ('Phoebe's Letter of Introduction').

2. *Textual History*, pp. 48f. See also D. Guthrie, *New Testament Introduction* (London: Tyndale, 1970), p. 401.

3. Bornkamm's suggestion that this list of greetings is appropriate as part of a letter in which Paul is saying farewell to the church at Ephesus (*Paul*, p. 247) is too speculative to be entertained seriously.

4. So Donfried, 'A Short Note on Romans 16', p. 56. Also Käsemann (*Romans*, p. 413), even though he regards ch. 16 as a separate letter written to an address other than Rome. See also Barrett, *Romans*, p. 283.

5. So Gamble, *Textual History*, p. 52.

6. So Donfried, 'A Short Note on Romans 16', p. 59.

7. Cf. Gamble, *Textual History*, pp. 52f.

study shows, a Pauline conclusion does not elsewhere contain only a peace-benediction. (5) Likewise, the suggestion that 16.1-2 serves as the introduction to a separate letter of recommendation is questionable. It is to be noted that the Greek letter of introduction, unlike these verses, usually begins by describing the person introduced as the 'deliverer of the letter'.[1] As Gamble notes, the evidence supporting 16.1-2 as part of an ancient letter of recommendation is too weak to uphold such an hypothesis.[2]

Therefore, the evidence in favour of the integrity of Rom. 16.1-23 is considered stronger than that for what must remain the more speculative 'Ephesian hypothesis'. For, as A.M. Hunter aptly states, 'in a case of this kind it is wise to prefer tradition to speculation'.[3]

The third issue which must be dealt with concerns the authenticity of 16.24. Modern scholarship has generally accepted the grace-benediction of 16.20b, while rejecting that of 16.24, on the grounds that only one benediction should occur in a Pauline conclusion. K. Aland, for example, proposes that 16.24 was added prior to the addition of the doxology as a means of closing the letter and adduces the verse's close resemblance to 2 Thess. 3.18 as support.[4] Corssen's opinion was that the benediction of 16.20b was originally found at 16.24 and that when the doxology was brought from the end of ch. 14 to the end of ch. 16, the benediction was moved to 16.20b in order to avoid an overabundance of concluding elements.[5]

Gamble, however, rightly finds both of these suggestions inadequate, asking, in response to Aland, why the doxology at 16.20b was not

1. So C.W. Keyes, 'The Greek Letter of Introduction', *American Journal of Philology* 56 (1935), pp. 28-44 (p. 39).
2. *Textual History*, p. 54.
3. *The Epistle to the Romans* (London: SCM, 1957), p. 129. Cf. F. Watson: 'The view that Rom. 16 like Rom. 1–15 is addressed to Rome is preferable to the cumbersome theory that without any break or explanation Paul suddenly addresses not Rome but Ephesus, and to the view that an entirely unrelated letter-fragment has unaccountably been attached by a later editor to the letter to the Romans. If Rom. 16 can be satisfactorily explained as an integral part of the letter to the Romans, the Ephesian theory collapses automatically' (*Paul, Judaism and the Gentiles*, pp. 98f.).
4. 'Glosse, Interpolation, Redaktion und Komposition in der Sicht der neutestamentlichen Textkritik', in *Studien zur Überlieferung des Neuen Testaments und seines Texts* (Berlin: De Gruyter, 1967), p. 46, cited from Gamble, *Textual History*, p. 130 n. 6.
5. See Gamble, *Textual History*, p. 130 n. 7, who cites Corssen, 'Zur Überlieferungsgeschichte des Römerbriefes', *ZNW* 10 (1909), pp. 10-45, esp. pp. 11-12.

simply moved to 16.24 to accomplish a formal close. He points out in response to Corssen that there clearly are two different forms of the benediction that have been passed down in the textual tradition,[1] and so concludes (1) that 'the benediction of 16.24 is lost (or displaced to 16.28) only when the doxology is found at the end of ch. 16', (2) that the omission of 16.24 is the direct result of the secondary addition of the doxology and (3) that '16.24 has to be judged an original reading'.[2] Gamble further suggests that the fact that this benediction was not simply dropped indicates its originality.[3] Only when the doxology became accepted at the end of ch. 16 did the benediction at 16.24 become problematic. So the MSS retained 16.20b and often displaced 16.24 to 16.28.

Beyond this, Gamble argues that the occurrence of two benedictions is not unusual in Hellenistic letters where the final wish is often duplicated and greetings appear between them. Gamble notes further that these final wishes were usually in different hands.[4] By analogy, Gamble suggests that Paul wrote 16.1-20 in his own hand: 'Paul originally meant to bring the letter to a close with the autograph, and so finished writing with the benediction of 16.20b, having reiterated the peace-wish just beforehand, as elsewhere. But then he decided to add the greetings of his associates in 21-23 (a postscript), after which it was necessary to repeat the final wish. As we have seen, all of this can be closely paralleled in extant ancient letters.'[5] I concur with Gamble's opinion that the grace-benediction of 16.24 is the original close of the conclusion of Romans.

The conclusion of Romans begins, as did the conclusion of Paul's two letters to the Thessalonians, with a peace-benediction (15.33).[6] On Gamble's theory, which we have accepted, the double occurrence of a peace-benediction (15.33 and 16.20a) is the result of Paul adding a postscript in his own hand at 16.1-20 and so writing something similar in 16.20a to what he had dictated in 15.33. So the epistolary boundaries of the conclusion of Romans are 15.33–16.24.

---

1. Gamble, *Textual History*, p. 130.
2. Gamble, *Textual History*, p. 130.
3. Gamble, *Textual History*, p. 132.
4. Gamble, *Textual History*, p. 59. Gamble cites: P. Lond. 413, 897; BGU 249, 665, 815, 1874; P. Oxy. 298; etc.
5. Gamble, *Textual History*, p. 94.
6. Cf. J.A. Ziesler, *Paul's Letter to the Romans*, p. 35.

C. *Analyses of the Respective Conclusions*

1. *The Conclusion of 1 Thessalonians*

The conclusion of 1 Thessalonians (5.23-28) includes four of the five functional units, missing only the χαίρω unit. It begins with a peace-benediction (unit J: 5.23-24). This peace-benediction is the lengthiest of any of those found in the Pauline conclusions. After the customary reference to the God of peace, which in this case is intensified by αὐτός, Paul goes on to describe his prayer for his readers. His prayer is that God would make the Thessalonians perfect in holiness so that no blame would be found in them when the Lord returns. The peace-benediction concludes with an affirmation that 'the one who calls' the Thessalonians is faithful and capable of doing all that Paul has prayed for.

The content of this peace-benediction echoes part of the thanksgiving of the letter. In the thanksgiving Paul makes reference to the election of his readers (1.4). In the peace-benediction of the letter's conclusion God is 'the one who calls'. The thanksgiving of 1 Thessalonians twice makes reference to the Holy Spirit's active presence when the Thessalonians received the gospel (1 Thess. 1.5, 6). In the peace-benediction Paul prays that the Thessalonians would be entirely sanctified—body, soul and spirit. In the letter's thanksgiving Paul affirms how the Thessalonians have taken the right stance in waiting for God's son who will come from heaven (1.10). In the concluding peace-benediction Paul's prayer is that his converts would be kept blameless for the coming of the Lord Jesus Christ. So, while all the aspects of the content of the thanksgiving of 1 Thessalonians are not echoed in the peace-benediction, all of the content of the peace-benediction is reflected in the letter's thanksgiving.

The thanksgiving affirms Paul's positive regard for his readers in part by describing his prayer for them. The peace-benediction of the letter's conclusion also describes the kernel of Paul's prayers and so closes the letter as it began, by affirming the caring relationship he has with his readers.

The hortatory unit (unit L) is in two parts (v. 25 and v. 27). Paul addresses his readers as 'brothers', which is, as we have noted, a standard feature of a hortatory unit of a letter conclusion. In 5.25 Paul implores his readers to pray for him and his companions. This is the only instance in a Pauline letter conclusion where Paul exhorts his readers to pray. In the second part of the hortatory unit Paul adjures his readers 'by the Lord' to have the letter read to all of the brothers (5.27). Neither part of the hortatory unit indicates that Paul was concerned over anything specific within the Thessalonian congregation. The hortatory passages rather serve to require the readers to focus on Paul, both through praying for him and by reading his letter to all the believers. Paul then provides the means whereby the relationship between himself and his readers may be maintained—through prayer and this letter. At the close of his letter Paul both affirms his care for his readers (the peace-benediction) and encourages their care in response (the hortatory unit).

The greetings unit of 1 Thessalonians (unit N: 5.26) is one of the briefest of all of the Pauline conclusions. In it Paul requests that his readers greet each other with a holy kiss. The other comparable sub-units of the greetings unit (1 Cor. 16.20; 2 Cor. 13.12; Rom. 16.16) use ἀλλήλους, whereas in 1 Thess. 5.26 Paul writes τοὺς ἀδελφοὺς πάντας. This may suggest a relatively united Christian community at Thessalonica.

The final unit of this letter, as of every other Pauline letter, is the grace-benediction (unit K: 5.28). Paul prays that the grace of the Lord Jesus Christ would be with all of his readers. The form of the grace-benediction found in 1 Thessalonians is of the most simple type. In the other letters the grace-benediction is either a longer form of this simple benediction, or it includes additional benedictions (see 1 Cor. 16.23-24; 2 Cor. 13.13).

Thus the function of the conclusion of 1 Thessalonians is to close the letter (1) on a note of intimacy, which calls the readers to maintain a vital relationship with Paul through prayer and his letter, and (2) on a note of apostolic encouragement, which focuses the readers' hope on the parousia and on their assurance of salvation (5.24).

2. *The Conclusion of 2 Thessalonians*

The conclusion of 2 Thessalonians (3.16-18) has only three functional units. It begins with a peace-benediction (unit J: 3.16) that uses κύριος as the subject. As in 1 Thessalonians, here the divine name is intensified with αὐτός. The concluding peace-benedictions of the two Thessalonian letters are also similar in the fact that they both use the optative mood. The peace-benediction of 2 Thessalonians closes with a prayer for the Lord's presence, which is more like a typical peace-benediction (cf. Phil. 4.9b; Rom. 15.33).

The greetings unit (unit N: 3.17) contains only the autograph. This autograph, with its two qualifying phrases, is the most extensive of the Pauline autographs, suggesting that his readers' recognition of his handwriting and so of an authentic letter from him, was a concern for Paul. Such a concern was signalled earlier in the letter when Paul asked his readers not to accept communications purporting to come from him that say that the day of the Lord has come (2.2). That in the 'greetings' unit Paul only speaks of his autograph and does not either convey greetings or ask his readers to greet people on his behalf indicates the importance of this matter to him.

The letter then closes with a standard grace-benediction (unit K: 3.18).

The function of the conclusion of 2 Thessalonians, therefore, is (1) to assure Paul's readers of the hope of peace (unit J) and (2) to display his signature so as to prevent them from accepting a forged apostolic letter.[1]

3. *The Conclusion of 1 Corinthians*

The conclusion of 1 Corinthians (16.13-24) contains four of the five possible functional units of a Pauline conclusion, lacking only the peace-benediction. It begins with a hortatory unit (unit L) in vv. 13-16, with then exhortation occurring again in v. 22. The first hortatory unit exhorts Paul's readers to stand firm and do everything in love (vv. 13-14), then gives certain Christian leaders his endorsement and commands his readers to obey them (vv. 15-16). The second part of the hortatory unit (v. 22) uses a typical hortatory construction comprised of a conditional clause followed by an imperative verb (cf. Rom. 13.14; 1 Cor. 16.10). This unit implies that the readers will be judged on their love for the Lord and that they may also judge the sincerity of others by this standard. The Aramaic expression *Marana tha* contains a note of warning, for the coming of the Lord is also the arrival of the day of judgment in which, to be sure, love for the Lord will be the standard of judgment. Together the hortatory units function as Paul's appeal to his readers to hold onto his teaching.

In the χαίρω unit (unit M: 16.17-18) Paul again authorizes certain Christians (Stephanas, Fortunatus and Achaicus) and exhorts his read-

---

1. Cf. Bahr: Paul 'probably added his postscript with the special purpose of guarding against further forgery of his letters' ('Paul and Letter Writing in the First Century', p. 466).

ers to recognize them also as their leaders. Unlike the χαίρω unit of Philippians, in 1 Corinthians Paul does not express gratitude for certain aspects of his relationship with his readers. This underlines the depth of the concern Paul has that his readers would obey his teachings. Paul is seeking to establish a leadership in Corinth that will guide the community in accordance with his own understanding of the gospel.

The greetings unit (unit N: 16.19-21) evidences three of the four possible functions: it conveys greetings; it exhorts the readers to greet one another with a holy kiss; and it gives Paul's autograph.

The letter closes with a grace-benediction (unit K: 16.23-24). This, along with that of 2 Corinthians, is the most extensive grace-benediction to be found in the Pauline conclusions. Unlike other grace-benedictions it assures the readers of Paul's love for his readers (v. 24).

So the function of the conclusion of 1 Corinthians is primarily to exhort the readers to accept leadership from those Christians whom Paul endorses, and thereby to remain within the bounds of Paul's authority. That Paul ends his letter by stating that his love is with all of them through Jesus Christ indicates further that the function of the letter's conclusion is to strengthen the bond between himself and his readers.

4. *The Conclusion of 2 Corinthians*

The conclusion of 2 Corinthians (13.11-13) has four functional units. The beginning hortatory unit (unit L: 13.11a) directly addresses the readers as 'brothers'. The following peace-benediction (unit J: 13.11b) begins with καί, which serves to make it conditional on the readers heeding the preceding exhortation. The peace-benediction describes God as the God of both love and peace.

The greetings unit (unit N: 13.12) exhorts the readers to greet one another with a holy kiss and conveys greetings from 'all the saints'. This, along with the greetings units of the Thessalonian letters, is one of the briefest of such units.

The conclusion of 2 Corinthians then ends with a grace-benediction (unit K: 13.13) which is the fullest and most carefully crafted of any of the comparable units. It is a remarkably compact and dense theological statement.

Thus the function of the conclusion of 2 Corinthians appears to be to remind the readers of their obligation to live in accordance with what

Paul has taught so that they may know God's peace and love. It functions further to underscore Paul's authority as the one whose prayers concern their proper appropriation of all that is offered by the Lord Jesus Christ, God and the Holy Spirit.

5. *The Conclusion of Philippians*
Paul concludes his letter to the Philippian church (4.8-23) with all the five functional units of a Pauline conclusion. This conclusion begins with a hortatory unit (unit L: 4.8-9a), which, like that of 2 Corinthians, directly addresses his readers as 'brothers'. Paul exhorts his Philippian readers to think only of those things that are good and pure (4.8) and to practise only those things that he has taught and modelled (4.9a). The following peace-benediction (unit J: 4.9b) beginning with καί, as does the comparable unit in 2 Corinthians (13.11b), is conditional upon compliance with Paul's exhortation.

The conclusion progresses to the χαίρω unit (unit M: 4.10-20). This is the most extensive of any to be found in the Pauline conclusions, and appears to be structured in part to resemble a thanksgiving period:

Principal verb	v. 10	Ἐχάρην δὲ
Manner		ἐν κυρίῳ
Manner		μεγάλως
Cause		ὅτι. . . φρονεῖν,
Cause		ἐφ' ᾧ. . . δέ.
Explanation 1	v. 11	οὐχ ὅτι καθ' ὑστέρησιν λέγω,
		ἐγὼ γὰρ ἔμαθον. . . εἶναι.
	v. 12	οἶδα καὶ. . .
		οἶδα καὶ . . .
		ἐν παντὶ καὶ ἐν πᾶσιν
		μεμύημαι;
		καὶ χορτάζεσθαι καὶ πεινᾶν
		καὶ περισσεύειν καὶ
		ὑστερεῖσθαι·
	v. 13	πάντα ἰσχύω ἐν τῷ
		ἐνδυναμοῦντί με.
Explanation 2	v. 14	πλὴν καλῶς ἐποιήσατε
		συγκοινωνήσαντές μου τῇ
		θλίψει.
	v. 15	Οἴδατε δὲ καὶ ὑμεῖς,
		Φιλιππήσιοι,
		ὅτι ἐν ἀρχῇ τοῦ εὐαγγελίου,
		ὅτε ἐξῆλθον ἀπὸ Μακεδονίας,

οὐδεμία μοι ἐκκλησία
ἐκοινώνησεν . . .
ὑμεῖς μόνοι,
v. 16   ὅτι καὶ ἐν Θεσσαλονίκῃ . . . ἐπέμψατε.

Explanation 3   v. 17   οὐχ ὅτι ἐπιζητῶ τὸ δόμα,
ἀλλὰ ἐπιζητῶ τὸν
καρπὸν . . . ὑμῶν.

v. 18   ἀπέχω δὲ πάντα καὶ περισσεύω·
πεπλήρωμαι δεξάμενος παρὰ
Ἐπαφροδίτου . . .
ὀσμὴν εὐωδίας, θυσίαν δεκτήν,
εὐάρεστον τῷ θεῷ.

The principal verb (ἐχάρην) is followed by two qualifying sub-units that describe the manner in which Paul rejoices (ἐν κυρίῳ; μεγάλως). These are followed by two causal sub-units (ὅτι and ἐφ' ᾧ).[1] Then follows what is best regarded as an explanatory sub-unit in three sections. The first and third explanatory sub-units begin with οὐχ ὅτι[2] and bear certain grammatical similarities. For both are dominated by first person singular present active verbs (οἶδα in the first unit functioning as a present); both contain one significant perfect passive first person singular verb that introduces the closing of the sub-unit (μεμύημαι and πεπλήρωμαι) and reinforces its point. And both exhibit similar symmetrical structures.

The first explanatory sub-unit is dominated by infinitives. There is a chiastic arrangement of passive infinitives and active infinitives, along with a semantic dynamic between 'lack' and 'fulfilment'.

v. 12c   χορτάζεσθαι
πεινᾶν
περισσεύειν
ὑστερεῖσθαι

---

1. While Zerwick makes ἐπί with the dative final (*Biblical Greek*, para. 129), Robertson makes it causal (*Grammar*, p. 963). Since this construction was causal in the thanksgiving period, I argue that it is also causal in the letter's concluding χαίρω unit.

2. Robertson notes that οὐχ ὅτι can be either objective, i.e. 'I do not mean to say that', or causal, i.e. 'I say this not because' (*Grammar*, p. 965). Paul uses this construction in an objective sense at the other point it occurs in Philippians outside the conclusion (3.12). Thus I view it as objective.

Notice also the whole of v. 12:

ταπεινοῦσθαι
περισσεύειν
περισσεύειν
ὑστερεῖσθαι.

Both of the infinitive configurations end with phrases in which πᾶς is dominant.

In the third explanatory sub-unit there is a grammatical configuration following the passive πεπλήρωμαι that alternates noun with adjective:

ὀσμὴν εὐωδίας,
θυσίαν δεκτήν.

The middle sentence reiterates two major terms from the first explanatory unit: πάντα and περισσεύω.

The second explanatory sub-unit is dominated by the second person plural, both aorist and present/perfect (ἐποιήσατε, οἴδατε, ἐπέμψατε). The dominant term in this unit is κοινωνία (συγκοινωνήσαντες and ἐκοινώνησεν).

The explanation contained in these three explanatory sub-units moves from explaining Paul's stand as regards material needs, to his readers' loyalty and generosity, to Paul's relationship to their gift, which is ultimately a sacrifice to God.

After acknowledging his gratitude for their gift, Paul assures his readers that God will also care for them as he has cared for Paul through them (4.19). He then rounds off this unit of his conclusion by ascribing glory to God (4.20). The last two sentences of this unit, then, function as a blessing and a doxology which set Paul's gratitude for the Philippians' gift in the perspective of God's care for both himself and them.

There is both a structural and a verbal relationship between the concluding χαίρω and the thanksgiving period of Philippians. Both are governed by a principal verb that is modified by adverbs of manner and by a prepositional qualifying phrase (cf. 1.4; πάντοτε and ὑπὲρ πάντων; and 4.10; μεγαλῶς and ἐν κυρίῳ). Both contain causal constructions using ἐπί with the dative and ὅτι. Likewise, both have a number of terms in common: φρονεῖν , συγκοινωνία, πᾶς, τὸ εὐαγγελίον, and Χριστὸς ' Ιησοῦς.

There are also other evidences of a relationship between these two units, which, while not so direct, nevertheless warrant comment. For example, there is a strong influence of πᾶς in both the thanksgiving and the χαίρω. The unusual addition of μετὰ χαρᾶς in the thanksgiving period (1.4) may be explained as foreshadowing what we learn of in the χαίρω unit—that Paul is full of joy regarding the Philippians since they have come to his aid. And both the thanksgiving and the χαίρω unit of the conclusion assure the Philippians of Paul's love and appreciation because of their loyalty to him from the very beginning of his ministry (1.5; 4.15).

The greetings unit (unit N: 4.21-22) performs two of the functions of a greetings unit: it both requests and conveys greetings. The conclusion of Philippians ends with a standard grace-benediction (unit K: 4.23).

The function of the conclusion of Philippians, therefore, is largely to express Paul's gratitude for the gift he has received from his readers by way of Epaphroditus. The note of gratitude is made more resonant by the structural and verbal echoes between the χαίρω unit and the thanksgiving section. The conclusion also functions to reinforce Paul's apostolic leadership over his readers by reminding them of the importance of attending to what he has taught and shown them.

6. *The Conclusion of Philemon*
The concluding section of Paul's letter to Philemon is, like the rest of this letter, short and to the point. In his conclusion Paul only conveys greetings (unit N: vv. 23-24) and rounds off the letter with the standard grace-benediction (unit K: v. 25).

In Chapter 3 it was suggested that in this letter, while Paul directly addresses Philemon, he also directs his words to readers (both specific and general) whom he wants to witness this personal conversation. This suggestion is strengthened by noting that the object of the concluding grace-benediction is plural (ὑμῶν).

Thus the function of the conclusion of Philemon appears to be to remind Paul's reader(s) of the personal bonds that they share by way of mutual friends and to affirm the foundation of their common faith—the grace of the Lord Jesus Christ.

7. *The Conclusion of Galatians*
Paul closes his letter to the Galatians with an unusual concluding section (6.11-18). It contains five functional units, but rather than a χαίρω unit it has a passage that functions as a warning (unit S: 6.12-15).

The conclusion of Galatians begins with a greetings unit (unit N: 6.11). This unit only provides Paul's autograph and is the one instance of an autograph in Paul's letters that appears in the imperative mood. It is the only occurrence of an autograph that is not described as a greeting (ὁ ἀσμασμός [cf. 2 Thess. 3.17]). The impersonal character of this unit is noteworthy.

Then follows a long section (unit S: 6.12-15) that leads up to a conditional peace-benediction (unit J: 6.16). The passage in 6.12-15 contains a number of significant opposing terms—εὐπροσωπῆσαι, περιτέμνεσθαι, ἀναγκάζουσιν, σάρξ, διώκωνται, καυχήσωνται, νόμος, φυλάσσουσιν, and κόσμος, being set in opposition to ἐν τῷ σταυρῷ τοῦ κυρίου ἡμῶν Ἰησοῦ Χριστοῦ, καινὴ κτίσις. The contrasts in these terms reflect the semantic and theological contrasts that Paul plays on throughout Galatians.

All of 6.12-16 (i.e. unit S and unit J) should be viewed together. This construction can be set out in three parts:

(1) v. 12 ὅσοι θέλουσιν εὐπροσωπῆσαι ἐν σαρκί,
          οὗτοι ἀναγκάζουσιν ὑμᾶς περιτέμνεσθαι,
          μόνον ἵνα τῷ σταυρῷ τοῦ Χριστοῦ μὴ διώκωνται.

   v. 13 οὐδὲ γὰρ οἱ περιτεμνόμενοι αὐτοὶ νόμον φυλάσσουσιν
          ἀλλὰ θέλουσιν ὑμᾶς περιτέμνεσθαι,
          ἵνα ἐν τῇ ὑμετέρᾳ σαρκὶ καυχήσωνται.

(2) v. 14 ἐμοὶ δὲ μὴ γένοιτο καυχᾶσθαι
          εἰ μὴ ἐν τῷ σταυρῷ τοῦ κυρίου ἡμῶν ᾿ Ἰησοῦ
          Χριστοῦ,
          δι' οὗ ἐμοὶ κόσμος ἐσταύρωται κἀγὼ κόσμῳ.

   v. 15 οὔτε γὰρ περιτομή τί ἐστιν
          οὔτε ἀκροβυστία
          ἀλλὰ καινὴ κτίσις.

(3) v. 16 καὶ ὅσοι τῷ κανόνι τούτῳ στοιχήσουσιν,
          εἰρήνη ἐπ' αὐτοὺς
          καὶ ἔλεος,
          καὶ ἐπὶ τὸν ᾿ Ἰσραὴλ τοῦ θεοῦ.

The first and third parts begin with the relative pronoun ὅσοι; the second begins with the first person personal pronoun ἐμοί. The grammatical similarity between ἵνα τῷ σταυρῷ τοῦ Χριστοῦ μὴ διώκωνται (v. 12) and ἵνα ἐν τῇ ὑμετέρᾳ σαρκὶ καυχήσωνται (v. 13) highlights the semantic contrast of these clauses.

The second part begins emphatically with ἐμοὶ δὲ μὴ γένοιτο καυχᾶσθαι, providing a direct contrast to the καυχήσωνται of v. 13b. It continues with εἰ μὴ ἐν τῷ σταυρῷ τοῦ κυρίου ἡμῶν Ἰησοῦ Χριστοῦ, which contrasts to μόνον ἵνα τῷ σταυρῷ τοῦ Χριστοῦ μὴ διώκωνται of v. 12. So Paul replaces himself in opposition to the group identified by ὅσοι in the first part (vv. 12-13).

The second part of this construction climaxes with the words καινὴ κτίσις (v. 15). Both the first two parts of this construction approach their close with a negated consecutive clause (οὐδὲ γάρ and οὔτε γάρ) followed by an adversative clause (ἀλλά), with these similar constructions highlighting the contrast set out in each—that is, between being circumcised (v. 13) and being a new creation (v. 15).

The third part of the construction (unit J: 6.16), as has been noted above, begins with the relative pronoun ὅσοι. It refers to those who, as opposed to the group of people referred to in vv. 12-13, follow Paul's rule (presumably not to be circumcised). It is at this point that a version of the peace-benediction is given: εἰρήνη ἐπ᾽ αὐτοὺς καὶ ἔλεος, καὶ ἐπὶ τὸν Ἰσραὴλ τοῦ θεοῦ (v. 16). While a typical Pauline peace-benediction identifies God as the God of peace (θεὸς τῆς εἰρήνης), such a description is absent in Galatians. Furthermore, it is clear that the peace-benediction of Galatians applies only to those who follow Paul's rule.[1]

The peace-benediction, then, is conditional on heeding the warning that precedes it.[2] A somewhat similar construction has been seen in the conclusions of 2 Corinthians and Philippians where the peace-benediction was conditional upon the preceding hortatory passage. In Galatians, however, the note of warning and the conditional nature of the peace-benediction is much more intense, straightforward and direct.

The conclusion of Galatians progresses to a hortatory unit (unit L: 16.17) that employs an imperative verb and includes an explanatory sub-unit. Paul says that he bears the marks of Jesus in his body and commands that no one trouble him. This statement serves to underscore Paul's authority to speak as he does, for it places him in contrast to those who shy away from the cross of Christ (v. 12) because they

1. Cf. the standard form in the other letters where the benediction applies to πάντων ὑμῶν.
2. The conditional character of this blessing is noted by P. Richardson, *Israel in the Apostolic Church* (Cambridge: Cambridge University Press, 1969), p. 76, and Betz, *Galatians*, pp. 320-21.

care about the flesh (σάρξ). Paul, however, has realized Christ's redeeming and demanding presence ἐν σώματι (v. 17). Paul's implied defence of the divine authorization of his apostleship here echoes his direct defence of such in the opening formula of this letter (1.1).

The letter closes with a grace-benediction (v. 18) which is exceptional in two ways. First, it addresses the readers as ἀδελφοί, which may be read as Paul's final conciliatory note, and second, it closes with ἀμήν. This latter feature is paralleled in the letter's opening formula where the doxology also ends with ἀμήν (1.5).

Thus the function of the conclusion of Galatians appears to be primarily to warn Paul's readers of the seriousness of accepting leadership from those who advocate circumcision. To be the 'Israel of God' does not require circumcision[1] but rather acceptance of the gift of being a new creation. The conclusion also functions as an appeal to Paul's readers to recognize the integrity and divine authorization of his apostleship, for he is the one who bears on his body the marks of Jesus. The implication here is that these marks (and not circumcision) are the signs of obedience to God's will. The absence of any reminder of mutual relationships in the greetings unit suggests either (1) that Paul and the Galatians no longer share such, or (2) that Paul considered his relationship with the Galatian churches so strained that mention of shared personal friends would do nothing to further his goal of re-establishing apostolic leadership with them.

8. *The Conclusion of Romans*

The conclusion of Romans contains all five units of a Pauline conclusion, along with an extra unit (unit S: 16.1-2). It begins with a peace-benediction (unit J: 15.33). The occurrence of 'amen' in this otherwise standard peace-benediction is very probably a secondary addition held over from its use as the conclusion of a shorter recension of Romans (chs. 1–15).

There follows then a unit in which Paul introduces and commends Phoebe, a leader of the church at Cenchrea,[2] to his Roman readers

---

1. As Betz notes, 'the Christian Galatians loyal to Paul must be the same group as the "Israel of God"' (*Galatians*, p. 322).

2. See E.E. Ellis, who understands διάκονοι in Paul to refer to workers in a local congregation whom the community has recognized and designated ('Paul and His Co-Workers', *NTS* 17 [1971], pp. 437-52 [p. 443]). D.C. Arichea argues that 'diakonos' should be understood to indicate Phoebe's role as a leader within her Christian community ('Who was Phoebe? Translating *diakonos* in Romans 16.1',

(unit S: 16.1-2). The recommendation of Phoebe contributes to the function of establishing personal links between Paul and his readers.

Following this recommendation is an extensive list of greetings that occurs in two parts (unit N: 16.3-16 and unit N: 16.21-23). This 'greetings' unit requests greetings on Paul's behalf, conveys greetings and exhorts the readers to greet one another with a holy kiss.

The most noteworthy feature of the 'greetings' unit is its length, which results both from the many people Paul asks his readers to greet and from Paul's unusual inclusion of descriptions for most of these individuals. There is only one other instance where Paul describes people in a 'greetings' unit (Phlm. 23-24) but this occurrence is in the context of Paul conveying the greetings of others. In such a context a description is, of course, appropriate, since readers can profit from knowing a little about the person whose greetings Paul is conveying. In the context of requesting readers to greet individuals in their midst, however, the function of the descriptions is more obscure. For in Romans Paul exhorts his readers to greet people whom his readers presumably know and yet whom Paul takes pains to describe. This suggests that the function of this 'greetings' unit is to promote Paul's credibility with his readers through highlighting the personal relationships he has with several people in their community.

Such a function is also suggested by the order in which Paul mentions specific individuals and by the corresponding nature of the descriptions he gives. The people whom Paul mentions first are Prisca and Aquila with whom he can claim a missionary partnership (16.3) and whose credentials highlight Paul's importance to the Gentile mission (16.4). The next person Paul asks his readers to greet is Epaenetus whose status as the 'first convert in Asia'[1] also underscores the success of Paul's Gentile mission (16.5b). In the next verses (16.6-9) Paul requests his readers to greet people who are described as having a relationship with him (e.g. τὸν ἀγαπητόν μου). This relationship often involves participation in Paul's missionary work (e.g. τὸν

BibT 39 [1988], pp. 401-409). P. Richardson suggests that the phrase 'deacon of the church in Cenchraea' very probably indicates 'a functional "office" of some sort' ('From Apostles to Virgins: Romans 16 and the Roles of Women in the Early Church', *TJT* 2 [1986], pp. 232-61 [p. 239]); and E. Schüssler Fiorenza argues that Phoebe should be called a minister (*In Memory of Her. A Feminist Theological Reconstruction of Christian Origins* [New York: Crossroads, 1983], p. 170).

1. So Donfried, 'A Short Note on Romans 16', p. 56.

συνεργὸν ἡμῶν).[1] After this category, Paul names persons whom he commends as having good standing in his eyes (16.10-15). The function of this 'greetings' unit, then, appears to be to identify specific individuals within the Roman Christian community so that Paul may more fully commend himself to his readers.[2]

In the greetings unit Paul exhorts the usual greeting of one another with a holy kiss (16.16a) and conveys greetings on behalf of all the churches of Christ (16.16b). This latter feature of the 'greetings' unit implies Paul's apostolic stature, for he is the one who has authority to convey such greetings. The only comparable greeting is in 1 Corinthians (16.19a) where Paul conveys greetings on behalf of the churches of Asia. His greeting in Rom. 16.16b, however, being much more comprehensive, implies his concern to present himself to his readers as one who has a particularly significant position in relationship to the churches of Christ.

The second part of the greetings unit (16.21-23) only conveys greetings. The unusual occurrence of a greeting by an amanuensis (16.22) suggests Paul's desire to establish a personal relationship between his readers, himself and his associates.

The hortatory unit of the Romans conclusion is also in two parts (vv. 17-18 and v. 19b), being divided by the χαίρω unit. The first part is introduced by a παρακαλῶ clause, which is followed by two types of command constructions: an infinitive construction and an imperative construction. This is then followed by an explanation in two parts. The structure can be laid out as follows:

v. 17   Παρακαλῶ δὲ ὑμᾶς, ἀδελφοί,
command   σκοπεῖν τοὺς τὰς διχοστασίας
            καὶ τὰ σκάνδαλα παρὰ τὴν διδαχὴν
            ἣν ὑμεῖς ἐμάθετε ποιοῦντας,

command   καὶ ἐκκλίνετε ἐπ᾽ αὐτῶν·

v. 18 explanation   οἱ γὰρ τοιοῦτοι τῷ κυρίῳ ἡμῶν Χριστῷ οὐ

---

1. It is interesting to note, in passing, the suggestion that the name Junia (16.7) may, in fact, be the abbreviation of a woman's name, perhaps Junias or Julia, thereby indicating a female apostle (e.g. V. Fabrega, 'War Junia(s), der hervorragende Apostel (Rom. 16, 7), eine Frau?', *JAC* 27 (1984), pp. 47-64; Richardson, 'From Apostles to Virgins', pp. 238-39; R.R. Schulz, 'Romans 16.7: Junia or Junias', *ExpT* 98 [1987], pp. 108-10).

2. Cf. Donfried who interprets these greetings as part of Paul's strategy to gain support for his specific views from part of the Roman Christian community ('A Short Note on Romans 16', p. 58).

δουλεύουσιν ἀλλὰ τῇ ἑαυτῶν κοιλίᾳ,

explanation   καὶ διὰ τῆς χρηστολογίας καὶ εὐλογίας
ἐξαπατῶσιν
τὰς καρδίας τῶν ἀκάκων.

The hortatory unit is to be distinguished from those of Paul's other letter conclusions in that it is a warning to steer clear of certain people. Paul appeals to his readers to avoid people who do not serve the Lord whom Paul and his readers serve. In this unit Paul both (1) affirms his readers' existing faith, for what they already know (v. 17) puts them in an entirely different category from these dangerous people who do not serve Christ,[1] and (2) places himself in a position to give advice and warning to his readers.

The next part of the hortatory unit follows the χαίρω section and uses a parallel construction built on contrasting terms:

v. 19b   θέλω δὲ ὑμᾶς
σοφοὺς εἶναι εἰς τὸ ἀγαθόν,
ἀκεραίους δὲ εἰς τὸ κακόν.

This is a general paraenetic saying that does not indicate concern over any specific issues in the community. Moreover, the use of θέλω suggests that Paul is simply expressing his views rather than exhorting.

So the hortatory unit is used primarily to describe a group that is an enemy of both Paul and the Romans. The unit functions to place Paul and his readers in one camp over against an enemy capable of deceiving and corrupting those who are unprepared and unwise. The dual function of warning his readers and siding with them is entirely different from the function of the other Pauline concluding hortatory units, for in those units Paul stands apart, giving counsel and commands. Yet in the course of Romans' hortatory unit, Paul affirms his respect for the faith of the Roman community, his identity with them and his authority to warn.

The χαίρω unit (unit M: 16.19a) occurs between the two parts of the hortatory unit. It is grammatically different from comparable units in 1 Corinthians and Philippians where the principal verb is followed by the postpositive δέ and then by causal and explanatory construc-

---

1. In comparison with 1 Thess. 4.1 (ἐρωτῶμεν ὑμᾶς καὶ παρακαλοῦμεν ἐν κυρίῳ Ἰησοῦ, ἵνα καθὼς παρελάβετε παρ' ἡμῶν τὸ πῶς δεῖ ὑμᾶς περιπατεῖν καὶ ἀρέσκειν θεῷ, καθὼς καὶ περιπατεῖτε) we can see that Paul is here exhorting his readers to cling to teaching which, in fact, is not his own.

tions. The χαίρω unit of Romans has a reverse order, beginning with an explanatory clause (ἡ γὰρ ὑμῶν ὑπακοὴ εἰς πάντας ἀφίκετο) that is followed by a causal phrase (ἐφ᾽ ὑμῖν) and then the principal verb (οὖν χαίρω). In comparison to its counterparts in 1 Corinthians and Philippians, the causal sub-unit of the Romans χαίρω is distinctly brief and pointed. It betrays no immediate or preceding relationship, indicating only a formal awareness of the Roman Christians. Likewise, the explanatory clause ἡ γὰρ ὑμῶν ὑπακοὴ εἰς πάντας ἀφίκετο refers to no personal relationship, but only a general knowledge in the churches of the Christian community at Rome.

Following the second hortatory unit is a second peace-benediction (unit J: 16.20a). This is a distinctive peace-benediction, for the others refer to an action that God will do for his readers (e.g. 1 Thess. 5.23, ἁγιάσαι ὑμᾶς ὁλοτελεῖς; 2 Thess. 3.16, δῴη ὑμῖν τὴν εἰρήνην; Phil. 4.9b, ἔσται μεθ᾽ ὑμῶν), whereas in Rom. 16.20a the verb (συντρίψει) refers to something God will do to Satan with the Romans as his agents. The focus of this peace-benediction is, then, not on what Paul prays that the God of peace will give to the Romans, but rather on what God will do by means of them. So once more it would seem that Paul is according respect to his readers.

Furthermore, Paul's identification of a common enemy (Satan) in 16.20a produces a recognizable dynamic by serving to place himself and his readers in the same camp. This dynamic was at work in the preceding hortatory section. Paul uses the peace-benediction of 16.20a to place himself again in a relationship with his readers.

The last unit of the conclusion of Romans is the grace-benediction (unit K: 16.24), which, as was noted earlier, is the second occurrence of the grace-benediction (the first being at 16.20b). With this blessing Paul finally brings the longest of his letters to a close.

Thus the conclusion of Romans focuses primarily on creating a relationship between Paul and his readers by singling out specific individuals among the Roman readership with whom there is a mutual personal bond. The establishment of personal links may also be seen as part of the function of Paul's commendation and sending of Phoebe.

This conclusion further functions to affirm Paul's respect for his readers, as can be seen both from the unit M and unit L, where Paul trusts that the teaching they have already received is adequate to withstand the intruders (16.17). Paul's respect for his readers is also highlighted in the unusual second peace-benediction (16.20a) where Paul states that God will conquer Satan through the involvement of the

Roman Christians. At the same time, the fact that he warns his readers in 16.17-18 implies Paul's special authority. This authority is also signalled when Paul conveys greetings on behalf of all the churches of Christ (16.16).

To sum up, it may be said that the conclusion of Romans functions chiefly to create the type of dynamics that Paul desires there to be in his relationship with his readers. Paul wants this relationship to be one that is: (1) based on a personal foundation, and so he recommends Phoebe and gives extensive greetings; and (2) based on mutual respect, and so he makes his respect for his readers plain—also indirectly reminding them of the respect that is due to him.

D. *Comparative Observations*

The conclusion of Romans stands out from the rest of the Pauline conclusions in several ways. First, it is the only conclusion that repeats the peace-benediction (unit J) and the grace-benediction (unit K). It has been suggested that this repetition resulted not from the function that the conclusion was meant to play, but rather from the circumstances of its composition—that Paul dictated up to 15.33, where he gave his usual peace-benediction; that then he added a postscript in his own writing in 16.1-20, ending with another peace-benediction (16.20a) and a standard grace-benediction (16.20b); and that finally a further postscript was added to the letter by Tertius (16.21-23), which ended with another grace-benediction (16.24). The only feature of this compositional structure that begs explanation in relation to the function of the conclusion is the placement and content of the second peace-benediction, for in no other letter does Paul place the peace-benediction just prior to the grace-benediction. This suggests that Paul was using the peace-benediction at 16.20a in a non-formulaic manner in order to convey something particular to his readers. In connection with this we note the unusual content of this peace-benediction, which I have interpreted as functioning primarily to affirm Paul's respect for his readers. If that was indeed Paul's intent in this unit, its exceptional placement might be explained as resulting from an attempt to highlight this function, i.e. to underscore Paul's high regard for his readers.

Second, the conclusion of Romans is unique among the Pauline conclusions in its introduction of someone to the readership (unit S: 16.1-2). Third, the extent and descriptive character of the greetings requested on Paul's behalf in the Romans conclusion are also unique. I

suggested above that these special features serve to place Paul's relationship with his readers on a more personal and immediate footing.
In all his other letters, which were written to communities which
know Paul well, such greetings are absent, for personal relationship
was established prior to the letter. Part of the function of the conclusion of Romans, however, is to achieve a semblance of the type of
relationship which Paul shared with those Christian communities
which he founded himself.

Fourth, and finally, certain aspects of the hortatory unit (unit L) and
the rejoicing unit (unit M) are distinctly different in Romans from
their comparable units in the other Pauline conclusions. Both of these
units display little familiarity with the readers and function to show
Paul in a respectful posture towards them while taking a stance of
authority. In the other comparable units Paul is less concerned to
accord respect (e.g. 1 Cor. 16.15-18) and more direct about his apostolic position with his readers (e.g. Phil. 4.9a). He may even imply
that the peace of God is conditional on following his exhortations (so 2
Cor. 13.11; and Phil. 4.8-9), and sometimes he even bluntly states this
(Gal. 6.16).

Paul's concern to encourage a personal basis for his relationship
with his addressees, through Phoebe and his requested greetings, suggests that he is seeking to simulate his personal presence by means of
this letter. We may see this concern in relation to certain features of
the thanksgiving and apostolic parousia which we have noted. For if,
as I have suggested, Paul is in fact presenting his understanding of the
faith to the Roman believers and not just establishing openness for a
later visit in which he will do such, then it would be to his advantage
to try to create, as far as he is able, conditions similar to those that
would obtain were he with them. By highlighting personal links
between himself and the Roman believers he may, through this letter,
be seeking to make himself as fully present as possible to his readers.

I have suggested that the greetings in the Romans conclusion also
function as Paul's self-recommendation, for he probably hopes that the
mutual respect he shares with some among them may extend to all.
Such a function is in harmony with the concern, already identified in
the other letter-enclosing sections, to communicate his apostolic
authority over and responsibility for the Roman Christians. For certainly Paul's claims would have a greater chance of being upheld if his
readers were well-disposed towards him.

Paul's concern both to affirm his readers in their existing faith, and to show himself as one who has a special authority in relation to them, resonates in the conclusion. Throughout the opening and closing sections of Romans, then, Paul's apostolic role is asserted in tandem with affirmations of the high regard in which he holds his readers. So we see that, while Paul knew himself to be 'the authorized apostle to the Gentiles (15.15-16)',[1] he considered that the best way to encourage acceptance of this among his Roman readers was by approaching them with a degree of gracious respect.

The function of the conclusion of Romans is to reinforce the fact that, while Paul acknowledges the quality of faith of his readers, he nevertheless has a certain responsibility for and authority over them. The conclusion of Romans appears also as an attempt, at the close of this extraordinary letter, to create the semblance of a face-to-face relationship between Paul and his readers so that his message may be heard within the context of a personal relationship.

---

1. Donfried, 'A Short Note on Romans 16', p. 58.

Chapter 7

TOWARDS A RESOLUTION OF THE ROMANS DEBATE

The foregoing comparative analysis has identified a number of distinctive features in the opening formula, the thanksgiving, the apostolic parousia and the conclusion of Romans. Some of these distinctive features result from what occurs within a particular letter structure section of Romans which does not occur within the comparable letter structure sections of Paul's other letters, while some of what makes the Romans opening and closing sections unique is what is missing that customarily appears in comparable Pauline sections.

Romans is the only letter that Paul sends in a solo capacity. This is all the more noteworthy since Timothy was with Paul at the time of writing (Rom. 16.21). This suggests that Paul's customary mention of a co-worker(s) at the start of the letter would divert attention from his particular purpose(s) in writing Romans.

In the opening formula of Romans Paul exhibits a clear concern to underscore his apostolic role (cf. 1.1). Paul wants his apostolic self-understanding to be plain from the start. The relationship he is interested in having with his readers involves their acceptance of his apostolic calling. Paul's stress on such a calling may indicate that he expected opposition to this self-presentation, although there is no other evidence of a self-defensive stance within the opening and closing sections.

Following the underscoring of his special call, Paul presents an understanding of the gospel that his readers also share (1.3-4). This confession appears to function as a means of gaining credibility with his readers at the outset of the letter. So Paul begins this letter by presenting himself as an authoritative voice for the faith (1.1) whom the Roman believers should regard as 'orthodox' (1.3-4).

In the 'identification of sender' unit Paul tells his readers that they fall within his apostolic purview, that he has a divinely-given responsibility for them (1.5-6). The other Pauline opening formulas exhibit nothing comparable—not within their 'identification of sender' units, nor in any other unit of this opening letter structure section. This irregularity suggests that the establishment of an apostolic relationship with the Roman readers is an important function of this letter.

Some of the terms of the relationship that it is this letter's function to establish seem to be: (1) the Roman Christians' acceptance of Paul's self-presentation as one with a particular God-given mission to evangelize Gentiles; (2) the reader's understanding that the gospel Paul preaches is in accordance with what the faithful in Rome believe; and (3) the readers' recognition that Paul regards all Gentiles, even those in Rome, as falling under his leadership.

Paul's concern to highlight his apostolic calling appears also in the thanksgiving period, where, as has been noted, Paul draws attention to Christ's authorization of his apostleship (1.8) and his service to the gospel (1.9). These instances stand out as distinctive since they occur within an epistolary unit that usually concerns only the manner in which Paul prays for his readers. Yet in the course of telling his addressees that his attitude towards them is one of thankful prayer, Paul highlights his apostolic position.

This same focus is evident at the end of the thanksgiving, where Paul says that his reasons for wanting to come to Rome are that he may impart a spiritual gift, encourage and be encouraged in the faith, reap some fruit among them, and preach the gospel. These stated intentions must not be read as Paul seeking to convert his readers, since in the same breath he affirms their faith ('through one another's faith' 1.12). It would seem rather that, in context, these statements function to present Paul as one who has particular authority to speak to them about Jesus Christ—to preach the gospel. They function more as a means of dictating the readers' attitude towards himself than as a straightforward statement of purpose for his visit. For his desire to preach to the Roman Christians was not out of concern for their conversion, but because he regards himself as one whose call to be the apostle to the Gentiles is appropriate also to their situation (1.9). It is this self-understanding that Paul wants his Roman readers to appreciate.

A corollary to the readers' acceptance of his apostolic self-understanding is their acceptance of his authority over them in matters of faith. This expectation on Paul's part is evident in the opening formula (1.5-6) and is implied in the thanksgiving. For when Paul writes that one of the purposes he has for his visit is that he may reap some fruit among the Roman Christians just as he has among the rest of the Gentiles (1.13), the clear implication is that he is seeking to include his readers among his apostolic charges.

The thanksgiving of Romans is peculiar especially because of its focus on a visit to the readers. The topic of a visit is generally confined to the apostolic parousia section of a Pauline letter. The double occurrence of mention of a visit suggests that Paul wanted his readers to know how important he considered his personal presence with them to be (1.10-11), and that his absence from Rome has not been for lack of good intentions but because he has been prevented (1.13).

When Paul again mentions a visit to Rome in the apostolic parousia he stresses that he has tried many times before to come (15.22), but not until now has this seemed a real possibility. He has, he says, no more reason to stay in the eastern empire (15.23) beyond his final obligation of delivering the collection at Jerusalem (15.25). Once that obligation has been fulfilled, however, he expects to be free to come to Rome (15.31-32).

Paul wants his readers to be aware that he has every intention of making a personal visit to them. Yet this is not the only function of his mention of a visit. Paul emphasizes that he cannot make Rome his next stop and, in fact, asks for his readers' prayerful support for his trip to Jerusalem (15.30), thereby implying that he wanted them to be participants within his apostolic orbit. This is another indication of Paul's intention to draw his readers under his leadership—an intention that appears first in the opening formula (1.5-6).

Paul also mentions his ambition to evangelize the western empire when he writes about his desire to visit Rome (15.23-24, 28). When he asks for his readers' help in reaching this goal (15.24) he is again implicitly requesting the privilege of being their apostolic leader in the service of the gospel.

Paul's emphasis on his desire to visit the Roman Christians, which appears both at the beginning and the end of the letter—either in conjunction with mention of his concern for the spiritual welfare of his readers or in tandem with a presentation of himself as the representative apostle to the Gentiles (see also 15.23-28)—functions as a request for his readers to regard him as their apostolic leader. The terms of the relationship which, through this letter, he is seeking to establish with the Roman Christians include their acceptance of him as the authorized apostle to the Gentiles.

The contingent nature of Paul's visit to Rome is plain from the letter's apostolic parousia section. For Paul will be able to come to Rome only if his Jerusalem mission is successful. The seriousness of his concern about the danger he faces when he makes the trip with the Gentile churches' collection is obvious (15.31-32). The fact that Paul knows that his personal presence in Rome is dependent on a happy outcome of that very risky venture is significant for the problem of the function of Romans. For if Paul considered there was a high probability that he would never reach Rome, it is not likely that his visit was the chief reason for his letter. There are, however, indications that the function of Romans goes beyond that of mere preparation.

One of the places where it is clearest that the function of Romans is more than that of merely setting the stage for a visit, but is in fact the accomplishing of some of Paul's goals for his readers, is in the apostolic parousia section. The apostolic parousia of Romans is unique in having what I called a 'purpose for writing' sub-unit, which tells the readers that Paul writes (1) in order that he might fulfil his calling to be a priest of Christ Jesus who ministers the gospel of God, and (2) so that the offering of the Gentiles might be acceptable, having been sanctified in the Holy Spirit (15.16).

This passage must be given its full weight in connection with the question of the function of Romans. Here it is clear that Paul feels responsibility for his readers and that they are among his apostolic charges. He evidently wants to include them among his 'offering' of the Gentiles. It is, then, highly likely that in writing his letter Paul sought to impart to the Roman Christians the understanding of the gospel that it was his privilege to communicate in an especially dynamic way (15.18-19). Not that Paul considered he needed to give them a complete gospel message covering all aspects of Christian faith and practice, nor, of course, a gospel message in abstract, nor that he viewed his interpretation to be entirely new to his readers, but that he was responsible to offer what he considered to be his particularly powerful presentation of the gospel to them. For Paul knew himself as one through whom Christ worked to accomplish the obedience (15.18) and sanctification (15.19) of Gentiles, and he considered the Christians at Rome should also be part of his offering of 'obedient' and 'sanctified' Gentiles (15.16). Paul hints that during the course of his visit he will address this concern (1.11; 1.15), but since that visit is at the moment still only a future probability, the letter itself functions largely to realize Paul's particular objective for his readers.

Paul is careful to emphasize that his presentation of himself to Roman Gentile believers as their apostle and his concern to incorporate them within his 'offering' is not a judgment on their faith. He says plainly that his principle is never to build on someone else's foundation (15.20). So he is not completing another's unfinished task, but rather he is seeking acceptance for and compliance with the rightful position he has as their apostle.

Paul consistently assures his readers that he admires and respects their faith. Romans, in fact, is the only letter in which the recipients are identified within the 'identification of sender' unit as those 'called to belong to Jesus Christ' (1.6). This irregularity highlights Paul's concern to express his respect for his readers, and that right after he tells them that he considers them to be among his charges (1.6).

That Paul wanted his readers to be assured of his respect for them is plain also in the apostolic parousia of Romans. Paul begins this section by describing his letter as largely a reminder to his readers and by assuring his readers that he considers them to be mature and responsible Christians (15.14-15). And this concern is also evident in the letter conclusion, where at different places Paul takes opportunity to imply his respect for his readers (e.g. 16.17-20).

Romans is the only letter besides Philemon in which Paul does not designate his readers as a 'church'.[1] It is also one of those letters in which Paul does not describe those to whom he writes as being 'in Christ/God'—though, as we noted earlier, the absence of the latter designation is tied in with the absence of the former. The omission of these customary descriptions for his readers could indicate either that Paul does not know them well enough to label them as such, or that he does not consider them worthy of these labels, or that he wishes to speak to them more personally as fellow individual Christians rather than address them as a group. In Romans Paul describes all of his readers as 'beloved of God' and 'called to be holy' (1.7). The only other letter in which these two descriptions appear is 1 Corinthians (1.2) where they occur in conjunction with the word 'church'. In the case of 1 Corinthians these terms probably function to qualify the church at Corinth as one comprised of many who are beloved and called. In Romans, these same descriptions, occurring apart from any connection with the word 'church', suggest that Paul's intention is to

1. In Philippians 'church' is implicit in the reference to bishops and deacons. Cf. Klein, 'Paul's Purpose in Writing the Epistle to the Romans', p. 47.

show that he regards his readership as comprised of divinely loved and called individuals. It may be that by omitting the term 'church' Paul is seeking to reach out to the separate persons among his addressees.

The last chapter of Romans functions chiefly to create the semblance of a face-to-face relationship with the readers by singling out individuals among the readership with whom Paul has a relationship or about whom he can claim some knowledge. I have suggested that the recommendation of Phoebe may also be a means of creating personal links between Paul and the Roman congregation. The creation of a sense of kinship with his readers would be particularly important if Paul's objective was to create in the readers' minds openness to accepting him as their apostle in order that they might accept his interpretation of the gospel message given in the letter.

Of the various theories concerning the purpose of Romans, my proposal stands at the furthest end of the spectrum from what I labelled the 'pastoral' purpose proposal. A comparative study of the opening and closing sections of Romans yields no evidence that Paul was concerned either with the doctrine or practice of his addressees. In fact, as has been seen, Paul stresses his respect for both these aspects of the Roman believers' faith.

My proposal stands closest to the category of theories that I labelled the 'missionary' purpose proposal. However, rather than regarding the letter primarily as a means of preparing for Paul's arrival when he will use Rome 'as a staging area for a mission to Spain',[1] my investigation has led me to propose that Paul was chiefly exercising his apostolic mandate in the letter.

My proposal bears a similarity to the 'theological' purpose proposal in that it regards Romans as Paul's setting forth of his gospel in written form. Rather than understanding Paul's intention to be either that of offering his interpretation of the good news for a general public,[2] or summarizing his theological understanding,[3] I have proposed that Paul's 'preaching the gospel in writing'[4] was intended specifically for the believers at Rome so that they too would become part of his 'offering' of 'sanctified' and 'obedient' Gentiles. That Paul chose to write to Rome for this purpose, as opposed to other cities in the em-

---

1. Aune, *The New Testament in Its Literary Environment*, p. 219.
2. E.g. Manson, 'To the Romans—And Others'.
3. E.g. Bornkamm, 'Paul's Last Will and Testament'.
4. Dahl, 'The Missionary Theology in the Epistle to the Romans', p. 75.

pire, is probably best explained as the result of its being the world capital and a city holding a strategic position in relation to his missionary goals. Yet, as I have suggested, it would appear that Paul did not write to Rome primarily in order to be able to spread his missionary net to the western empire. The main function of the letter was to allow the Christians at Rome to hear the power of the gospel from him, since he knew himself to be their divinely commissioned apostle.

The function of Romans is to preach the gospel by letter to the Christian converts at Rome. The letter necessarily serves also as a self-introduction. Yet the function of the letter goes far beyond Paul's self-presentation, whether for the purposes of furthering his missionary activity, or of preparing for a visit by setting forth a particular understanding of the faith and/or of Christian behaviour. Paul created this letter to be capable of standing on its own; to function so as to accomplish his present goals for the believing community at Rome. While he concerns of the letter involve Paul's missionary plans and his desire to establish himself as the Roman Christians' leader in the faith, the primary concern of Romans is for this apostle to the Gentiles to make available to Christians at this particular locale the good news in all of its power. Paul's overriding concern is that the Roman believers hear what he considers is his particularly powerful and effective presentation of the gospel. For Paul knows his preaching to be capable of establishing gentile believers in obedience.

The function of Romans is to encourage the Roman believers to enter Paul's apostolic orbit so that they may be included within his 'offering' through having heard his preaching. Paul hoped that his life would be spared long enough that his letter to the Romans would also work to prepare them for a strategic support role. The letter, however, is not focused on his future relationship with the readers, but rather on Paul's present apostolic obligation for them. Romans is written to fulfill Paul's mandate to establish and nurture his Roman readers in a life of faith marked by obedience and holiness—to preach the gospel to them.

BIBLIOGRAPHY

Abraham, M.V., 'Paul: The Unique Apostle', *IJT* 26 (1977), pp. 62-72.

Aletti, J.-N., 'L'autorité apostolique de Paul. Théorie et pratique', in *L'Apôtre Paul. Personnalité, style et conception du ministère* (ed. A. Vanhoye; Leuven: Leuven University Press, 1986), pp. 229-46.

Althaus, P., *Der Brief an Die Römer* (Göttingen: Vandenhoeck & Ruprecht, 1946).

Arichea, D.C., 'Who was Phoebe? Translating *diakonos* in Romans 16.1', *BibT* 39 (1988), pp. 401-409.

Audet, J.-P. 'Literary Forms and Contents of a Normal Εὐχαριστία in the First Century', *Studia Evangelica* 1 (ed. F.L. Cross, K. Aland, *et al.*; Berlin: Akademie, 1959), pp. 632-43.

Aune, D.E., 'Review of H.D. Betz, *Galatians*', *RelSRev* 7 (1981), pp. 323-28.

—*The New Testament in Its Literary Environment* (Philadelphia: Westminster, 1987).

Augustine on Romans: Propositions From the Epistle to the Romans, Unfinished Commentary on the Epistle to the Romans (trans. P.F. Landes; Chico, CA: Scholars Press, 1982).

Aus, R., 'Paul's Travel Plans to Spain and the "Full Number of the Gentiles" of Rom. xi 25', *NovT* 21 (1979), pp. 232-61.

Bahr, G.J., 'Paul and Letter Writing in the First Century', *CBQ* 28 (1966), pp. 465-77.

—'The Subscriptions in the Pauline Letters', *JBL* 87 (1968), pp. 27-41.

Bailey, J.A., 'Who Wrote II Thessalonians?', *NTS* 25 (1978–79), pp. 131-45.

Barrett, C.K., *The Epistle to the Romans* (New York: Harper, 1957).

—*The First Epistle to the Corinthians* (London: Black, 1968).

—*The Signs of an Apostle* (London: Epworth, 1970).

—'I am Not Ashamed of the Gospel', *AnBib* 42 (Rome: Institut Biblique Pontificial, 1970), pp. 19-50.

—'Paul's Opponents in II Corinthians', *NTS* 17 (1971), pp. 233-54.

—*A Commentary on the Second Epistle to the Corinthians* (London: Black, 1973).

—'Galatians as an "Apologetic Letter"', *Int* 34 (1980), pp. 414-17.

Barth, G., *Der Brief an die Philipper* (Zürich: Theologischer Verlag, 1979).

Barth, K., *The Epistle to the Romans* (trans. E.C. Hoskyns; London: Oxford University Press, 1933).

—*The Epistle to the Philippians* (trans. J.W. Leitch; London: SCM, 1962).

Bartsch, H.-W., 'The Historical Situation of Romans', *Encounter* 33 (1972), pp. 329-39.

Bassler, J.M., *Divine Impartiality. Paul and a Theological Axiom* (Chico, CA: Scholars Press, 1982).

Bates, W.H., 'The Integrity of II Corinthians', *NTS* 12 (1965–66), pp. 56-69.

Batey, R., 'Paul's Interactions with the Corinthians', *JBL* 84 (1965), pp. 139-46.

Baur, F.C., *Paul The Apostle of Jesus Christ* I (trans. from 2nd German edn; ed. E. Zeller, rev. A. Menzies; London: Williams & Norgate, 1876).

Beare, F.W., *A Commentary on the Epistle to the Philippians* (London: Black, 1959).

—*St Paul and His Letters* (London: Black, 1962).

Beker, J.C., 'Contingency and Coherence in the Letters of Paul', *USQR* 33 (1978), pp. 141-51.

—*Paul The Apostle. The Triumph of God in Life and Thought* (Philadelphia: Fortress, 1980).

—'Paul's Theology: Consistent or Inconsistent?', *NTS* 34 (1988), pp. 364-77.

Belleville, L.L., 'Continuity or Discontinuity: A Fresh Look at 1 Corinthians in the Light of First-Century Epistolary Forms and Conventions', *EQ* 59 (1987), pp. 15-37.

Bengel, J.A., *Gnomon of the New Testament* (trans., rev. and ed. A.R. Fausset; Edinburgh: T. & T. Clark, 1873).

Bergen, R.D., 'Text as a Guide to Authorial Intention: An Introduction to Discourse Criticism', *JETS* 30 (1987), pp. 327-36.

Berger, K., 'Apostelbrief und apostolische Rede: Zum Formular frühchristler Briefe', *ZNW* 65 (1974), pp. 190-231.

Best, E., *The Letter of Paul to the Romans* (Cambridge: Cambridge University Press, 1967).

—*A Commentary on the First and Second Epistles to the Thessalonians* (London: Black, 1977).

—'The Revelation to Evangelize the Gentiles', *JTS* 35 (1984), pp. 1-30.

—'Paul's Apostolic Authority—?', *JSNT* 27 (1986), pp. 3-25.

—*Second Corinthians* (Atlanta: John Knox, 1987).

Betz, H.D., '2 Cor. 6.14–7.1: An Anti-Pauline Fragment?', *JBL* 92 (1973), p. 88-108.

—'The Literary Composition and Function of Paul's Letter to the Galatians', *NTS* 21 (1975), pp. 353-79.

—'Galatians, Letter to the', *IDB* Supp. (1976), pp. 352-53.

—*Galatians. A Commentary on Paul's Letter to the Churches in Galatia* (Philadelphia: Fortress, 1979).

—*2 Corinthians 8 & 9* (ed. G.W. MacRae; Philadelphia: Fortress, 1985).

Bjerkelund, C.J., *Parakalo: Form, Funktion und Sinn der parakalo-Satze in den paulinischen Briefen* ('Bibliotheca Theologica Norvegica', 1; Oslo: Universitetsforlaget, 1967).

Black, M., *Romans* (London: Marshall, Morgan & Scott, 1973).

Bligh, J., *Galatians. A Discussion of St Paul's Epistle* (London: St. Paul, 1969).

Boers, H., 'Form Critical Study of Paul's Letters', *NTS* 22 (1975–76), pp. 140-58.

Bonnard, P., *L'Epître de Saint Paul aux Galates* (Paris: Delachaux et Niestlé, 1972).

Bornkamm, G., 'Der Philipperbrief als paulinische Briefsammlung', in *Neotestamentica et Patristica. Eine Freundesgabe, Herrn Professor Dr. Oscar Cullmann zu seinem 60. Geburtstag Überreicht* (Leiden: Brill, 1962), pp. 192-202.

—'The History of the Origin of the So-Called Second Letter to the Corinthians', in *The Authorship and Integrity of the New Testament* (London: SPCK, 1965), pp. 73-81.

—*Paul* (trans. D.M.G. Stalker; New York: Harper & Row, 1971).

—'Paul's Last Will and Testament', in *The Romans Debate* (ed. K.P. Donfried; Minneapolis, MN: Augsburg, 1977), pp. 17-31.

Bowers, P., 'Fulfilling the Gospel: The Scope of the Pauline Mission', *JETS* 30 (1987), pp. 185-98.

Bradley, D.G., 'The *Topos* as a Form in the Pauline Paraenesis', *JBL* 72 (1953), pp. 238-46.

Bring, R., *Commentary on Galatians* (trans. E. Wahlstom; Philadelphia: Muhlenberg, 1961).

—'Die Gerechtigkeit Gottes und das alttestamentlich Gesetz. Eine Untersuchung von Röm. 10, 4', in *Christus und das Gesetz. Die Bedeutung des Gesetzes des Alten Testaments nach Paulus und sein Glauben an Christus* (Leiden: Brill, 1969), pp. 35-72.

Brinsmead, B.H., *Galatians—Dialogical Response to Opponents* (Chico, CA: Scholars Press, 1982).

Broer, I., ' "Antisemitismus" und Judenpolemik im Neuen Testament. Ein Beitrag zum besseren Verständnis von I Thess. 2, 14-16', *BN* 20 (1983), pp. 59-91.

Brooks, J.A., and C.L. Winbery, *Syntax of New Testament Greek* (Washington, DC: University Press of America, 1979).

Brown, G., and G. Yule, *Discourse Analysis* (Cambridge: Cambridge University Press, 1983).

Brown, R.E., and J.P. Meier, *Antioch and Rome: New Testament Cradles of Christianity* (New York: Paulist, 1982).

Brown, S., *The Origins of Christianity. A Historical Introduction to the New Testament* (Oxford: Oxford University Press, 1984).

—'Reader Response: Demythologizing the Text', *NTS* 34 (1988), pp. 232-37.

Bruce, F.F., *1 & 2 Corinthians* (London: Oliphants, 1971).

—*Paul: Apostle of the Heart Set Free* (Grand Rapids: Eerdmans, 1977).

—*The Epistle to the Galatians* (Exeter: Paternoster, 1982).

Brunner, E., *The Letter to the Romans* (trans. based on one made by H.A. Kennedy from 1956 German edn; London: Lutterworth, 1959).

Bultmann, R., *The Theology of the New Testament* (2 vols.; trans. K. Grobel; New York: Scribner's, 1951).

—*The Second Letter to the Corinthians* (Minneapolis, MN: Augsburg, 1985).

Burton, E.D., *Moods and Tenses of New Testament Greek* (Edinburgh: T. & T. Clark, 1898).

—*A Critical and Exegetical Commentary on the Epistle to the Galatians* (Edinburgh: T. & T. Clark, 1921).

Calvin, J., *The Epistle of Paul the Apostle to the Romans and to the Thessalonians* (trans. R. MacKenzie; Grand Rapids: Eerdmans, 1961).

Campbell, W.S., 'Why Did Paul Write Romans?', *ExpT* 85 (1974), pp. 264-69.

Caird, G.B., *Paul's Letters from Prison* (Oxford: Oxford University Press, 1976).

—*The Language and Imagery of the Bible* (London: Duckworth, 1980).

Cha, Jin Soon, *Linguistic Cohesion in Texts: Theory and Description* (Seoul, Korea: Daehan Textbook, 1985).

Cherry, C., *On Human Communication: A Review, A Survey, and A Criticism* (Cambridge, MA: M.I.T. Press, 1966).

Chrysostom, J., *The Homilies of St John Chrysostom on the Epistle of St Paul the Apostle to the Romans* (trans. J.B. Morris; Oxford: Parker, 1841).

Church, F.F., 'Rhetorical Structure and Design in Paul's Letter to Philemon', *HTR* 71 (1978), pp. 17-33.

Collange, J.-F., *Enigmes de la deuxième épître aux Corinthiens* (Cambridge: Cambridge University Press, 1972).

—*L'Epître de Saint Paul aux Philippiens* (Neuchatel: Delachaux et Niestlé, 1973).

Coneybeare, W.J., and J.W. Howson, *The Life and Epistle of St Paul* (London: Longmans, Green, 1873).

Conzelmann, H., *An Outline of the Theology of the New Testament* (trans. J. Bowden from the 2nd German edn, 1968; New York: Harper & Row, 1969).

—*I Corinthians* (trans. J.W. Leitch; Philadelphia: Fortress, 1975).

Cook, D., 'Stephanus Le Moyne and the Dissection of Philippians', *JTS* 32 (1981), pp. 138-42.

Cope, L., 'On Rethinking the Philemon–Colossians Connection', *BR* 30 (1985), pp. 45-50.

Coppens, J., 'Miscellanées bibliques. LXXX. Une diatribe antijuive dans I Thess, II, 13-16', *ETL* 51 (1975), pp. 90-95.

Coulthard, M., *An Introduction to Discourse Analysis* (London: Longman, 1977).

Coursar, C.B., *Galatians* (Atlanta: John Knox, 1982).

Craddock, F.B., *Philippians* (Atlanta: John Knox, 1985).

Cranfield, C.E.B., *A Commentary on Romans 12–13* (Edinburgh: Oliver & Boyd, 1965).

—*The Epistle to the Romans* (2 vols.; Edinburgh: T. & T. Clark, 1975, 1979).

—*Romans: A Shorter Commentary* (Grand Rapids: Eerdmans, 1985).

Cullmann, O., *The Earliest Christian Confessions* (trans. J.K.S. Reid; London: Lutterworth, 1949).

—*The New Testament: An Introduction for the General Reader* (trans. J. Bowden; Philadelphia: Westminster, 1966).

Cuming, G.J., 'Service-endings in the Epistles', *NTS* 22 (1975), pp. 110-13.

Dahl, N.A., 'Two Notes on Romans 5', *ST* 5 (1951), pp. 37-48.

—'The Particularity of the Pauline Epistles as a Problem in the Ancient Church', in *Neotestamentica et Patristica. Eine Freundesgabe, Herrn Professor Dr. Oscar Cullmann zu Seinem 60. Geburtstag überreicht* (Leiden: Brill, 1962), pp. 261-71.

—'On the Literary Integrity of 2 Corinthians 1–9', in *Studies in Paul* (Minneapolis, MN: Augsburg, 1977), pp. 38-39.

—'A Fragment and Its Context: 2 Cor. 6.14–7.1', in *Studies in Paul* (Minneapolis, MN: Augsburg, 1977), pp. 62-69.

—'The Missionary Theology in the Epistle to the Romans', in *Studies in Paul* (Minneapolis, MN: Augsburg, 1977), pp. 70-87.

Dalton, W.J., 'The Integrity of Philippians', *Bib* 60 (1979), pp. 97-102.

Danker, F.W., 'Under Contract: A Form–Critical Study of Linguistic Adaptation in Romans' in *Festschrift to Honor F. Wilbur Gingrich* (ed. E.H. Barth and R.E. Cocroft; Leiden: Brill, 1972), pp. 91-114.

Deissmann, G.A., *Bible Studies* (trans. A. Grieve; Edinburgh: T. & T. Clark, 1901).

—*St. Paul: A Study in Social and Religious History* (trans. L.R.M. Strachan; London: Hodder & Stoughton, 1912).

—*The Religion of Jesus and the Faith of Paul* (trans. W.E. Wilson; London: Hodder & Stoughton, 1923).

—*Light from the Ancient East* (rev. edn; trans. L.R.M. Strachan; London: Hodder & Stoughton, 1927).

Deschamps, A., 'La structure de Rom. 1–11', in *Studiorum Paulinorum Congressus* I, *AnBib* 17, pp. 3-14.

Dibelius, M., *A Commentary on the Epistle of James* (11th rev. edn prepared H. Greeven; ed. H. Koester, trans. M.A. Williams; Philadelphia: Fortress, 1976).

—*A Fresh Approach to the New Testament and Early Christian Literature* (London: Nicholson & Watson, 1936).

—*An die Thessalonicher I. II an die Philipper* (Tübingen: Mohr/Siebeck, 1937).

—*An die Kolosser, Epheser, an Philemon* (3rd rev. edn; Tübingen: Mohr/Siebeck, 1953).

Dinkler, E., 'Corinthians, First Letter to the' in *Hastings Dictionary of the Bible* (rev. and ed. F.C. Grant and H.H. Rowley; Edinburgh: T. & T. Clark, 1963).

Dion, P.E., 'The Aramaic "Family Letter" and Related Epistolary Forms in Other Oriental Languages and in Hellenistic Greek', *Semeia* 22 (1981), pp. 59-76.

Dodd, C.H., *The Epistle of Paul to the Romans* (London: Hodder & Stoughton, 1932).

—'The Mind of Paul: I', in *New Testament Studies* (Manchester: Manchester University Press, 1953), pp. 67-82.

Donfried, K.P., 'A Short Note on Romans 16', in *The Romans Debate* (ed. K.P. Donfried; Minneapolis, MN: Augsburg, 1977), pp. 50-60.

—'False Assumptions in the Study of Romans', in *The Romans Debate* (ed. K.P. Donfried; Minneapolis, MN: Augsburg, 1977), pp. 120-48.

—'The Cults of Thessalonica and the Thessalonian Correspondence', *NTS* 31 (1985), pp. 336-56.

Dorsey, D., 'Paul's use of Ἀπόστολος', *RQ* 28 (1986), pp. 193-99.

Doty, W., 'The Epistle in Late Hellenism and Early Christianity: Developments, Influences and Literary Form' (PhD dissertation; Drew University, Madison, NJ, 1966).

—*Letters in Primitive Christianity* (Philadelphia: Fortress, 1973).

Drane, J.W., 'Why Did Paul Write Romans?', in *Pauline Studies: Essays Presented to F.F. Bruce on his 70th Birthday* (ed. D.A. Hagner and M.J. Harris; Exeter: Paternoster, 1980), pp. 208-27.

Dunn, J.D.G., *Romans1-8* (Dallas, TX: Word, 1988).

Dupont, J., 'Appel aux faibles et aux forts dans la communauté romaine (Rom. 14, 1–15, 13)', *Studiorum Paulinorum Congressus Internationalis Catholicus 1961* (Rome: Pontificio Instituto Biblico, 1963), pp. 357-66.

Eckart, K.-G., 'Der zweite echte Brief des Apostel Paulus an die Thessalonicher', *ZThK* 58 (1961), pp. 30-44.

Ellis, E.E., 'Paul and His Co-Workers', *NTS* 17 (1971), pp. 437-52.

Ellis, P.F., *Seven Pauline Letters* (Collegeville, MN: Liturgical Press, 1982).

Erdman, C.R., *The Epistle of Paul to the Romans* (Philadelphia: Westminster, 1925).

Eschlimann, A., 'La rédaction des epîtres pauliniennes', *RB* 53 (1946), pp. 185-96.

Exler, F.X.J., 'The Form of the Ancient Greek Letter: A Study in Greek Epistolography' (PhD dissertation; Catholic University of America, 1923).

Fabrega, V., 'War Junia(s), der hervorragende Apostel (Rom. 16, 7), eine Frau?', *JAC* 27 (1984), pp. 47-64.

Faw, C.E., 'The Anomaly of Galatians', *BR* 5 (1960), pp. 25-38.

Feine, P. and J. Behm, *Introduction to the New Testament* (14th rev. edn completely re-edited by W.G. Kümmel, trans. A.J. Mattill, Jr; Nashville: Abingdon, 1966).

Feuillet, A., 'Le Plan salvifique de Dieu d'après l'Epître aux Romans: essai sur la structure litteraire de l'Epître et sa significance theologique', *RB* 52 (1950), pp. 336-87; 489-529.

Finegan, J., 'The Original Form of the Pauline Collection', *HTR* 49 (1956), pp. 85-103.

Fitzmyer, J.A., 'Qumran and the Interpolated Paragraph in 2 Cor 6, 14–7, 1', *CBQ* (1961), pp. 271-80.

—'New Testament Epistles', in *The Jerome Biblical Commentary* (ed. R.E. Brown, *et al.*; Englewood Cliffs, NJ: Prentice–Hall, 1968), pp. 223-26.

—'The Letter to the Galatians', in *The Jerome Biblical Commentary* (Englewood Cliffs, NJ: Prentice–Hall, 1968), pp. 236-46.

—'The Letter to the Romans', in *The Jerome Biblical Commentary* (Englewood Cliffs, NJ: Prentice–Hall, 1968), pp. 291-331.

—'Some Notes on Aramaic Epistolography', *JBL* 93 (1974), pp. 201-25.

Fowler, R., *Linguistic Criticism* (Oxford: Oxford University Press, 1986).

Francis, F.O., and J.P. Sampley (eds.), *Pauline Parallels* (Philadelphia: Fortress, 1984).

Friedrich, G., 'Die Gegner des Paulus im 2. Korintherbrief', in *Abraham unser Vater. Juden und Christen im Gespräch über die Bibel. Festschrift für Otto Michel* (ed. O. Betz, *et al.*; Leiden: Brill, 1963), pp. 181-215.

Fridrichsen, A., 'The Apostle and His Message', *Uppsala Universitets Årsskrift* 3 (1947), pp. 1-23.

Fuchs, E., *Hermeneutik* (Bad Canstatt: Müllershön, 1954).

Funk, R.W., *Language, Hermeneutic, and Word of God* (New York: Harper & Row, 1966).

—'Saying and Seeing: Phenomenology of Language and the New Testament', *JBR* 34 (1966), pp. 197-213.

—'The Apostolic "Parousia": Form and Significance" in *Christian History and Interpretation: Studies Presented to John Knox* (ed. W.R. Farmer, C.F.D. Moule, and R.R. Niebuhr; Cambridge: Cambridge University Press, 1967), pp. 249-68.

—'Form and Structure of II and III John', *JBL* 86 (1967), pp. 424-30.

—*Parables and Presence. Forms of the New Testament Tradition* (Philadelphia: Fortess, 1982).

Furnish, V.P., 'The Place and Purpose of Philippians iii', *NTS* 10 (1963), pp. 80-88.

—*II Corinthians* (Garden City, NY: Doubleday, 1984).

Gamble, H. *The Textual History of the Letter to the Romans* (Grand Rapids: Eerdmans, 1977).

Gaston, L., *No Stone on Another. Studies in the Significance of the Fall of Jerusalem in the Synoptic Gospels* (Suppl. *NovT* 23; Leiden: Brill, 1970).

—*Paul and the Torah* (Vancouver: University of British Columbia Press, 1987).

Georgi, D., *Die Gegner des Paulus im 2. Korintherbrief. Studien zur Religiösen Propaganda in der Spätantike* (Neukirchen-Vluyn: Neukirchener, 1964).

Gnilka, J., '2 Cor. 6.14–7.1 in the Light of the Qumran Texts and the Testaments of the Twelve Patriarchs', in *Paul and Qumran. Studies in New Testament Exegesis* (ed. J. Murphy-O'Connor; London: Chapman, 1968), pp. 48-68.

—*Der Philipperbrief* (Freiburg: Herder, 1980).

Godet, F., *Commentary on St Paul's Epistle to the Romans* (trans. A. Cusin; New York: Funk & Wagnalls, 1883).

Goguel, M., *The Birth of Christianity* (trans. H.C. Snape; London: Allen & Unwin, 1953).

Goodspeed, E.J., *Paul* (Nashville: Abingdon, 1947).

— 'Phoebe's Letter of Introduction', *HTR* 44 (1951), pp. 55-57.

Gore, C., *St Paul's Epistle to the Romans* (London: Murray, 1899).

Grayston, K., ' "Not ashamed of the Gospel". Romans 1. 16a and the Structure of the Epistle', in *Studia Evangelica*, II (Berlin: Akademie, 1964), pp. 569-73.

—*The Letters of Paul to the Philippians and to the Thessalonians* (Cambridge: Cambridge University Press, 1967).

Grosheide, F.W., *Commentary on the First Epistle to the Corinthians* (Grand Rapids: Eerdmans, 1953).

Grossouw, W.K., 'The Dead Sea Scrolls and the New Testament. A Preliminary Survey', *SC* 26 (1951), pp. 289-99.

Gunther, J.J. '2 Corinthians 6.14–7.1', in *St. Paul's Opponents and their Background. A Study of Apocalyptic and Jewish Sectarian Teaching* (Leiden: Brill, 1973), pp. 308-13.

Guthrie, D., *Galatians* (London: Nelson, 1969).

—*New Testament Introduction* (London: Tyndale, 1970).

Hahn, F., *Mission in the New Testament* (trans. F. Clarke; London: SCM, 1965).

Haldane, R., *Exposition of the Epistle to the Romans* (Edinburgh: Oliphant, 1874).

Hall, R.G., 'The Rhetorical Outline for Galatians: A Reconsideration', *JBL* 106 (1987), pp. 277-87.

Harder, G., 'Der konkrete Anlass des Römerbriefes', *ThV* 6 (1954), pp. 13-24.

Harrison, J., 'St Paul's Letters to the Corinthians', *ExpT* 77 (1966), pp. 285-86.

Hausrath, A., *Der Vier-Capitel-Brief des Paulus an die Korinther* (Heidelberg: Bassermann, 1870).

Hawkins, R.M., 'Romans: A Reinterpretation', *JBL* 60 (1941), pp. 129-50.

Heil, J.P., *Romans—Paul's Letter of Hope* (Rome: Biblical Institute Press, 1987).

Hemer, C.J., 'The Name of Paul', *TB* 36 (1985), pp. 179-83.

Hengel, M., *Der Sohn Gottes. Die Entstehung der Christologie und die jüdisch-hellenistische Religionsgeschichte* (Tübingen: Mohr/Siebeck, 1975).

Héring, J., *La premier épître de saint Paul aux Corinthiens* (Neuchâtel: Delachaux & Niestlé, 1949).

—*The Second Epistle of Saint Paul to the Corinthians* (trans. A.W. Heathcote and P.J. Allcock; London: Epworth, 1967).

Hort, F.J.A., *Prolegomena to St Paul's Epistles to the Romans and the Ephesians* (London: Macmillan, 1895).

Holland, G.S., *The Tradition that You Received from Us: 2 Thessalonians in the Pauline Tradition* (Tübingen: Mohr/Siebeck, 1988).

Houlden, J.L., *Paul's Letters from Prison: Philippians, Colossians, Philemon and Ephesians* (London: SCM, 1977).

Hughes, P., *Paul's Second Epistle to the Corinthians* (Grand Rapids: Eerdmans, 1962).
Hunter, A.M., *Paul and His Predecessors* (London: Nicholson and Watson, 1940).
—*The Epistle to the Romans* (London: SCM, 1957).
Hurd, J.C., *The Origin of I Corinthians* (New York: Seabury, 1965).
—'Concerning the Structure of 1 Thessalonians' (Unpublished paper for *SBL* Annual Meeting, 1972).
Hyldahl, N., 'Die Frage nach der literarischen Einheit des Zweiten Korintherbriefes', *ZNW* 64 (1973), pp. 289-306.
Jervell, J., 'The Letter to Jerusalem', in *The Romans Debate* (ed. K.P. Donfried; Minneapolis, MN: Augsburg, 1977), pp. 61-74.
Jewett, R., 'The Form and Function of the Homiletic Benediction', *ATR* 51 (1969), pp. 18-34.
—'The Epistolary Thanksgiving and the Integrity of Philippians', *NovT* 12 (1970), pp. 40-53.
—*Paul's Anthropological Terms* (Leiden: Brill, 1971).
—'Enthusiastic Radicalism and the Thessalonian Correspondence', in *Proceedings of the 1972 SBL Annual Meeting*, pp. 181-232.
—'Romans as an Ambassadorial Letter', *Int* 36 (1982), pp. 5-20.
—'The Redaction and Use of an Early Christian Confession in Romans 1.3-4', in *The Living Text: Essays in Honor of Ernest W. Saunders* (ed. R. Jewett and D.E. Groh; Washington, DC: University Press of America, 1985), pp. 99-122.
Johnston, G., *Ephesians, Philippians, Colossians and Philemon* (London; Nelson, 1967).
Jülicher, A., *An Introduction to the New Testament* (trans. J.P. Ward; London: Smith & Elder, 1904).
Kamlah, E., *Die Form der katalogischen Paränese im Neuen Testament* (Tübingen: Mohr/Siebeck, 1964).
Karris, R.J., 'Romans 14.1–15.13 and the Occasion of Romans', in *The Romans Debate* (ed. K.P. Donfried; Minneapolis, MN: Augsburg, 1977), pp. 75-99.
Käsemann, E., *New Testament Questions of Today* (trans. W.J. Montague; Philadelphia: Fortress, 1969).
—*Perspectives on Paul* (trans. M. Kohl; Philadelphia: Fortress, 1971).
—*Commentary on Romans* (trans. and ed. G.W. Bromiley; Grand Rapids: Eerdmans, 1980).
Kaye, B.N., ' "To the Romans and Others" Revisited', *NovT* 18 (1976), pp. 37-77.
Kennedy, J.H., *The Second and Third Epistles of St. Paul to the Corinthians* (London: Methuen, 1900).
Keyes, C.W., 'The Greek Letter of Introduction', *American Journal of Philology* 56 (1935), pp. 28-44.
Kim, Chan-Hie, *Form and Structure of the Familiar Greek Letter of Recommendation* (Missoula, MT: University of Montana, 1972).
Kinoshita, J., 'Romans—Two Writings Combined', *NovT* 7 (1964), pp. 258-77.
Kirk, J.A., 'Apostleship since Rengstorf: Towards a Synthesis', *NTS* 21 (1975), pp. 249-64.
Kirk, K.E., *The Epistle to the Romans* (Oxford: Clarendon, 1937).
Klein, G., 'Paul's Purpose in Writing the Epistle to the Romans', in *The Romans Debate* (ed. K.P. Donfried; Minneapolis, MN: Augsburg, 1977), pp. 32-49.
Klijn, A.F.J., *An Introduction to the New Testament* (trans. M. van der Vathorst–Smit; Leiden: Brill, 1967).
Knox, J., 'A Conjecture as to the Original Status of II Corinthians and II Thessalonians in the Pauline Corpus', *JBL* 55 (1936), pp. 145-53.
—'Philemon and the Authenticity of Colossians', *JR* 18 (1938), pp. 144-60.
—*Chapters in a Life of Paul* (New York: Abingdon–Cokesbury, 1950).

—'Romans. Introduction', *IB* IX (New York: Abingdon–Cokesbury, 1954), pp. 355-72.
—*Philemon Among the Letters of Paul* (Nashville: Abingdon, 1959).
—'Galatians, Letter to the', in *IDB* (New York: Abingdon, 1962), pp. 338-43.
—'Romans 15.14-33 and Paul's Conception of his Apostolic Mission', *JBL* 83 (1964), pp. 1-11.
Knox, W.L., *St Paul and the Church of Jerusalem* (Cambridge: Cambridge University Press, 1925).
Koester, H., 'Philippians, Letter to the', in *IDB* Suppl. (Nashville: Abingdon, 1976), pp. 665-66.
—*History and Literature of Early Christianity* (Philadelphia: Fortress, 1983).
Koskenniemi, H., *Studien zur Idee und Phraseologie des griechischen Briefes bis 400 n. Chr.* (Helsinki: Suomalaisen Kirjallisuuden Kirjapaino Oy, 1956).
Krodel, G., 'The 2 Letter to the Thessalonians', in *Ephesians, Colossians, 2 Thessalonians, the Pastoral Epistles* (Philadelphia: Fortress, 1978), pp. 73-96.
Kruger, M.A., '*Tina Karpon*, "Some Fruit" in Romans 1.13', *WTJ* 49 (1987), pp. 167-73.
Kühl, E., *Der Brief des Paulus an die Römer* (Leipzig: Quelle & Meyer, 1913).
Kümmel, W.G., 'Das literarische und geschichtliche Problem des ersten Thessalonicherbriefes', in *Neotestamentica et Patristica. Freundesgabe Oscar Cullmann* (ed. W.C. van Unnik; Leiden: Brill, 1962), pp. 213-27.
—*The New Testament: The History of the Investigation of Its Problems* (trans. S.M. Gilmour and H.C. Kee; London: SCM, 1973).
—*Introduction to the New Testament* (rev., ed., and trans. H.C. Kee; Nashville: Abingdon, 1975).
Kuss, O., *Der Römerbrief* (Regensburg: Pustet, 1963).
Lagrange, M.-J., *Saint Paul: L'Epître aux Romans* (Paris: Gabalda, 1950).
Lake, K., *The Earlier Epistles of St Paul* (London: Rivingtons, 1930).
Lambrecht, J., 'The Fragment 2 Cor. VI 14-VII 1. A Plea for Its Authenticity', in *Miscellanea Neotestamentica* (ed. T. Baarda, *et al.*; Suppl. *NovT*. 23; Leiden: Brill, 1978), pp. 143-61.
Leenardt, F.J., *The Epistle to the Romans: A Commentary* (trans. H. Knight; London: Lutterworth, 1961).
Léon–Dufour, X., 'Situation Littéraire de Rom. V', *RSR* 51 (1963), pp. 83-93.
Lietzmann, H., *Einführung in die Textgeschichte der Paulusbriefe: An die Römer* (Tübingen: Mohr, 1919).
—*An die Korinther I, II* (enlarged by W.G. Kümmel; Tübingen: Mohr/Siebeck, 1969).
Lieu, J.M., '"Grace to you and Peace": The Apostolic Greeting', *BJRL* 68 (1985), pp. 161-78.
Lightfoot, J.B., *St Paul's Epistle to the Galatians* (London: Macmillan, 1865).
—*Biblical Essays* (London: Macmillan, 1893).
—*Saint Paul's Epistles to the Colossians and to Philemon* (Grand Rapids: Zondervan, 1961 [repr.]).
Lips, H. von, 'Der Apostolat des Paulus—ein Charisma? Semantische Aspekte zu *charis–charisma* und anderen Wortpaaren im Sprachgebrauch des Paulus', *Bib* 66 (1985), pp. 305-43.
Lipsius, R.A., *Briefe an die Galater, Römer, Philipper* (Freiburg: Mohr, 1891).
Lohmeyer, E., *Die Briefe an die Philipper, an die Kolosser und an Philemon* (Göttingen: Vandenhoeck & Ruprecht, 1930).
Lohse, E., *A Commentary on the Epistles to the Colossians and to Philemon* (trans. W.R. Poehlmann and R.J. Karris; ed. H. Koester; Philadelphia: Fortress, 1971).
Longacre, R.E., 'Interpreting Biblical Stories' in *Discourse and Literature* (ed. T.A. Van Dijk; Amsterdam: Benjamins, 1985), pp. 169-86.
Longenecker, R.N., *Paul, Apostle of Liberty* (New York: Harper & Row, 1964).

—*The Christology of Early Jewish Christianity* (London: SCM, 1970).

—'Ancient Amanuenses and the Pauline Epistles' in *New Dimensions in New Testament Study* (ed. R.N. Longenecker and M.C. Tenney; Grand Rapids: Zondervan, 1974), pp. 218-97.

Lührmann, D., *Der Brief an die Galater* (Zürich: Theologischer Verlag, 1978).

Lütgert, W., *Der Römerbrief als historisches Problem* (Gütersloh: Bertelsmann, 1913).

Luther's Works. Lectures on Romans, XXV (ed. H.C. Oswald; St. Louis: Concordia, 1972).

Lüthi, W., *The Letter to the Romans* (trans. K. Schoenenberger; Edinburgh: Oliver & Boyd, 1961).

Lyons, G., *Pauline Autobiography. Toward a New Understanding* (Atlanta: Scholars Press, 1985).

Mack, B.L., *A Myth of Innocence. Mark and Christian Origins* (Philadelphia: Fortress, 1988).

Mackay, B.S., 'Further Thoughts on Philippians', *NTS* 7 (1960), pp. 161-70.

MacRory, J., 'The Occasion and Object of the Epistle to the Romans', *ITQ* 9 (1914), pp. 21-32.

McDonald, J.I.H., 'Was Romans XVI a Separate Letter?', *NTS* 16 (1970), pp. 369-72.

McKenzie, J., *Light on the Epistle* (Chicago: Thomas More, 1975).

Malherbe, A.J., 'Ancient Epistolary Theorists', *OJRS* 5 (1977), pp. 3-77.

Manson, T.W., 'The Corinthian Correspondence (1)', in *Studies in the Gospels and Epistles* (ed. H. Black; Manchester: Manchester University Press, 1962), pp. 190-209.

—'To the Romans—And Others', in *The Romans Debate* (ed. K.P. Donfried: Minneapolis, MN: Augsburg, 1977), pp. 1-16.

Marcus, J., 'The Circumcision and the Uncircumcision in Rome', *NTS* 35 (1989), pp. 67-81.

Marshall, I.H., *1 & 2 Thessalonians* (Grand Rapids: Eerdmans, 1983).

Martin, R.P., *Carmen Christi. Philippians ii.5-11 in Recent Interpretation and in the Setting of Early Christian Worship* (Cambridge: Cambridge University Press, 1967).

—*Colossians and Philemon* (London: Oliphants, 1974).

—*Philippians* (London: Oliphants, 1976).

—*Reconciliation: A Study of Paul's Theology* (London: Marshall, Morgan & Scott, 1981).

Marxsen, W., *Introduction to the New Testament* (trans. G. Buswell; Philadelphia: Fortress, 1968).

Masson, C., *Les Deux Epîtres de Saint Paul aux Thessaloniciens* (Neuchâtel: Delachaux et Niestlé, 1957).

Melanchthon on Christian Doctrine (trans. and ed. C.L. Manschreck; New York: Oxford, 1965).

Merk, O., 'Der Beginn der Paränese im Galaterbrief', *ZNW* 60 (1969), pp. 83-104.

Merklein, H., 'Die Einheitlichkeit des ersten Korintherbriefes', *ZNW* 75 (1984), pp. 153-83.

Metzger, B.M., *A Textual Commentary on the Greek New Testament* (London: United Bible Societies, 1975).

Meyer, P.W., 'Review of H.D. Betz, *Galatians*', *RelSRev* 7 (1981), pp. 318-23.

Michel, O., *Der Brief an die Römer* (Göttingen: Vandenhoeck & Ruprecht, 1963).

Milligan, G., *Selections from the Greek Papyri* (Cambridge: Cambridge University Press, 1910).

Minear, P.S., 'Church, idea of', in *IDB* (New York: Abingdon, 1962), pp. 607-17.

—*The Obedience of Faith* (London: SCM, 1971).

Morris, L., *The First and Second Epistles to the Thessalonians* (Grand Rapids: Eerdmans, 1959).

—*The First Epistle of Paul to the Corinthians* (Grand Rapids: Eerdmans, 1963).

—*The Epistle to the Romans* (Grand Rapids: Eerdmans, 1988).

Moule, C.F.D., *An Idiom-Book of New Testament Greek* (Cambridge: Cambridge University Press, 1977).

—'Form Criticism and Philological Studies", *LQHR* (1958), pp. 87-92.

—*The Epistles of Paul the Apostle to the Colossians and to Philemon* (Cambridge: Cambridge University Press, 1968).

Moulton, J.H., *From Egyptian Rubbish Heaps* (London: Kelly, 1916).

Müller, J.J., *The Epistles of Paul to the Philippians and to Philemon* (Grand Rapids: Eerdmans, 1978).

Müller–Bardorff, J., 'Zur Frage der literarischen Einheit des Philipperbriefes', in *Wissenschaftliche Zeitschrift der Universität Jena* (1957–58), pp. 591-604.

Mullins, T.Y., 'Petition as a Literary Form', *NovT* 5 (1962), pp. 46-54.

—'Disclosure: A Literary Form in the New Testament', *NovT* 7 (1964), pp. 44-50.

—'Greeting as a New Testament Form', *JBL* 87 (1968), pp. 418-26.

—'Formulas in New Testament Epistles', *JBL* 91 (1972), pp. 380-90.

—'Ascription as a Literary Form', *NTS* 19 (1973), pp. 194-205.

—'Visit Talk in the New Testament Letters', *CBQ* 35 (1973), pp. 350-58.

—'Benediction as a New Testament Form', *AUSS* 15 (1977), pp. 59-64.

Munck, J., *Christ and Israel* (trans. I. Nixon: Philadelphia: Fortress, 1967).

—*Paul and the Salvation of Mankind* (trans. F. Clarke; London: SCM, 1959).

Murphy-O'Connor, J., 'Interpolations in 1 Corinthians', *CBQ* 48 (1986), pp. 81-94.

Mussner, F., *Der Galaterbrief* (Freiburg: Herder, 1974).

Neil, W., *The Letter of Paul to the Galatians* (Cambridge: Cambridge University Press, 1967).

Neufeld, V.H., *The Earliest Christian Confessions* (Grand Rapids: Eerdmans, 1963).

Nickle, K.F., *The Collection. A Study in Paul's Strategy* (London: SCM, 1966).

Nida, E.A., 'Implications of Contemporary Linguistics for Biblical Scholarship', *JBL* 91 (1972), pp. 73-89.

Noack, B., 'Current and Backwater in the Epistle to the Romans', *ST* 19 (1965), pp. 155-66.

Nygren, A., *Commentary on Romans* (Philadelphia: Muhlenberg, 1949).

O'Brien, P.T., 'Thanksgiving and Gospel in Paul', *NTS* 21 (1974), pp. 144-55.

—*Introductory Thanksgivings in the Letters of Paul* (Leiden: Brill, 1977).

Oepke, D.A., *Der Brief des Paulus an die Galater* (Berlin: Evangelische Verlagsanstalt, 1960).

Okeke, G.E., 'I Thess. ii. 13.16. The Fate of the Unbelieving Jews', *NTS* 27 (1980), pp. 127-36.

Olson, S.N., 'Epistolary Uses of Expressions of Self-Confidence', *JBL* 103 (1984), pp. 585-97.

—'Pauline Expressions of Confidence in His Addressees', *CBQ* 47 (1985), pp. 282-95.

Orchard, B., 'Galatians', in *A Catholic Commentary on Holy Scripture* (New York: Nelson, 1953), pp. 1112-18.

Parker, T.H.L., *Commentaries on The Epistle to the Romans 1532–1542* (Edinburgh: T. & T. Clark, 1986).

Patte, D., *Paul's Faith and the Power of the Gospel* (Philadelphia: Fortress, 1983).

Pearson, B.A., 'I Thessalonians 2.13-16: A Deutero-Pauline Interpolation', *HTR* 64 (1971), pp. 79-94.

Pfeifer, C.J., 'Three Letters in One', *BT* 23 (1985), pp. 363-68.

Perrin, N., *The New Testament: An Introduction* (New York: Harcourt, Brace, Jovanovich, 1974).

Petersen, N., *Literary Criticism for New Testament Critics* (Philadelphia: Fortress, 1978).

Pollard, T.E., 'The Integrity of Philippians', *NTS* 13 (1966), pp. 57-66.

Ponthot, J., 'L'expression cultuelle du ministère paulinien selon Rom. 15, 16' in *L'Apôtre Paul. Personnalité, Style et Conception du Ministère* (ed. A. Vanhoye; Leuven: Leuven University Press, 1986), pp. 254-62.

Preisker, H., 'Das historische Problem des Römerbriefes', *Wissenschaftliche Zeitschrift der Friedrich-Schiller Universität Jena* 2 (1952–53), pp. 25-30.

Pritchard, J.P., *A Literary Approach to the New Testament* (Norman, OK: University of Oklahoma Press, 1972).

Prümm, K., 'Zur Struktur des Römerbriefes', *ZKT* 72 (1950), pp. 333-49.

Rahtjen, B.J., 'The Three Letters of Paul to the Philippians', *NTS* 6 (1959), pp. 167-73.

Ramsay, W.M., *A Historical Commentary on St. Paul's Epistle to the Galatians* (Grand Rapids: Baker, 1965 [repr.]).

Reinhartz, A., 'On the Meaning of the Pauline Exhortation: *"mimetai mou ginesthe*—Become Imitators of Me"', *SR* 16 (1987), pp. 393-403.

Renan, E., *Saint Paul* (trans. I. Lockwood; New York: Carleton, 1869).

Rengstorf, K.H., 'ἀπόστολος' in *Theological Dictionary of the New Testament*, I (ed. G. Kittel; trans. and ed. G.W. Bromiley; Grand Rapids: Eerdmans, 1964), pp. 407-47.

Richardson, P., *Israel in the Apostolic Church* (Cambridge: Cambridge University Press, 1969).

—'From Apostles to Virgins: Romans 16 and the Roles of Women in the Early Church', *TJT* 2 (1986), pp. 232-61.

Ridderbos, H.N., *The Epistle of Paul to the Churches of Galatia* (Grand Rapids: Eerdmans, 1956).

—*Paul. An Outline of His Theology* (trans. J.R. de Witt; Grand Rapids: Eerdmans, 1966, 1975).

Riddle, D.W., *Paul, Man of Conflict* (Nashville: Cokesbury, 1940).

Rigaux, B., *Saint Paul: Les Epîtres aux Thessaloniciens* (Paris: Gabalda, 1956).

—*The Letters of St Paul. Modern Studies* (ed. and trans. S. Yonick; Chicago: Franciscan Herald, 1968).

Robert, J.H., 'The Eschatological Transitions to the Pauline Letter Body', *Neotestamentica* 29 (1986), pp. 29-35.

Robertson, A.T., *A Grammar of the Greek New Testament in the Light of Historical Research* (New York: Hodder & Stoughton, 1914).

Robinson, J.A.T., *Wrestling with Romans* (London: SCM, 1979).

Robinson, J.M., 'The Historicality of Biblical Language' in *The Old Testament and Christian Faith* (ed. B.W. Anderson; New York: Harper & Row, 1963), pp. 124-58.

Roetzel, C.J., 'I Thess 5.12-28: A Case Study' in *SBL Seminar Papers*, II (1972), pp. 367-83.

—*The Letters of Paul: Conversations in Context* (Atlanta: John Knox, 1975).

Roller, O., *Das Formular der paulinischen Briefe. Ein Beitrag zur Lehre vom antiken Briefe* (Stuttgart: Kohlhammer, 1933).

Roosen, A., 'Le genre littéraire de L'Epître aux Romains' in *Studia Evangelica*, II.I: The New Testament Scriptures (ed. F.L. Cross; Berlin: Akademie, 1964), pp. 465-71.

Ropes, J.H., *The Singular Problem of the Epistle to the Galatians* (Cambridge, MA: Harvard University Press, 1929).

Russell, R., 'Pauline Letter Structure in Philippians', *JETS* 25 (1982), pp. 295-306.

Russell, W.B., 'An Alternative Suggestion for the Purpose of Romans', *BS* 145 (1988), pp. 174-84.

St John Parry, R., *The Epistle of Paul the Apostle to the Romans* (Cambridge: Cambridge University Press, 1921).

Sanday, W. and A.C. Headlam, *The Epistle to the Romans* (New York: Scribner's, 1920).

Sanders, E.P., *Paul and Palestinian Judaism* (Philadelphia: Fortress, 1977).

Sanders, J.N., 'Galatians', in *Peake's Commentary on the Bible* (London: Nelson, 1962), pp. 973-79.

Sanders, J.T., 'The Transition from Opening Epistolary Thanksgiving to Body in the Letters of the Pauline Corpus', *JBL* 81 (1962), pp. 348-62.

—*The New Testament Christological Hymns* (Cambridge: Cambridge University Press, 1971).

Sandmel, S., *A Jewish Understanding of the New Testament* (Cincinnati: Hebrew Union College Press, 1957).

Schelke, K.H., *Der zweite Brief an die Korinther* (Düsseldorf: Patmos, 1964).

—*An Introduction to the New Testament* (trans. G. Kirstein from the 3rd edn; Cork: Mercier, 1969).

Schenk, W., 'Der I Korintherbrief als Briefsammlung', *ZNW* 60 (1969), pp. 219-43.

—*Die Philipperbriefe des Paulus* (Stuttgart: Kohlhammer, 1984).

Schlatter, A., *Gottes Gerechtigkeit: Ein Kommentar zum Römerbrief* (Stuttgart: Calwer, 1952).

Schmidt, D., 'I Thess. 2, 13-16. Linguistic Evidence for an Interpolation', *JBL* 102 (1983), pp. 269-79.

Schmithals, W., *Gnosticism in Corinth* (trans. J.E. Steely; Nashville: Abingdon, 1971).

—'Die Thessalonicherbriefe als Briefkompositionen' in *Zeit und Geschichte. Dankesgabe an Rudolf Bultmann zum 80. Geburtstag* (ed. E. Dinkler; Tübingen: Mohr, 1964), pp. 295-315.

—*Paul and the Gnostics* (trans. J.E. Steely; Nashville: Abingdon, 1972).

—*Der Römerbrief als historisches Problem* (Gütersloh: Mohn, 1975).

Schubert, P., 'Form and Function of the Pauline Letters', *JR* 19 (1939), pp. 365-77.

—*Form and Function of the Pauline Thanksgivings* (Berlin: Töpelmann, 1939).

Schulz, R.R., 'Romans 16.7: Junia or Junias?', *ExpT* 98 (1987), pp. 108-10.

Schüssler Fiorenza, E., *In Memory of Her. A Feminist Theological Reconstruction of Christian Origins* (New York: Crossroads, 1983).

Schütz, J.H., *Paul and the Anatomy of Apostolic Authority* (Cambridge: Cambridge University Press, 1975).

Schweitzer, A., *The Mysticism of Paul the Apostle* (trans. W. Montgomery; New York: Macmillan, 1955).

Scott, C.A.A., *Saint Paul: The Man and the Teacher* (Cambridge: Cambridge University Press, 1936).

Scott, E.F., *The Literature of the New Testament* (New York: Columbia University Press, 1932).

Selby, D.J., *Toward the Understanding of St Paul* (Englewood Cliffs, NJ: Prentice–Hall, 1962).

Sellin, G., 'Hauptprobleme des Ersten Korintherbriefes', *ANRW* II.25., (1988), pp. 2940-3044.

Shedd, W.G.T., *A Critical and Doctrinal Commentary on the Epistle of St. Paul to the Romans* (Grand Rapids: Zondervan, 1967 [repr.]).

Steen, H.A., 'Les clichés epistolaires dans les lettres au Papyrus Grecque', *Classica et Mediaevalia* 1 (1938), pp. 119-76.

Stegemann, W., 'War der Apostel Paulus ein römischer Bürger?' *ZNW* 78 (1987), pp. 200-99.

Stendahl, K., 'The Apostle Paul and the Introspective Conscience of the West', *HTR* 61 (1963), pp. 199-215.

—*Paul among Jews and Gentiles* (Philadelphia: Fortress, 1980).

Stephenson, A.M.G., 'Partition Theories on II Corinthians', in *Studia Evangelica*, II.I: The NT Scriptures (ed. F.L. Cross; Berlin: Akademie, 1964), pp. 639-46.

—'A Defense of the Integrity of 2 Corinthians', in *The Authorship and Integrity of the New Testament* (London: SPCK, 1965), pp. 82-97.

Stirewalt, M.L., 'Paul's Evaluation of Letter-Writing' in *Search the Scriptures* (ed. J.M. Myers, *et al.*; Leiden: Brill, 1969), pp. 179-96.

—'The Form and Function of the Greek Letter-Essay' in *The Romans Debate* (ed. K.P. Donfried; Minneapolis, MN: Augsburg, 1977), pp. 175-206.

Stowers, S.K., *The Diatribe and Paul's Letter to the Romans* (Chico, CA: Scholars Press, 1981).

—*Letter Writing in Greco-Roman Antiquity* (Philadelphia: Westminster, 1986).

Stuhlmacher, P., *Der Brief an Philemon* (Zürich: Benziger, 1975).

—'Der Abfassungszweck des Römerbriefes', *ZNW* 77 (1986), pp. 180-93.

Suggs, M.J., ' "The Word is Near You": Rom. 10.6-10 Within the Purpose of the Letter', in *Christian History and Interpretation* (ed. W.R. Farmer, C.F.D. Moule and R.R. Niebuhr; Cambridge: Cambridge University Press, 1967), pp. 289-312.

Suhl, A., 'Der konkrete Anlass des Römerbriefez', *Kairos* 13 (1971), pp. 119-50.

Sundberg, A.C., 'Enabling Language in Paul', *HTR* 79 (1986), pp. 270-77.

Sykutris, J., 'Epistolographie', *Realencyclopadie der classischen Altertumswissenschaft.* Suppl. 5 (ed. A. Pauly, G. Wissowa, *et al.*; Stuttgart: Metzler, 1931), pp. 186-220.

Taylor, V., *The Epistle to the Romans* (London: Epworth, 1955).

Tenney, M.C., *Galatians: The Charter of Christian Liberty* (Grand Rapids: Eerdmans, 1964).

Thieme, K., 'Die Struktur des Ersten Thessalonicher-Briefes' in *Abraham Unser Vater. Festschrift für O. Michel* (ed. O. Betz, *et al.*; Leiden: Brill, 1963), pp. 450-58.

Thompson, G.H.P., *The Letters of Paul to the Ephesians, to the Colossians and to Philemon* (Cambridge: Cambridge University Press, 1967).

Thraede, K., *Gründzuge griechisch-römisher Brieftopik* (Munich: Beck, 1970).

Thrall, M.E., *The First and Second Letters of Paul to the Corinthians* (Cambridge: Cambridge University Press, 1965).

—'A Second Thanksgiving Period in II Corinthians', *JSNT* 16 (1982), pp. 101-24.

Trilling, W., *Der zweite Brief an die Thessalonicher* (Neukirchen–Vluyn: Neukirchener, 1980).

Turner, N., *Syntax*, in *A Grammar of New Testament Greek*, III (Edinburgh: T. & T. Clark , 1963).

Van Dijk, T.A. (ed.), *Discourse and Literature* (Amsterdam: Benjamins, 1985).

Violi, P., 'Letters', in *Discourse and Literature* (ed. T.A. Van Dijk; Amsterdam: Benjamins, 1985), pp. 149-68.

Watson, D.F., 'A Rhetorical Analysis of Philippians and its Implications for the Unity Question', *NovT* 30 (1988), pp. 57-88.

Watson, F., *Paul, Judaism and the Gentiles. A Sociological Approach* (Cambridge: Cambridge University Press, 1986).

Wedderburn, A.J.M., *The Reasons for Romans* (ed. J. Riches; Edinburgh: T. & T. Clark, 1988).

Weiss, B., *Kritisch-exegetisches Handbuch über den Brief des Paulus an die Römer* (Göttingen: Vandenhoeck & Ruprecht, 1886).

—*A Commentary on the New Testament*, III (trans. G.H. Schodde and E. Wilson; New York: Funk & Wagnalls, 1906).

Weiss, J., *Earliest Christianity. A History of the Period AD 30–150*, I (trans. and ed. F.C. Grant; New York: Harper, 1959).

Weiss, K., 'Paulus—Priester der christlichen Kultgemeinde', *ThLZ* 79 (1954), pp. 355-64.

Welleck, R., and A. Warren, *Theory of Literature* (3rd edn; New York: Harcourt, Brace and World, 1956).

Wetherill, P.M., *The Literary Text: An Examination of Critical Methods* (Berkeley: University of California Press, 1974).

Wendland, H.-D., *Die Briefe an die Korinther* (Göttingen: Vandenhoeck & Ruprecht, 1962).
Wendland, P., 'Die urchristlichen literaturformen', in *HNT* 1.3 (Tübingen: Mohr/Siebeck, 1912), pp. 191-357.
White, J.L., 'The Structural Analysis of Philemon: A Point of Departure in the Formal Analysis of the Pauline Letter', in *SBL* I (1971), pp. 1-48.
—'Introductory Formulae in the Body of the Pauline Letter', *JBL* 90 (1971), pp. 91-97.
—*The Form and Function of the Body of the Greek Letter: A Study of the Letter-Body in the Non-Literary Papyri and in Paul the Apostle* (Missoula, MT: University of Montana, 1972).
—*The Form and Structure of the Official Petition* (Missoula, MT: University of Montana, 1972).
—'Epistolary Formulas and Clichés in Greek Papyrus Letters', *SBL Seminar Papers 2* (1978), pp. 289-319.
—'The Ancient Epistolography Group in Retrospect', *Semeia* 22 (1981), pp. 1-14.
—'Saint Paul and the Apostolic Letter Tradition', *CBQ* 45 (1983), pp. 433-44.
—'New Testament Epistolary Literature in the Framework of Ancient Epistolography', *ANRW* Series II.25.2 (1984), pp. 1730-56.
—*Light from Ancient Letters* (Philadelphia: Fortress, 1986).
—'Ancient Greek Letters', in *Greco-Roman Literature and the New Testament* (ed. D.E. Aune; Atlanta: Scholars, 1988), pp. 85-106.
White, J.L. and K. Kensinger, 'Categories of Greek Papyrus Letters' in *SBL 1976 Seminar Papers* (ed. G. MacRae; Missoula, MT: Scholars Press, 1976), pp. 79-92.
Wiefel, W., 'The Jewish Community in Ancient Rome and the Origins of Roman Christianity', in *The Romans Debate* (ed. K.P. Donfried; Minneapolis, MN: Augsburg, 1977), pp. 100-19.
Wikenhauser, A., *New Testament Introduction* (trans. J. Cunningham; Freiburg: Herder-Druck, 1958).
—*Pauline Mysticism. Christ in the Mystical Teaching of St. Paul* (trans. J. Cunningham; Freiburg: Herder & Herder, 1960).
Wilckens, U., 'Uber Abfassungzweck und Aufbau des Römerbriefes' in *Rechtfertigung als Freiheit: Paulusstudien* (Neukirchen-Vluyn: Neukirchener, 1974), pp. 110-70.
Wiles, G.P., *Paul's Intercessory Prayers* (Cambridge: Cambridge University Press, 1973).
Williams, C.B., *A Commentary on the Pauline Epistles* (Chicago: Moody, 1953).
Williams, S.K., 'The "Righteousness of God" in Romans', *JBL* 99 (1980), pp. 241-90.
Wimsatt, W.K., Jr, and M.C. Beardsley, *The Verbal Icon. Studies in the Meaning of Poetry* (Lexington, KY: University of Kentucky Press, 1954).
Windisch, H., *Der zweite Korintherbrief* (Göttingen: Vandenhoeck & Ruprecht, 1924).
Winer, G.B., *A Treatise of the Grammar of New Testament Greek Regarded as the Basis of New Testament Exegesis* (trans., with large additions and full indices by W.F. Moulton; Edinburgh: T. & T. Clark, 1870).
Winter, C.S., 'Paul's Letter to Philemon', *NTS* 33 (1987), pp. 1-15.
Wrede, W., *Die Echtheit des zweiten Thessalonicherbriefes* (Leipzig: Hinrichs, 1903).
Wuellner, W., 'Paul's Rhetoric of Argumentation in Romans: An Alternative to the Donfried–Karris Debate over Romans', in *The Romans Debate* (ed. K.P. Donfried; Minneapolis, MN: Augsburg, 1977), pp. 152-74.
Zahn, T., *Introduction to the New Testament*, I (trans. J.M. Trout *et al.*, supervised by M.W. Jacobus, assisted by C.S. Thayer; Edinburgh: T. & T. Clark, 1909).
—*Der Brief des Paulus an die Römer* (Leipzig: Deichert, 1910).
Zeller, D., *Der Brief an die Römer, übersetzt und erklärt* (Regensburg: Pustet, 1985).
Zerwick, M., *Biblical Greek* (English edn adapted from the 4th Latin edn by J. Smith; Rome: Scripta Pontificii Instituti Biblici, 1963).

Ziesler, J.A., *The Meaning of Righteousness in Paul. A Linguistic and Theological Inquiry* (Cambridge: Cambridge University Press, 1972).

—*Paul's Letter to the Romans* (London: SCM, and Philadelphia: Trinity Press International, 1989).

Zuntz, G., *The Text of the Epistles. A Disquisition upon the Corpus Paulinum* (London: Oxford University Press, 1953).

INDEXES

INDEX OF BIBLICAL REFERENCES

NEW TESTAMENT

Acts
18.18f.   136
18.26   136

Romans
1.1–16.23 17
1–15   138, 150
1.1–
  15.33   17
1.1–
  15.13   17, 36
1.1–4.25 26
1   27
1.1-3   75
1.1   72,78,79,
           158
1.2   74
1.3-4   74, 77,
           85, 158
1.3   74, 75
1.4   77, 75,
           78
1.5-6   76, 77,
           108, 158,
           159, 160
1.5   75, 76,
           82, 85,
           104, 121,
           122
1.6   77, 78,
           79, 104,
           162

1.7   17, 81,
           162
1.8ff.   51, 88
1.8-17   19, 105
1.8-15   102, 107
1.8-9   108
1.8   40, 97,
           102, 159
1.9   107, 159
1.10ff.   88
1.10-15   19
1.10-11   160
1.10   90, 102,
           103, 108
1.11-12   105, 106,
           108
1.11   103, 104,
           161
1.12   159
1.13-15   82
1.13f.   104
1.13   103, 105,
           106, 108,
           109, 160
1.14-15   106
1.14   104, 108
1.15   17, 19,
           81, 104,
           108, 122,
           129, 161
1.16–
  2.10   107

1.16-17   85, 105,
           106
1.16   75, 107
1.18   106
2.6-16   27
3.21-26   27
5-8   75
5.1-11   27
5.2   75
5.12–
  11.36   26
8   27
10.6-10   136
11.13   82, 104
12–.1
  15.13   136
12   27
12.1-21   20
13   27, 46
13.8-10   26
13.14   142
14–15   22
14.1–
  15.4a   26
14   136, 138
14.23   135
15   136
15.5f.   26
15.5   121
15.7   26
15.8-13   26
15.13   75

15.14-33	27, 53, 105, 110, 112, 123, 124	15.33–16.24	139	1.4	98	
		15.33	1, 26, 11, 135, 136, 137, 139, 141, 150, 155	1.8	100	
				1.9-11	100	
				1.9	78, 97, 98	
15.14-32	19, 26, 120, 127			1.10ff.	58	
15.14-21	120			1.10	97, 106	
15.14-15	120, 162	16	135-139	3.6	121	
15.14	112	16.1-23	135-138	3.9	121	
15.15-21	82, 129	16.1-20	139, 155	3.10	121	
15.15-16	157	16.1-2	136, 138, 150, 151, 155	4.14-21	110, 116, 127	
15.15	104, 129			4.14-16	116	
15.16	121, 122, 129, 130, 161	16.3-16	136, 137, 151	4.14	116, 120	
				4.15	116	
15.17-21	122	16.3	151	4.16	113, 116, 117, 125	
15.17	122, 123	16.4	151			
15.18-19	123, 161	16.5	136, 151	4.17	113, 114, 116	
15.18	123	16.6-9	151			
15.19	75, 123, 127	16.7	72, 152, 153	4.18-21	116-118	
				4.18-19	117	
15.20	26, 124, 162	16.10-15	152	4.19-21	117	
		16.16	141, 152, 155	4.19	93, 114	
15.21-23	26			4.21	117	
15.22-32	120	16.17-20	136, 137, 162	5.1–15.58	110	
15.22-29	19					
15.22-23	93	16.17-18	152, 155	5.9	57	
15.22	125, 160	16.17	154	6.12-20	57	
15.23-28	160	16.19	152, 153	6.14–7.1	57	
15.23-24	160	16.20	54, 138, 139, 154, 155	8–10	58	
15.23	125, 130, 160			8	58	
				9	58	
15.24	19, 124, 125, 160	16.21-23	139, 151, 152, 155	9.1-18	58	
				9.1	58	
15.25-28	122, 130	16.21	158	9.24-27	57	
15.25-27	126, 129	16.22	152	10.1–22(23)	57	
15.25	125, 160	16.23	135			
15.28-29	124	16.24	135, 138, 139, 154, 155	10.1-22	58	
15.28	125, 127, 160			10.23-33	58	
				11.2-34	57, 58	
15.29	127	16.25-27	135	11.18ff.	58	
15.30-32	125	16.28	139	11.18	58	
15.30-31	130			12.14	58	
15.30	93, 160	*1 Corinthians*		15.1-58	57	
15.31-32	160, 161	1–4	58, 59	15.5	72	
15.31	126	1.1	70-72	15.58	66	
15.32	112, 124, 129, 130	1.2	116, 162	16.1-11	110	
		1.4-9	98	16.1-4	126	

16.1-11   134
16.10   142
16.12   134
16.13-24   57, 134,
         142
16.13-16   134, 142
16.13-14   142
16.15-18   156
16.15-16   142
16.17-18   142
16.19-21   143
16.19   136
16.20   141
16.22   142
16.23-24   141, 143
16.24   143

2 Corinthians
1-13   64
1-8   63
1.1   71
1.10-11   98
1.12-13   61
2.13   61, 63
2.14-7.4   61, 62,
         64
2.14-6.2   60
2.14ff.   61
2.14-17   63
2.14   63
6.1-13   60
6.13   60
6.14-7.4   60
6.14-7.1   58, 60,
         61, 64
6.16-18   60
7.2f.   60
7.2   60
7.5   61
8   63, 64,
         126
8.16-24   112
9   63, 64,
         126
9.1-5   112
9.15   64
10-13   62, 64
10.1-

13.14   57
10.1-
    13.10   63
10.1   64
12.11   72
12.16-18   64
13.10   64
13.11-13   135, 143
13.11   143, 144,
         156
13.12   141, 143
13.13   141, 143

Galatians
1.1   120, 150
1.2   84
1.4   29, 82
1.5   84, 150
1.6-7   120
1.16   104
1.17   72
2.7f.   104
2.10   126
4.11-20   112, 127
4.11-19   119
4.11   112, 119
4.12   125
4.14-15   119
4.16   120
4.17   119
4.10   93
4.20   119
6.10   66, 135
6.11-18   147
6.11   135, 148
6.12-16   148
6.12-15   147, 148
6.12-13   149
6.15   149
6.16   148, 149,
         156
6.17   149, 150
6.18   135, 150

Philippians
1.1-3.1   65
1.1   71, 118
1.3-11   68

1.3   40, 67
1.4   146, 147
1.5   97, 147
1.9   90, 102
1.12   100, 106
2.6-11   29
2.19-30   112
2.19-24   127
2.19-23   117
2.19   112-114,
         117
2.20-22   113, 117
2.23   113, 117
2.24   112, 117,
         118
2.25-30   112
2.25   72
2.26   67
3.1-4.2   66
3.1-9   65
3.1   66
3.2-4.1   65, 66
3.2ff.   65
3.2   65
3.12   145
4.8-23   135, 144
4.8-9   135, 144,
         156
4.8   135
4.9   135, 141,
         154, 156
4.10-20   65, 67,
         68, 99,
         144
4.10   146
4.11   144
4.12   144, 145,
         146
4.13   144
4.14   144
4.15   144, 147
4.16   145
4.17   145
4.18   145
4.19   146
4.20   146
4.21-23   65, 67
4.21-22   66, 147

4.23	147	3.9-10	115	1.10	94-96
		3.9	92, 114	1.11	90, 95,
1 Thessalonians		3.10	114, 115		102
1.2–		3.11-13	115	1.12	95
3.13	92	3.11	92	2.1	95
1.2ff.	86	3.12	92	2.2	142
1.2-10	93	3.13	93, 115	2.13–	
1.3-5	107	4.1–		3.5	96
1.3	97	5.22	134	2.13ff.	96
1.5	93	4.1	110, 153	2.13-20	93
1.5	140	4.9–		2.13-14	96
1.6-7	93	5.11	46	2.13	96
1.6	93, 140	5.23-28	134, 140	3.1-5	110
1.8-10	93	5.23-24	78, 140	3.1	93
1.10	93, 140	5.23	54, 115,	3.6-15	134
1.25	140		134, 154	3.16-18	134, 141
1.27	140	5.24	141	3.16	134, 141,
2.1-12	93	5.25	140		154
2.1	92, 93	5.26	141	3.17	54, 142,
2.13	92	5.27	141		148
2.17–		5.28	141		
3.13	114, 127			*Philemon*	
2.17-18	114, 125	*2 Thessalonians*		1	70
2.17	110	1.3-12	96	5	97, 107
2.19-20	93, 114	1.3	97, 107	7	101
2.20	116	1.4-10	95	8	101
3.1-13	93	1.4	94, 95	19	135
3.1-2	113, 115	1.5	94	21-22	112, 127,
3.2-5	113, 115	1.6-7	94		135
3.2	113, 115	1.6	94, 97	21	93, 118-
3.3-4	115	1.7-10	94, 95,		120, 125
3.6-8	115		96	22	93, 14,
3.7	93	1.7	94		118
3.8	116	1.8	95	23-25	135
3.9-13	92, 93	1.9	97	23-24	147, 151

INDEX OF AUTHORS

Abraham, M.V. 72, 104
Aland, K. 138
Aletti, J.-N. 74
Arichea, D.C. 150
Audet, J.-P. 51
Aune, D.E. 19, 43, 130, 163
Aus, R. 21

Bahr, G.J. 55, 142
Bailey, J.A., 56
Barrett, C.K. 59, 61, 62, 64, 73,
  74, 135-137
Barth, G. 67
Barth, K. 15, 66, 122
Bartsch, H.-W. 25, 26
Bassler, J.M. 106, 107, 125, 126
Bates, W.H. 64
Batey, R. 64
Baur, F.C. 11-14, 24
Beardsley M.C. 30
Beare, F.W. 21 66, 67
Behm, J. 19
Beker, J.C. 13, 15, 16, 22, 27, 55,
  82
Belleville, L.L. 59
Bengel, J.A. 15
Bergen, R.D. 32-34
Berger, K. 48
Best, E., 22 56, 79
Betz, H.D. 63, 71, 149, 150
Bjerkelund, C.J. 20, 41, 45, 46,
  105
Black, M. 18
Boers, H. 110
Boobyer, G.H. 41
Bornkamm, G. 17, 56, 62-64, 66,
  67, 74, 136, 137, 163

Bowers, P. 109, 124
Bradley, D.G. 46
Brown, G. 31-33
Brown, R.E. 18
Brown, S. 30, 31, 85
Bruce, F.F. 21, 59, 61, 62, 64
Brunner, E. 15
Bultmann, R. 16, 56, 63, 64
Burton, E.D., 102

Caird, G.B. 30, 66, 68
Campbell, W.S. 25, 26
Cha, Jin Soon 34
Champion, L. 41
Cherry, C. 33
Collange, J.-F. 60, 67
Coneybeare, W.J. 24
Conzelmann, H. 58
Cook, D. 65
Cope, L. 55
Corssen, 135, 138, 139
Coulthard, M. 33
Craddock, F.B. 67
Cranfield, C.E.B. 11, 20, 81, 82,
  122, 135
Cullman, O. 19, 73
Cuming, J.G. 54

Dahl, N.A. 16, 21, 47, 61, 63, 77,
  81, 104, 124-26, 129, 130,
  163
Dalton, W.J. 68
Deissmann, G.A. 12, 13, 36, 37,
  122, 136
Dibelius, M. 20, 44, 45
Dinkler, E. 57, 58, 61, 64
Dion, P.E. 71

Dodd, C.H. 21, 67
Donfried, K.P. 56, 126, 136, 137, 151, 152, 157
Dorsey, C. 72
Doty, W. 13, 38, 41, 48, 97, 100
Doubrovsky, S.,= 31
Drane, J.W.,= 21
Dunn, J.D.G.,= 73, 107
Dupont, J. 26

Ellis, E.E. 150
Ellis, P.F. 62, 66
Erdman, C.R. 21
Eschlimann, A. 55
Exler, F.X.J. 37, 38, 47, 48

Fabrega, V. 152
Feine, P. 19
Feuillet, A. 15
Finegan, J. 23
Fitzmyer, J.A. 39, 52, 60, 136
Francis, F.O. 105
Friedrich, G. 62
Fridrichsen, A. 26, 73
Fuchs, E. 18
Funk, R.W. 14, 29, 36, 40, 41, 43, 44, 46, 52, 53, 97, 101, 105, 110, 112, 113, 127
Furnish, V.P. 60, 62, 64, 66

Gamble, H. 36, 41, 53, 54, 66, 105, 134, 135, 137, 138, 139
Gaston, L. 24, 60, 82
Georgi, D. 61, 62, 64
Gnilka, J. 60, 65, 66
Godet, F. 21, 26
Goguel, M. 21, 22
Goodspeed, E.J. 18, 136, 137
Gore, C. 18
Grayston, K. 68
Grenfell, B. 12
Grosheide, F.W. 58
Grossouw, W.K. 60
Gunther, J.J. 60
Guthrie, D. 137

Haldane, R. 15
Harder, G. 24

Harnack, A. von 135
Harris, Z. 32
Harrison, J. 57
Hausrath, A. 63
Hawkins, R.M. 21
Headlam, A.C. 18, 78, 82
Hemer, C.J. 69
Héring, J. 58, 63, 64, 71
Holland, G.S. 56
Hort, F.J.A. 11, 18
Houlden, J.L. 66, 68
Howson, J.W. 24
Hughes, P. 24
Hunt, A.S.,12
Hunter, A.M. 22, 74, 138
Hurd, J.C. 56, 57, 59, 60
Hyldahl, N. 62, 64

Jervell, J. 18
Jewett, R. 17, 20, 39, 54, 56, 65-68, 74, 75, 105
Johnston, G. 65
Jülicher, A. 24

Kamlah, E. 46
Käsemann, E. 16, 20, 74, 105, 122, 137
Kay, B.N. 19
Kennedy, J.H. 63
Kensinger, K. 39
Kenyon, F.G. 12
Keyes, C.W. 138
Kim, Chan-Hie 39
Kinoshita, J. 27, 139
Kirk, J.A. 72
Kirk, K.E. 21
Klein, G. 26, 82, 130, 162
Klijn, A.F.J. 19
Knox, J. 22, 55, 64, 69, 70, 73, 80, 123, 124, 126
Knox, W.L. 22
Koester, H. 66, 126
Koskenniemi, H. 38
Krodel, G. 56, 96
Kruger, M.A. 109
Kümmel, W.G. 23, 24, 56, 58, 59, 60, 61, 62, 64, 82, 135, 136
Kuss, O. 75

Labov, W. 33
Lake, K. 24, 63
Lambrecht, J. 61
Lietzmann, H. 21, 58, 64
Lieu, J.M. 83
Lightfoot J.B. 16, 17
Lips, H. von 76
Lipsius, R.A. 19
Lohmeyer, E. 30, 66
Lohse, E. 80, 101, 118
Longacre, R.E. 31, 32
Longenecker, R.N., 12, 16, 74
Lütgert, W. 24
Lüthi, W. 15
Lyons, G. 42

Mackay, B.S. 67
MacRory, J. 23
McDonald, J.I.H. 136
McKenzie, J. 22
Malherbe, A.J. 38
Manson, T.W. 17, 64, 80, 136, 163
Marcus, J. 24
Marshall, I.H. 56
Martin, R.P. 22, 30, 55, 65-67, 99
Marxsen, W. 25, 45, 47, 56, 60,
    63, 64, 67, 136
Masson, C. 56
Meier, J.P. 18
Merklein, H. 57, 59
Metzger, B. 81
Michel, O. 105
Milligan, G. 12
Minear, P.S. 25
Morris, L. 58, 96
Moule, C.F.D. 12, 104
Moulton, J.H. 12
Müller-Bardorff, J. 66
Mullins, T.Y. 35, 40, 41, 45, 54
Munck, J. 64, 73
Murphy–O'Connor, J. 57

Neufeld, V.H. 75
Nickle, K.F. 63, 122, 126
Nida, E.A. 76-78
Nygren, A. 15-16

O'Brien, P.T. 50, 51, 96, 101, 105
Olbrechts-Tyteca L. 20
Olson, S.N. 35, 107, 119, 121,
    122

Parker, T.H.L. 15
Patte, D. 24
Perelman, C. 20
Perrin, N. 18
Pfeifer, C.J. 65
Pollard, T.E. 65-67
Ponthot, J. 121
Preisker, H. 23
Pritchard, J.P. 21

Rahtjen, B.J. 65
Reinhartz, A. 117
Renan, E. 16
Rengstorf, K.H. 73, 77
Richardson, P. 149, 151, 152
Ridderbos, H.N. 16
Riddle, D.W. 18
Rigaux, B. 48, 49, 56, 57
Roberts, J.H. 98, 107
Robertson, A.T. 76, 97, 99, 102,
    104, 145
Robinson, J.A.T. 19
Robinson, J.M. 50, 51
Roetzel, C.J. 22, 36, 45
Roller, O. 41, 47, 48, 55
Russell, W.B. 25

St John Parry, R. 21
Sampley, J.P. 105
Sanday, W. 18, 78, 82
Sanders, E.P. 16
Sanders, J.T. 30, 43, 50, 51, 96,
    105
Sandmel, S. 15
Schelke, K.H. 19, 64
Schenk, W. 57
Schlatter, A. 15
Schmithals, W. 26, 57, 58, 62-64,
    66, 67
Schrader, K. 65
Schubert, P. 35, 36, 41, 42, 49,
    50, 68, 86-87, 89-93, 96, 98,
    99, 101, 104, 106

Schültz, R. 49
Schülz, D. 136
Schulz, R.R. 152
Schüssler Fiorenza, E. 151
Schütz, J.H. 74, 123, 124
Schweitzer, A. 16
Scott, C.A.A. 15
Scott, E.F. 21
Selby, D.J. 13, 21
Sellin, G. 57
Semler, J.S. 63
Shedd, W.G.T. 15
Steen, H.A. 37
Stegemann, W. 69
Stephenson, A.M.G. 64
Stirewalt, M.L. 13, 39
Stowers, S.K. 20, 21
Suggs, M.H. 136
Suhl, A. 20
Sundberg, A.C. 89, 98
Sykutris, J. 38

Taylor, V. 21
Thraede, K. 38
Thrall, M.E. 58, 61, 63
Trilling, W. 56

Vetschara, R. 45
Violi, P., 32

Watson, D.F. 68
Watson, F. 24, 25, 82, 126, 138

Wedderburn, A.J.M. 22, 27, 103, 121, 122
Weiss, B. 19
Weiss, J. 63
Weiss, K. 121
Wendland, P. 40, 45, 48
Wetherill, P.M. 31
White, J.L. 35, 36, 39, 41-44, 47, 48, 50, 52, 54, 55, 69, 71, 75, 83, 92, 100, 101, 105, 110, 112, 128, 129, 132, 135
Wiefel, W. 25, 26
Wikenhauser, A. 19
Wilckens, U. 18
Wiles, G.P. 22, 51, 54, 135
Williams, C.B. 21
Williams, S.K. 19
Wimsatt, W.K. Jr 30
Windisch, H. 63
Winer, G.B. 90
Winter, C.S. 80
Wrede, W. 56
Wuellner, W. 20, 39

Yule, G. 31, 32, 33

Zahn, T. 21
Zerwick, M. 102, 103, 145
Ziemann, 37
Ziesler, J.A. 22, 81, 107, 121, 139
Zuntz, G. 136

JOURNAL FOR THE STUDY OF THE NEW TESTAMENT

Supplement Series

1   THE BARREN TEMPLE AND THE WITHERED TREE
    William R. Telford
2   STUDIA BIBLICA 1978
    II. PAPERS ON THE GOSPELS
    Edited by E.A. Livingstone
3   STUDIA BIBLICA 1978
    III. PAPERS ON PAUL AND OTHER NEW TESTAMENT AUTHORS
    Edited by E.A. Livingstone
4   FOLLOWING JESUS
    DISCIPLESHIP IN MARK'S GOSPEL
    Ernest Best
5   THE PEOPLE OF GOD
    Markus Barth
6   PERSECUTION AND MARTYRDOM IN THE THEOLOGY OF PAUL
    John S. Pobee
7   SYNOPTIC STUDIES
    THE AMPLEFORTH CONFERENCE 1982 AND 1983
    Edited by C.M. Tuckett
8   JESUS ON THE MOUNTAIN
    A STUDY IN MATTHEAN THEOLOGY
    Terence L. Donaldson
9   THE HYMNS OF LUKE'S INFANCY NARRATIVES
    THEIR ORIGIN, MEANING AND SIGNIFICANCE
    Stephen Farris
10 CHRIST THE END OF THE LAW
    ROMANS 10.4 IN PAULINE PERSPECTIVE
    Robert Badenas
12 THE LETTERS TO THE SEVEN CHURCHES OF ASIA IN THEIR LOCAL
    SETTING
    Colin J. Hemer
13 JESUS AND THE LAWS OF PURITY
    TRADITION HISTORY AND LEGAL HISTORY IN MARK 7
    Roger P. Booth
14 THE PASSION ACCORDING TO LUKE
    THE SPECIAL MATERIAL OF LUKE 22
    Marion L. Soards
15 HOSTILITY TO WEALTH IN THE SYNOPTIC GOSPELS
    T.E. Schmidt
16 MATTHEW'S COMMUNITY
    THE EVIDENCE OF HIS SPECIAL SAYINGS MATERIAL
    S.H. Brooks

17 THE PARADOX OF THE CROSS IN THE THOUGHT OF ST PAUL
    A.T. Hanson
18 HIDDEN WISDOM AND THE EASY YOKE
    WISDOM, TORAH AND DISCIPLESHIP IN MATTHEW 11.25–30
    C. Deutsch
19 JESUS AND GOD IN PAUL'S ESCHATOLOGY
    L.J. Kreitzer
20 LUKE: A NEW PARADIGM
    M.D. Goulder
21 THE DEPARTURE OF JESUS IN LUKE–ACTS
    THE ASCENSION NARRATIVES IN CONTEXT
    M.C. PARSONS
22 THE DEFEAT OF DEATH
    APOCALYPTIC ESCHATOLOGY IN 1 CORINTHIANS 15 AND ROMANS 5
    M.C. De Boer
23 PAUL THE LETTER-WRITER
    AND THE SECOND LETTER TO TIMOTHY
    M. Prior
24 APOCALYPTIC AND THE NEW TESTAMENT
    ESSAYS IN HONOR OF J. LOUIS MARTYN
    Edited by J. Marcus & M.L. Soards
25 THE UNDERSTANDING SCRIBE
    MATTHEW AND THE APOCALYPTIC IDEAL
    D.E. Orton
26 WATCHWORDS
    MARK 13 IN MARKAN ESCHATOLOGY
    T. Geddert
27 THE DISCIPLES ACCORDING TO MARK
    MARKAN REDACTION IN CURRENT DEBATE
    C.C. Black
28 THE NOBLE DEATH
    GRAECO-ROMAN MARTYROLOGY AND
    PAUL'S CONCEPT OF SALVATION
    D. Seeley
29 ABRAHAM IN GALATIANS
    EPISTOLARY AND RHETORICAL CONTEXTS
    G.W. Hansen
30 EARLY CHRISTIAN RHETORIC AND 2 THESSALONIANS
    F.W. Hughes
31 THE STRUCTURE OF MATTHEW'S GOSPEL
    A STUDY IN LITERARY DESIGN
    D.R. Bauer
32 PETER AND THE BELOVED DISCIPLE
    FIGURES FOR A COMMUNITY IN CRISIS
    K.B. Quast

33 MARK'S AUDIENCE
    THE LITERARY AND SOCIAL SETTING OF MARK 4.11–12
    M.A. Beavis
34 THE GOAL OF OUR INSTRUCTION
    THE STRUCTURE OF THEOLOGY AND ETHICS IN THE PASTORAL
    EPISTLES
    P.H. Towner
35 THE PROVERBS OF JESUS
    ISSUES OF HISTORY AND RHETORIC
    A.P. Winton
36 THE STORY OF CHRIST IN THE ETHICS OF PAUL
    AN ANALYSIS OF THE FUNCTION OF THE HYMNIC MATERIAL
    IN THE PAULINE CORPUS
    S.E. Fowl
37 PAUL AND JESUS
    COLLECTED ESSAYS
    A.J.M. Wedderburn
38 MATTHEW'S MISSIONARY DISCOURSE
    A LITERARY CRITICAL ANALYSIS
    D.J. Weaver
39 FAITH AND OBEDIENCE IN ROMANS
    A STUDY IN ROMANS 1–4
    G.N. Davies
40 IDENTIFYING PAUL'S OPPONENTS
    THE QUESTION OF METHOD IN 2 CORINTHIANS
    J.L. Sumney
41 HUMAN AGENTS OF COSMIC POWER IN HELLENISTIC
    JUDAISM AND THE SYNOPTIC TRADITION
    M.E. Mills
42 MATTHEW'S INCLUSIVE STORY
    A STUDY IN THE NARRATIVE RHETORIC OF THE FIRST GOSPEL
    D.B. Howell
43 JESUS, PAUL AND TORAH
    COLLECTED ESSAYS
    H. Räisänen
44 THE NEW COVENANT IN HEBREWS
    S. Lehne
45 THE RHETORIC OF ROMANS
    ARGUMENTATIVE CONSTRAINT AND STRATEGY AND PAUL'S
    'DIALOGUE WITH JUDAISM'
    N. Elliot
46 THE LAST SHALL BE FIRST
    THE RHETORIC OF REVERSAL IN LUKE
    J.O. York

47   JAMES AND THE 'Q' SAYINGS OF JESUS
Patrick J. Hartin

48   TEMPLUM AMICITIAE:
ESSAYS ON THE SECOND TEMPLE PRESENTED TO ERNST BAMMEL
Edited by W. Horbury

49   PROLEPTIC PRIESTS
AN INVESTIGATION OF THE PRIESTHOOD IN HEBREWS
J.M. Scholer

50   PERSUASIVE ARTISTRY
STUDIES IN NEW TESTAMENT RHETORIC
IN HONOR OF GEORGE A. KENNEDY
Edited by Duane F. Watson

51   THE AGENCY OF THE APOSTLE
A DRAMATISTIC ANALYSIS OF PAUL'S RESPONSES TO CONFLICT IN
2 CORINTHIANS
Jeffrey A. Crafton

52   REFLECTIONS OF GLORY
PAUL'S POLEMICAL USE OF THE MOSES–DOXA TRADITION IN
2 CORINTHIANS 3.1-18
Linda L. Belleville

53   REVELATION AND REDEMPTION AT COLOSSAE
Thomas J. Sappington

54   THE DEVELOPMENT OF EARLY CHRISTIAN PNEUMATOLOGY
WITH SPECIAL REFERENCE TO LUKE–ACTS
Robert P. Menzies

55   THE PURPOSE OF ROMANS
A COMPARATIVE LETTER INVESTIGATION
L. Ann Jervis

56   THE SON OF THE MAN IN THE GOSPEL OF JOHN
Delbert Burkett

57   ESCHATOLOGY AND THE COVENANT
A COMPARISON OF 4 EZRA AND ROMANS 1-11
Bruce W. Longenecker

58   'NONE BUT THE SINNERS'
RELIGIOUS CATEGORIES IN THE GOSPEL OF LUKE
David A. Neale